THE C
with
THREE
PASSPORTS

THE CAT
with
THREE
PASSPORTS

What a Japanese cat taught me about an old culture and new beginnings

CJ Fentiman

Silver Vine Press

Printed in Australia

First Printing, October 2020

ISBN 978-0-6488519-0-5

Silver Vine Press
PO Box 418, Strawberry Hills, NSW 2012 Australia

NATIONAL
LIBRARY
OF AUSTRALIA

A catalogue record for this
book is available from the
National Library of Australia

Table of Contents

New Beginnings

They say cats choose their owners. Gershwin chose me. If it weren't for him, my life would have taken a very different course. I certainly would not have stayed in Japan.

When I first arrived in the country a year earlier, you could have described the look on my face by a Japanese saying, *neko ga cha o fuku you na*, which roughly translates as 'like the face of a cat blowing tea, as if to cool it.'

It's not that I didn't like Japan during my first encounters. It was more that it wasn't living up to my expectations, or at least the expectations I had derived from the glossy travel brochures.

The beautiful timber Samurai houses I'd been dreaming about were nowhere to be seen in the busy city of Osaka. My shoebox apartment was literally bento-sized. Even Marie Kondo would have had difficulty decluttering that space. My computer-based job was uninspiring and the complete foreignness of everything, plagued me with doubt.

When I stepped out of the apartment that first morning in Osaka, cutting through the maze-like streets en-route to my new job, I became overwhelmed. I felt uncharacteristically subdued, '*like a borrowed cat*,' as the Japanese say. As I battled the stifling heat and swarming streets, I felt like I was an extra in the film *Lost in Translation*. The daily sounds of the city were far from the serenity I had imagined. The pulsating rhythms of the pachinko parlours and the singing traffic lights that alerted you if it was safe to cross the road, in a city that seemed to be constantly talking at you, abused my senses.

I didn't enjoy being a borrowed cat. I'd rather borrow one. All this made me wish that someone would just let me borrow a cat to soothe my anxiety…or at least give me directions to the nearest cat cafe.

Over a hundred years ago, when famed Japanese writer Natsume Soseki arrived in London, the Brits made him feel under-dressed and awkward, like 'a shaggy dog among gentlemen.' As far as I was concerned, he had enjoyed a stroll in the park compared to my experience through Osaka's streets.

Had we really signed a one year contract? Ryan, my partner, and I, had looked forward to taking up our respective positions in Japan's largest language school.

The opportunity to work with a mixture of different nationalities was the driving force behind my decision to come to this school, since they had French, Spanish and Mandarin instructors. But immediately I got dumped on the 'Anglo' table, and never got to speak to my European or Chinese counterparts...which was disappointing.

As the days passed, I realised I had landed here because I was running from something elsewhere. I didn't want to go back to England so I'd try my best to make the most of it. After all, there were elements of the city I enjoyed such as the order and cleanliness. Unlike Western stations where commuters have to negotiate a maze of rubbish, I could walk through the subway station without worrying that a disposed fast-food bag would pin itself to my heel, or a wad of gum would stick to the sole of my shoe. Even though it was filled to capacity like neat sardines positioned just so in a purpose-built can, standing to attention to take up less room, the Japanese commuters filed through the steel barriers in an orderly fashion, with none of the aggravation, pushing, and shoving I was used to at home.

No sooner had that thought crossed my mind, than my days at work began, shunting me back to reality. I was an employee at one of the biggest language schools in Japan.

The forty-minute lessons felt like they took more like the historic forty days and forty nights. I struggled trying to navigate the teleconferencing system and I didn't see the point of this remote style of teaching that I could have been doing from the comfort of my own home. I had been excited about being based in the headquarters of the school's multimedia centre but what I didn't realise, was that it would feel more like working in a call centre than an education hub. Every forty-five minutes, three fresh Japanese faces appeared on my monitor with the cyclical precision of a revolving sushi train. I had new students each day. There was no continuity. I never came to really know anybody.

I could list on my fingers all the ways in which the organisation seemed to now own me. One, they had selected my apartment for me. Two, they had dictated what flight I'd take. Three, they had mandated the type of mobile phone I would use. Every moment and aspect of my life had been laid out, imposing a predetermined destination. I was used to making these sorts of choices by myself. I felt like a screen actor obeying a script, at the whim of a remote control button that someone else controlled.

The corporate rigidity and factory-style teaching were already making me think twice. If I quit working at the school, I'd have to go home, and there were reasons why I didn't want to return to England. Painful reasons.

While munching on seaweed crisps, Ryan and I decided we'd had enough.

After just one week in Osaka, we decided to chuck it in and go back to England.

What I didn't tell Ryan was that constantly running away from my life, first to Australia a year earlier and then to Japan, was beginning to feel uncomfortable. I thought that maybe I should go back to England and grow up.

On the day we booked our return flights home, I saw something that would have a dramatic effect on me, although I didn't realise it at the time. Just ahead, in the midst of the city, I saw a mass of pedestrians slowing down for something, like when you can't help but linger to look at the aftermath of a road accident. It surprised me, as usually nothing dared to interrupt the flow of Japanese throngs.

It was then that I saw a robed, bald man wearing sandals and ambling along the street, followed by a small calico cat. The man was walking slowly in a city where people usually galloped. This Zen Buddhist monk, comfortably defiant in his gait, made a clear yet wordless statement about the city's rat race.

I wanted to follow him and ask how he retained such calm in a place where everything else moved so quickly. But I was afraid to put myself forward, so watched as the back of his grey kimono wafted down a side street and vanished, with his disciple the calico cat, marching in meditative silence behind.

The next day, Ryan and I made our final preparations to leave. In the back of my mind however, I was plagued by the thought that maybe this was a bad idea. Maybe the monk was a sign I would be missing out on a profound experience if I left. But I was locked in and on my way back to good ole England.

I didn't realise it then but a month following my arrival home in England, I'd be lured back to Japan by two cats.

Chapter 1: Like a Borrowed Cat

借りてきた猫のよう / karite kita neko no you.

When we arrived at Kansai International Airport in Osaka for the second time, on an early morning in December, it was 180 degrees different from our first arrival a month earlier.

Firstly, Ryan and I knew what to expect. There was no culture shock. No bewilderment. No frustration. No internecine fighting. Just vast crowds of Japanese travellers, overly bright lights and colours, continuous public announcements, and the roar of jet engines.

Secondly, we knew that Osaka – that great metropolis of blinding neon colours, packed streets, and ear drum-rattling noise – was not our final destination. Thirdly, neither of us wanted to turn around and leave. This time, we believed we'd got it right.

We were being met at the airport by a real, live human being who spoke English, was glad to see us, and would act as our guide. Most important of all was that the staff apartment came with two house cats. I had grown up with cats and knew they had the ability to make an unhappy place feel more like home. Perhaps these Japanese cats would make me feel more settled in this new city?

We had found the job after trawling through websites in England but this one felt almost too good to be true.

Keith – that big, cheerful Aussie, and owner of our new school, was waiting for us at an airport restaurant. He was taller than I expected, seeming to tower over both Ryan and me. He had a shiny bald head that gleamed under the airport's bright lights, steely deep-set blue eyes behind thin-rimmed glasses, a goatee, and a beaming smile. He was dressed casually in black leather boots and a white shirt tucked into stone-washed blue jeans. Not your typical business owner, or educator. Just looking at him, I felt more at ease.

The first words out of his mouth were 'Youse look better in the flesh than in your photos,' and he winked. He was the human manifestation of a bear hug. I knew I was going to like him immensely.

Keith helped us stow our luggage in the back of the compact SUV, then I jumped into the back seat and let Ryan ride shotgun up front with Keith.

The owner of the school was chauffeuring us to our new home, the remote city of Hida-Takayama in the Gifu Prefecture in the Japanese Alps, about 312 kilometres north of Osaka on the western side of Honshu Island, basically a four-hour drive, where two cats we would be inheriting with the apartment were waiting for us.

Even though it was late December, the cold Siberian air mass had not yet crossed the Sea of Japan, picking up mammoth amounts of moisture along the way, to unleash days and weeks of unrelenting snowstorms, so the road was dry and, to my enormous relief, safe as we climbed into the mountains. Unfortunately, by the time we reached Gifu Prefecture, I had succumbed fully to jet lag. I was exhausted, disoriented, and doing my very best not to vomit in Keith's maroon Toyota Rav 4.

More than four hours after we'd begun, with mountains all around touching the grey sky, Keith finally drove us into Takayama.

Oh! *This* was the Japan I had envisaged when Ryan and I had first started talking about teaching in this country. Low-rise timber residential and commercial buildings dominated the structures lining the town's narrow streets. No traffic jams, no crowds rushing up and down the pavements. Everything was quiet and peaceful.

Keith parked beside the two-storey building that housed our new home. The building had originally held the proctology practise of the now-deceased husband of our new landlady. To help make ends meet, she had converted part of the upper floor into a large rental apartment now used exclusively by the teachers of our new school.

To reach our new apartment, we had to lug our suitcases up a steep concrete staircase that ended on a balcony in front of a pair of sliding glass doors that led into the kitchen. Keith rang the doorbell.

The front door swung open and suddenly two people were crowding onto the balcony with us, hugging Keith, and welcoming him back. This was the couple who were transferring the teaching torch to Ryan and me, and the people with whom we would be living for the next five days until they ended their term and flew home to Canada.

'These are the Pommies I told you about,' Keith said with a grin to the Canadians. It was the only introduction he gave us.

'It's great to meet you.' Kath said enthusiastically. 'And thank you so much for taking the cats!'

Well, I thought, that was an odd remark . . . until I considered the stress involved with packing up your lives, moving across an ocean, *and* finding a home for beloved pets. I would eventually learn just how arduous that task could be myself.

'We're happy to,' I said warmly. 'They're why I came.'

We shook hands all around and walked into the apartment.

Kath and Jake were newlyweds in their early thirties from Toronto. They had been teaching at the school for the last year. Kath was a larger than life blonde with pale skin and a laugh that could pierce walls. Her husband Jake was the yin to her yang. A quiet, soft-spoken man with a gentle smile, he had longish brown hair parted on the side and a neatly trimmed goatee. Like Ryan and me, they had come to Japan to earn some money while immersing themselves in a different culture for a bit before getting on with their careers; she in accounting, he as an engineer.

I liked them immediately, and I was curious about them, because I might have been Canadian myself. My grandparents had emigrated to Canada with their two daughters – my future mother and Aunt Cora – when they were young. My grandparents only lasted a year, because they couldn't endure an Ontario winter. So, back to England they, my future mother, and Aunt Cora had gone. If they had chosen to settle in British Columbia instead of Ontario, who knows? I might have been Canadian, too, and my first twenty-nine years might have been significantly different.

Kath and Jake helped us carry our luggage into the apartment, which didn't feel much warmer than the outside. I began to understand why the Canadians were bundled up in jackets and fleeces.

At first sight, the apartment was significantly bigger. It was nothing like the cramped conditions we'd experienced in Osaka.

We faced a long, dark, tiled hallway. Opening onto the right of the hallway were the only bedroom and the lounge where Ryan and I would be staying until Kath and Jake moved out in five days.

As we moved further into the apartment, the tatty kitchen had ugly reddish brown vinyl flooring, but the sliding glass doors let in abundant natural daylight. The kitchen also had a spacious aluminium countertop that instantly conjured images of nights after work when Ryan and I would actually cook and chat together. I couldn't wait to sit there with Ryan and eat dinner like grown-ups, something that had been impossible in our miniscule living spaces in Osaka and London.

All in all, the apartment furniture looked like it had been found in a dump. It had obviously been accumulated over the years by previous tenants – teachers like us. Truth be told, I didn't give a damn.

The only things missing were two of the main reasons I had agreed to take this new teaching job: the cats. They didn't like all of the hustle and bustle, they didn't trust the two strangers in their midst, and they disliked our strange scents and accents, so they kept themselves hidden out of sight for most of that first day. The only evidence they lived there was the blue litter box and bowls in the corner of the kitchen.

Kath and Jake had been giving us the grand tour of the apartment during their afternoon break from school. Duty, however, soon called, so they trooped back to the school and Keith left to check into his hotel.

Finally able to utter huge sighs of relief, Ryan and I had the apartment to ourselves and the leisure to shower, recuperate from our seventeen hours of travel from London to Takayama, and chat. The cats – two grey females – occasionally peeked out at us from under furniture or from behind curtains before skittering away.

That night, to honour our arrival, Keith took Ryan and me and Kath and Jake out to dinner at a cosy family restaurant just a brief walk from the apartment, the first of what would be several dinners out together.

Keith held open the timber door and we walked into the compact dining room, which was warm. As was typical of many Japanese restaurants, the chef was working in the dining room behind a plain wooden counter, knives moving at lightning speed.

We sat down, perused the menu, and then our middle-aged waitress came up to take our orders. To my horror, Keith, Kath, and Jake ordered *basashi*, raw horsemeat, for their entrées! I love horses. I was raised with them. I couldn't believe they would be chowing on *Pharlap*.

It felt like a challenge, like a slap in the face. It triggered all of my doubts. Would there be anything I could actually eat in Takayama? Would Ryan and I have to leave Japan too soon *again* to prevent starvation?

My stomach heaving, I picked at some edamame (soybeans), which instantly drew my hosts' attention.

'Aren't you hungry?' Kath asked.

My face was burning. 'Oh no, it's not that. It's a lovely dinner,' I said hurriedly. 'I'm just jet-lagged and my stomach is a little unsettled, that's all. I'm so sorry. Please don't worry about me.'

The last thing I wanted was to make a fuss in front of my new employer. Refusing the food Keith had so generously provided was a terrible first impression. Ryan gave me a reassuring, sympathetic smile – he knew what I was going through – but it didn't help. I sat at that table restless and flushed and praying for the dinner to end.

It seemed, of course, to go on forever. Finally, back at the apartment, I collapsed with Ryan on our makeshift bed in the lounge.

The next morning, Ryan and I dressed in layers: jumpers to keep us warm with shirts over them to make us look presentable, and plain black trousers. Then, Keith, Kath, and Jake took us to the school about a ten-minute drive away at the southern end of town.

The school was unprepossessing. Outside, it was a nondescript grey concrete block on a main road. Inside, it was just one floor divided into a small equally nondescript reception area and three classrooms, which were decorated with colourful ABC pictures and posters of English pronunciation on the walls.

Keith introduced us to Kimiko, a slender, neatly turned out thirty-something woman who had lived in New Zealand nearly two years and would be our receptionist and assistant. She was polite and slightly evasive. (Keith loved to tease her about her slight Kiwi accent, but she never actually responded.) Then, classes began. Sort of.

We had arrived just before Christmas. Like many other countries that enjoy celebrating as many international, national, or frankly made-up holidays as possible, Japan goes absolutely mad for Halloween, and Christmas. These are two Western celebrations with which the Japanese are totally on board. So on board in fact that I'd heard about the bizarre custom of KFC™ at Christmas, where hoards of Japanese across the country queue to purchase some 'finger lickin' good' chicken at Christmastime. With a lack of suitable roasting ovens to cook a turkey, a clever marketing campaign was devised in the 1970's, which led to this time of year being synonymous with KFC™, and as a result the holiday was forever associated with Colonel Sanders.

At our new school, classes were pretty informal as the night for Father Christmas's international night-time journey drew near. Ryan and I helped out that first day making Christmas cards and decorations and playing games with the children. With the adult students, we got to eat cake, which students had brought in, both to welcome us to the school and as a farewell to Kath and Jake.

The school had an unusual schedule. Classes began at ten in the morning and ended at noon. There was then a four hour break. Classes picked up at four in the afternoon and continued until eight o'clock at night.

'Why?' was the natural question.

'It's all about supply and demand,' Keith replied vaguely.

The truth was, some of our adult students had jobs and could only come to class after work. The teenagers, of course, could only come when their high school classes ended.

The next day, our third day in Takayama, Ryan and I met our school's Japanese co-owner.

The school's proprietor, Mr. Iwaki, was second in command after Keith and our new boss. He owned the Takayama school franchise and he was an investor in the overall business. Still, he didn't really get involved in things. He left the hiring and firing to Keith, as long as the students didn't complain, he was happy.

Mr. Iwaki was a likeable guy in his fifties who wore glasses, smoked too much, and never went anywhere without his white Maltese Terrier, *Momo.*

I warmed immediately to our new chain-smoking boss. As far as I'm concerned, if you're a dog lover, that means you're affectionate and loyal, two great qualities in any employer.

During our first five days in Takayama, Ryan and I did our best to learn the ropes from the ever-helpful Canadians. We had to learn not only the school's policies and procedures, but also how to administer and maintain the school. In fact, every aspect of the school was going to be our responsibility. Keith was already on his way back to Kani City in Gifu Prefecture where he lived and ran his network of schools. Mr. Iwaki was pre-occupied with his other businesses. Kath and Jake were already mentally back in Canada. In just a few days, Ryan and I would be completely on our own.

It was an overwhelming thought for both of us. It fed into my anxiety about starting a new job in a new place, and soured my initial excitement of coming to Takayama. I was certain I would never learn everything in time.

Back at the apartment, Kath and Jake focussed on packing a multitude of cardboard boxes and shipping their things back to Canada. It both helped to keep us from feeling like we were living on top of each other – straining Commonwealth goodwill – and made things feel claustrophobic in the apartment.

In their last week in Takayama they spent most evenings away at *sayonara* parties, leaving the apartment to Ryan and me. We could cook and eat together in glorious solitude, or, to save money, go out to a nearby McDonald's Kath and Jake had pointed out to me after our first disastrous dinner. It had salads.

After Kath and Jake flew back to Canada, we could finally settle fully into our new home.

In Takayama, Nature was just a short walk away. The still active volcano of Mount Norikura loomed over Takayama with snow-covered threatening grace, generating a perpetual undercurrent of awe in us everywhere we went. Being awed by Nature's daunting achievements beat being oppressed by Mankind's supposed structural achievements.

My first jaunt out to Japan had been sweaty and oppressive, whereas Takayama was icy cold and magical. The only thing I'd wanted to do the first time around was to run. I'd got much further this time.

Except I had never been so cold in my life.

Even though Takayama, which translates to 'high mountains,' was situated in the middle of Japan, as far as I was concerned, Ryan and I might just as well have settled in the Arctic Circle. The freezing Siberian air mass did cross the Sea of Japan, burying Takayama under thick, heavy snow that continued to fall almost every day.

The apartment had two sources of heat: a small gas heater in the kitchen that was extremely proficient at slightly warming an area one metre in front of it.

The two feline sisters we had inherited with our new apartment snuggled contentedly under the apartment's other source of heat: a small *kotatsu*, a traditional Japanese (i.e., low) wooden table with an electric heater attached under the table top and a nice thick blanket draped from the four sides of the table to the floor.

Whether big or small, basic or luxurious, many Japanese families in the winter basically centre their lives around their *kotatsu*. Certainly, our new cats did.

Our two grey happily baking one-year-old female kitties had been found nine months earlier tied to a lamppost outside the local leisure centre's gym by Kath and Jake, who had named them Iko and Niko, which means One and Two in English. They were tiny bundles of cute that made even the frigid temperature in the apartment bearable. After their initial shyness, Iko and Niko had claimed us as their own. They didn't seem to care that it was Ryan and me and not their original Canadian rescuers.

Iko was a little plump and definitely heavy-footed. Whichever poet had celebrated the light tread of cats' paws had got it all wrong. We always knew when Iko was on the move. She was both strong-willed and lazy. Each morning, her meows thundered unrelentingly through the apartment until we got up and fed her. Iko's main interests were food, trying to escape the apartment, and cuddling with Ryan or me or both for warmth. She would play, a little, if we dangled a feathered toy near her, and then quickly become bored.

Niko was her opposite. Niko was slender and gentle and a bit timid. If she wanted my attention, she would pat my leg, being careful to keep her claws retracted. She was a rabid player of fetch. Ryan or I would throw a hair band and she would go tearing off after it, snagging it in her teeth, and then carrying it immediately back and dropping it at our feet to throw again and again and again.

The cats had a basic daily routine: wake us up in the morning, eat, try to escape the apartment when we went to work, greet us at the front door when we returned from work, demand dinner, and then cuddle with us for warmth when we were working on our computer at the kotatsu, or reading a book or watching TV in bed. In fact, Iko and Niko loved to snuggle with us in bed, and it wasn't long before Ryan and I and the cats were all sleeping together to keep warm.

Of course, I fell in love with Iko and Niko at first sight. Ryan was a bit more guarded. He wasn't sure it was a good idea to take on the responsibility of caring for two cats in a foreign country. Therefore, Iko and Niko, as cats always do, launched a charm offensive on the person who showed them the least attention, tapping at Ryan's leg with their paws at breakfast and jumping on his lap after dinner.

After just a week of their unrelenting kitty cuteness, Ryan succumbed unconditionally. Iko and Niko had made the apartment a home.

Despite the winter weather, whenever Ryan and I found the gumption (and the super thick clothing) to explore our new town we found a multitude of treasures, including an old saké brewery, several ancient shrines and temples, and plenty of museums.

Often called 'Little Kyoto,' because of the centuries-old wooden houses and purveyors of handmade arts and crafts, it emanates a calmness and historic charm that so many other places have traded (or demolished). Strolling through the wintry streets with Ryan, I felt like I was back in the seventeenth century, not the twenty-first.

It was the comfortable feel of the place with its slower pace of life as well as the cats that drew us to Takayama.

Ryan and I had got it right this time. Or had we?

Chapter 2: A Good Cat Doesn't Need a Collar of Gold

良い猫は金の首輪を必要としない / Yoi Neko Wa Kin No Kubiwa Wo Hitsuyō To Shinai

Spring sneaks up on you in Takayama, like a cat stalking a ping-pong ball through the house.

Not only is the season celebrated in Japan for its natural beauty, it is celebrated as the season of rejuvenation and change. The season quickly swept me up and I went eagerly, gratefully, and was rewarded with a most unexpected silver blessing that further helped transform my life.

The sun always shines in Japan, whatever the season, unlike England where it can hide for weeks in the spring and summer. So, it always surprised me to walk out of our Takayama apartment into a sunny day that was freezing cold with snow and ice that demanded heavy boots and at least three or four layers of clothes. Slowly, however, the sun grew warmer and the snow and ice started to melt, and with it my unease about the decision to return to Japan.

In other cities and countries, the melting of several metres of snow leaves you in several metres of mud that is tracked into classrooms, offices, and homes. But not in Japan and not in Takayama. In my neighbourhood, the elderly residents spent most of their waking hours shovelling snow and ice off driveways and pavements to prevent even a hint of mud wherever human feet might tread, which at times seemed like a futile battle of Man (and Woman) versus Nature.

By late March, purple and white spring cabbages were filling the tiny gardens in front of homes throughout the city. But every time I said 'It's spring!' snowflakes would fall from the sky again, long cold evenings would send us scurrying indoors, and Ryan and I would once again be huddled around the kerosene heater in the kitchen, shivering, while Iko and Niko baked happily under the royal blue *kotatsu*.

Then one April day, I realised I was only wearing a sweater to stay warm outside the apartment, and I was bicycling, not driving, to school. The mountain peaks all around Takayama were still blindingly white with snow, the nights could still be cold, but the city had finally, fully, laid claim

14

to spring and would not go back.

In the mornings, when I bicycled to work, the warm air felt like velvet on my skin as I crossed over the train tracks on the southern outskirts of town and rode past beautiful traditional Japanese gardens with their koi-filled ponds and large decorative stones covered with thick green moss, the sound of rippling water soothing me before I began each work day.

On our long afternoon breaks, Ryan and I would walk along the blowy banks of the Miyagawa River and watch the eagles fly in formation over the icy water of the river looking for their lunches while children, still rugged up in warm clothing that made them look twice their size, fed the golden koi that lived in the shallow rock pools. I loved watching housewives run along the grassy riverbanks with their beloved *Shiba Inus*, the fox-like dog breed that is so popular in Japanese mountain cities because of its ability to cope with the bitter cold and heavy snows of winter.

Sometimes, Ryan and I would sit together on a wooden bench near the Yayoi Bridge on the northern end of the city and just breathe in deep gulps of the rich spring air as we listened to the Miyagawa River rush through the city with its mountain snow runoff, and watched a white heron posed in artistic stillness as it looked for its next meal.

Ryan heaved a happy sigh. 'It's nice to be surrounded by Nature instead of skyscrapers, don't you think?'

'It's heaven,' I said with an equally happy sigh.

Rather than being engulfed by massive man-made concrete structures as we'd been in Osaka, here we were surrounded by cedar forests and snow-capped mountains that stretched skyward, making us tilt our heads all the way back just so we could see the top of them. The alpine air was crisp and abundant and life-affirming.

For all the beauty and fun of Takayama, the companionship of Iko and Niko, unease still dampened my and Ryan's spirits. We were in charge of the school now. Besides extensive preparation of lesson plans and the actual classroom teaching, we had to work a very odd schedule.

Three times a week, we had to visit the local public Kindergarten to teach the English alphabet, the English names for colours, and the English names for animals to tiny children, one of whom cried the first time she saw me. She had never seen a 'yellow-haired' foreigner before.

Ryan and I had never taught such young children before, which worried us. Most of all, we worried about meeting the high benchmark set by the enormously popular Kath and Jake, who, it was immediately clear, were a very tough act to follow.

And then there were the high school and adult classes back at Let's English. The high schools students, in particular, were tough to handle. They'd been sent to this school by their parents to give them an edge over their peers. The problem was, they didn't give a damn about an edge, let alone English.

Anger mixed with unease. Something was wrong, and it had nothing to do with performance anxiety at Let's English. Something was wrong and it had been wrong from the moment I had stepped out of Keith's maroon Toyota Rav 4 and breathed in Takayama's bracingly cold air. I just didn't know *what* was wrong and that made me increasingly troubled. Kath and Jake had been so incredibly upbeat about their year-long sojourn in Takayama, but I couldn't feel the same enthusiasm.

'*What is wrong with me?*' I asked myself again and again. Why did I seem to be failing where Kath and Jake and now Ryan had succeeded?

I had known that the first few weeks at work were going to be a challenge for me. They always are at a new job. I can be a bit of a perfectionist and being a rookie on the job means mistakes are going to be made. I don't suppose many people really enjoy starting a new job, but I really hated it. I obsessed over every mistake, big and small, that I made, from mispronouncing Japanese names to thinking a young teenaged girl student was actually a boy and repeatedly calling her 'him' for an entire week. But I'd been at the school for a while, so that was no longer an excuse.

I didn't like the fact that Mr. Iwaki had insisted on keeping an entire class open even though it only had one student, which meant I had to give up my evenings just to teach her.

I felt . . . ancy. Like I needed to be doing something else, be somewhere else.

16

'I'm not sure I'm enjoying this,' I said to Ryan.

'It'll get better, you'll see,' he assured me.

'When?' I snapped.

'Just give it some time.'

One morning, about ten days into running Let's English, as I was teaching the infinitive to a group of middle-aged housewives, I turned from the white board to find a sea of blank faces. Some of the women even avoided eye contact.

This was perhaps the one Japanese cultural behaviour I struggled with most. I'd always associated being direct and forthright with being honest, but the Japanese, while valuing honesty, seem to have a horror of confrontation or even just speaking their minds.

'What's the matter?' I demanded in far from an inviting tone.

They looked a little guilty, a little tentative, but also determined. They'd clearly been discussing their worries together away from the classroom. All of their eyes darted and finally settled on one woman. She was taller than the rest of the group with shoulder length hair dyed several shades lighter than her natural black. Her husband was some kind of surgeon and I always felt that she had an air of privilege and superiority about her. If she had lived in England, she'd have worn a Barbour jacket and had a house in Surrey. She always made me feel inferior and the other students had elected *her* their spokeswoman. Wonderful.

'The other teacher didn't teach grammar,' she said. 'We like talk, no grammar.'

I felt like someone who had given a gold coin to a cat, as the Japanese say, which enjoyed playing with the shiny object but was ignorant and unappreciative of its purpose.

I took my glasses off and glared at them, bristling at being compared to Kath and furious that they dared to question my knowledge.

I crossed my arms and shifted my weight. 'What would you like to study then?' I heard the sharpness in my voice and saw the effect it had on their faces. They were scared. I was angry. There was silence.

I was not exhibiting good Japanese etiquette and I just didn't give a damn. They didn't want a teacher, they wanted a performing monkey!

They wanted someone they could order around and have a *chat* with.

I stalked out of the classroom and headed for Kimiko in the reception area.

'None of those women want to learn grammar!' I snapped. 'I am doing my best to teach them and they just aren't responding.'

'I'll talk to them after the lesson and find out what the problem is,' Kimiko said.

I stalked back to my classroom, ended the lesson early, and told my rebellious know-it-all students to speak to Kimiko on their way out.

'That's it! I'm done.' I growled to myself as I drove back to the apartment on my afternoon break by myself. Ryan had stayed at the school to finish up some work.

A word I couldn't quite hear pounded at my temples and set my heart to racing. I was vibrating with barely suppressed energy.

I stormed into the apartment, threw my coat and boots wherever they chose to land, plopped myself down in front of the computer set up on the *kotatsu*, wrapped the royal blue blanket over the lower half of my body and, shivering with more than the cold, I got to work. I'd always wanted to ride the Trans-Siberian Railway and this felt like the *perfect* time to give it a go. I'd be free of know-it-all Japanese housewives and responsibilities I'd never wanted in the first place. I'd be adventuring. Of course, deep down I knew that I was seriously overreacting to something trivial but could not work out what was making me respond in such a way. Why was I overreacting to this?

I began looking for tickets online.

Iko and Niko were cuddled together between my legs beneath the *kotatsu* and purring happily, sounding like full-throttled twelve-valve race cars.

Wait a minute. The cats. It hadn't taken me long to fall deeply in love with them. I couldn't leave them behind. I just couldn't. They'd have to come with Ryan and me. Yes, that was it. They'd come with us while we rode the Trans-Siberian Railway.

My fingers suddenly stilled on the computer keyboard. Stunned, I stared at the screen. I couldn't catch my breath.

Was I seriously planning on dragging two cats 9,289 kilometres across Russia, completely ignoring the enormous technicalities involved in quarantining them across borders, let alone where the hell we were going to end up? What was I going to do? Teach English in Moscow?

That's when I heard it. That's when I heard the word that had been drumming against my temples for three weeks. RUN!

A voice was screaming at me: 'Run, run, run, run, run!' and for the first time in my twenty-nine years I finally heard and recognised that voice. It had been driving me, controlling me, *my entire life.*

Shivering, I stared at my computer screen as I traced all the tendrils of that word through every vein in my body to its root. I found it at last in an ugly little parasite embedded deep within my mind, as comfy and cosy as Iko and Niko beneath the *kotatsu*, and similarly disinclined to vacate the premises.

This ugly, squirming parasite, I realised, had taken up residence in my troubled childhood and had been controlling me ever since. I regularly ran away to the stables seeking refuge with the animals. If things were really bad, I would sleep overnight in the barn with the barn cats.

Still, there had been times when the parasite had actually served me well. Whenever my mother was committed to a psychiatric hospital for having 'an episode' – it happened off and on from the time I was around five through my teenage years – I had gone running to my Aunt Cora for comfort and distraction. She was a journalist and the owner of the riding stables and given me a lifelong love of horses.

When my mother remarried and emigrated to South Africa, I was placed with my Grandmother, and then a foster family, I ran as often as I could to the stables. Eventually, I ran to Social Services and they gave me my own apartment when I was fifteen.

Many times, however, my ugly parasite had done a great deal of harm. At university, I had run away from classes that made me feel like a fraud, and at work had held me back running away from the best jobs that would have both paid me well and helped me excel.

In fact, whenever things got a little too tricky, the parasite would whisper at me from its nasty little nest inside my mind. One word. One familiar word uttered so quietly, so insidiously, that I didn't even hear it. I just felt the urge.

RUN.

It had hovered under everything I did, everything I thought, and the worst part of it was that I hadn't even known it was there. I was a puppet to an invisible internalised creature. That damn parasite had merged with me so well that I had never actually heard the word. I had just felt the discomfort, the itch, the galvanising desire. All it needed was just the slightest trigger to pain me into action. I'd be overtaken with the overwhelming need to be somewhere else, anywhere else, and then BOOM. I ran.

I hadn't controlled it in my adult life, because I hadn't even know it was there. You can't solve a problem you don't know you have. The parasite had played its part there, too, by whispering lies in my unconscious ears.

It had told me that I wasn't someone who ran away. Quite the opposite. I was someone who was seeking growth and a better life. I was being brave by constantly moving. In fact, I wasn't running: I was adventuring.

Maybe it was brave of me at first to leave my roots, the roots that could have pulled me down with my parents and my grandmother, but something had changed along the way. Somewhere between London and Australia, the parasite had become far too comfortable in its nest. It needed me to keep running, because, like a shark, the parasite could only survive if I kept moving and kept feeding it with my fears.

Sitting there, stunned, in my Japanese apartment, I realised that this parasite had been in most of the other females in my family, too, causing them to run from their problems across oceans and continents. My grandmother had tried to put the Atlantic Ocean between her and her troubled marriages and past by emigrating to Canada. But, of course, her troubles had followed her, so she returned to England less than a year later, blaming the harsh Ontario winter weather.

When my mother had emigrated to South Africa with her new husband she had also returned a year later, tail between her legs.

Was I about to give in and follow their decades-old pattern?

It was this, perhaps more than anything else that made me stop. I knew this pattern well. I knew how it would end if I continued it.

Sitting at the *kotatsu*, Iko and Niko baking happily between my legs, the phrase 'Keep the cats, keep the faith' suddenly marched in and took up residence in my brain.

Screaming in agony, the parasite slowly withered and died in my mind.

Sitting on the cold bedroom floor, I was swamped by a rush of emotion as I realised that I was finally far enough away from my childhood pain to stop running, that I could finally stand still, that I was beginning to claim true freedom.

Because of two stray cats, an ancient town, and a looming mountain teaching me about real perspective, about a deeper current of life, I broke down. I sobbed, and wept, and sobbed again. I was a flood of joy and pain.

The release and freedom I claimed that afternoon nudged my entire life onto a new course. A Zen proverb says 'No snowflake ever falls in the wrong place.' Despite my rebellious students, maybe, just maybe, I had drifted down into the right place after all.

Chapter 3: A Cat's Resentment (toward those who help it)

猫の逆恨み / Neko No Sakaurami

In just a few months, I had undergone some significant changes. I was more relaxed, more satisfied, and much happier than I had ever been. Much of this progress could be squarely laid at the paws of two little cats.

I had successfully nudged my unwilling teen students into learning English by getting rid of my former rigidity, throwing out the grammar book, and instead conducting conversations with them, often while playing the card games they liked. I had made similar changes with the housewives, who had forgiven me my earlier antagonism.

If it weren't for Iko and Niko, I probably wouldn't have stayed in Takayama, or in Japan for that matter. But on my bad days, those furry balls of fluff had given me a reason to stay and keep going. I loved them and they needed me. I couldn't run away from a job, a country, let alone myself like I'd done in the past. They had made me more responsible and, in turn, more stable and less likely to take off because things weren't going well. I was now more able to stare down my obstacles rather than run.

Before Takayama and Iko and Niko, my life had seemed like an endless grey winter with an occasional sprinkle of good times. The cats, and now the bright shimmer of spring, had put happiness and confidence back in my life and I felt more able to embrace and enjoy the good times.

Although it didn't always feel like it at the time, the transient nature of *Haru*, spring was about to signal a new chapter of my life and a new cat.

This season is so important for the Japanese, that their rugby team named itself the Brave Blossoms. Japanese television and radio stations provide daily news reports on *hanami* (flower viewing), telling their viewers and listeners the best locations to enjoy lush, beautiful blooms after a cold white winter. *Sakura* (cherry blossoms), of course, get the major coverage, because they are so popular and so fleeting.

One Tuesday, I was driving home from work on my afternoon break. I had just finished teaching kindergarten, which meant spending the morning being *kanchoed* by delightful cherub-faced children doing their best to insert their tiny fingers up my anal region whenever I wasn't looking.

Suddenly, when I was only a few minutes from the apartment, I got a frantic call from Ryan on my mobile phone. I pulled over on the side of the road with a view of the secretive *Sukyo Mahikari* sect's world headquarters and shrine – a massive white building topped with a gleaming gold roof. (The sect believes that Jesus died in Japan.)

'CJ! CJ! You have to come right now! You have to help.' Ryan shouted at me.

'What?' I said, stunned as cars whizzed by me. 'What's wrong? Are you hurt?'

'No, no, no! It's a kitten. He was trying to cross Tenman-cho. I grabbed some *niboshi* [dried fish] from the supermarket and managed to lure him back to the pavement, but he's scared and he's got claws and he keeps trying to escape. I need your help and some kind of basket and *you*.'

My heart was pounding frenetically in my chest. Tenman-cho is a very busy street. Ryan had saved that kitten from certain death, and now it was trying to dash back out into the traffic.

I rushed to the apartment, grabbed Iko and Niko's cat carrier and some more *niboshi*, ran downstairs, and kept running past the tiny shrine at the end of our street and through a narrow lane to Tenman-cho.

Sweating, heart pounding, and out of breath, I ran towards Ryan, who was kneeling on the pavement trying to coax the kitten out from under a drain sandwiched between a house and a smallish temple as cars and lorries roared down the street.

'Ryan! I'm here.' I yelled as I ran to him.

He looked up, relief written all over him. 'Thank God!' he said. 'He's under here and I can't get him out.'

'Don't worry. I've got more *niboshi*,' I said, kneeling down beside him. I peered into the concrete drain and was met by a startling pair of emerald green eyes lined in black, like the eyes of an Egyptian pharaoh.

On his grey forehead was black fur in the shape of an M. He had a pink nose. The rest of him was silver wire-haired tabby. He was tiny, no more than five weeks old. A baby. He was scared and suspicious and uncertain which way to run.

Fortunately, he was also hungry. The strong smell of the dried fish I waved in front of him was too much for the starving kitten. Ryan was able to scoop him up and set him into the carrier I had brought, along with a supply of *niboshi*. The kitten emitted a loud 'Meow' of protest which made a young couple on the other side of the street stare at us suspiciously. I smiled back so they wouldn't think we were hurting him.

'Let's get him back to the apartment.' Ryan said.

'He's so cute,' I cooed, staring into the carrier.

'Try not to get too attached, CJ. Remember: we already have two cats at home.'

'Right,' I said . . . unconvincingly.

With Ryan carrying the cat carrier, we walked back to the apartment with the kitten. I kept squeezing pieces of *niboshi* through the carrier door, which he guzzled in between infuriated meows at his incarceration.

'Thank God you saw him and saved him,' I said gratefully. 'He's so tiny. He wouldn't have lasted long out there by himself.'

'I saw him trying to negotiate that traffic and I was never so scared in my life.'

'You did a brilliant job.' I peered into the carrier at the angry kitten and then grinned up at Ryan. 'You're becoming quite the cat magnet, aren't you?'

'He must be someone's cat, he looks like a pedigree not a stray,' Ryan said as we walked through the lane.

'How could anyone let such a wonderful kitten roam the streets?' I demanded.

The Japanese generally do not de-sex their cats and dogs. They consider such procedures an artificial interference in the natural order of things, which was true enough. The only problem with this philosophy, however, is the fact that one female cat can reproduce two to three times a year, bearing one to eight kittens per litter. A single unaltered female cat and her offspring can generate around 370,000 cats in only seven years.

The tragedy of unwanted and unloved cats and dogs in Japan's cities and countryside always saddened me and I knew, from the feeling in the pit of my stomach, that the kitten filling the air with angry yowls was just one of thousands of abandoned cats in Takayama.

'What are we going to do, Ryan?' I asked as we climbed the concrete stairs to our apartment. 'We don't have room for another cat, and I'm pretty sure Iko and Niko won't want a step-brother.'

'He's a good-looking cat. Someone is bound to want him if we can't find his owners,' Ryan reassured me.

'Of course. We must know someone who will want him. He's special.'

'Yes, he is special,' Ryan said as we walked into the apartment.

Iko and Niko took one look at their cat carrier, heard the angry yowl that was coming from it, and darted into the bedroom.

Ryan and I looked at each other.

'They're not going to like this,' he said.

'Clearly,' I said with a grimace. 'Where should we put him?'

When introducing a new kitten or cat to an existing feline household, it's important to separate the newcomer from the established cats for a week or two, so they can all get accustomed to each other's scents and energy and presence and the newcomer learns that he is entering an established territory, rather than laying claim to his own territory.

Ryan and I decided that the laundry room with its large window and sunshine and door would be a good place to lodge the kitten for now. We got a saucer of water, found a fluffy blanket, and arranged them on the floor.

With the door securely fastened, Ryan and I finally let the kitten out of the carrier. He darted out, scurried around frantically, his body low to the floor, looking desperately for a place to hide. He suddenly saw what he wanted, headed straight for the washing machine, squeezed himself under it, and stayed there.

Ryan and I tried coaxing him out, but the terrified and infuriated kitten would not budge.

'Let's give him some time to settle down and get used to the laundry room,' Ryan suggested.

I hated giving up. I wanted the kitten to throw himself into my arms and purr in ecstatic gratitude and love for the person who had helped rescue him from certain death. But he had other ideas.

So, Ryan and I left him to his new, albeit temporary, home, carefully closing the door behind us. Iko and Niko hid themselves away in our bedroom for the best part of that day. It was clear they were giving us the cold shoulder. I caught a single glimpse of Iko walking carefully past the laundry room door *en route* to the kitchen, hissing and looking accusingly at me.

'He could have been killed.' I explained.

She didn't care.

All during my late afternoon and evening classes, I could barely focus on my students. My brain was crowded with thoughts and images of the green-eyed kitten, my heart filled with worry. He was just a baby, all alone in the world, and now thrown into a strange new environment with hostile cats beyond the door and towering humans trying to get him to do what he did not want to do.

As Ryan and I drove home together that night all we talked about was the kitten. When we got home, we were careful to give Iko and Niko their usual evening routine, along with dinner and lots of attention, but they knew and we knew we were eager to get to the kitten in the laundry room.

We opened the door carefully, in case he tried to bolt for freedom. To our relief, it appeared that he had eaten the food we had left him, and drunk some of the water. But he was not curled up contentedly sleeping in his basket. Despite its much greater weight and size, he had dragged a bath towel under the old washing machine, made a nest for himself there, and was now hissing angrily at us, warning us to back off.

Ryan and I are no fools. We backed off.

But in my heart of hearts, I couldn't understand it. Iko and Niko had had no problems accepting us as their new caregivers. This kitten, however, refused to come out from under the washing machine and interact with Ryan and me for the best part of a *week*.

'If food doesn't work, and beaming love and goodwill at him doesn't work, let's try playing with him,' Ryan said. 'Cats love to play.'

'Play with him? We can't even get him out from under the washing machine.' I said.

'So, find a toy to entice him back out into the world.'

I ransacked the apartment until I found the perfect enticement: a ping pong ball.

With Ryan sitting on the floor beside me, I leaned down and rolled the ping pong ball slowly past the washing machine. Nothing. I walked over to the ball and rolled it past the washing machine again and back to Ryan. A single silvery paw edged out, and then the other paw emerged. Ryan threw the ball again. Some whiskers emerged. Suddenly, one of the paws swatted the ball and it skittered across the floor. Success.

When we rolled the ball a fourth time, the kitten couldn't resist. He darted out, batted the ball across the grey mosaic tiles, and ran across the room to hide behind the rack that we used to dry our clothes on (currently covered in sweaters and jumpers) so he could leap out and surprise the ping pong ball.

Ryan and I kept playing with him, but eventually necessity intervened. I needed to have a bath, so I opened the connecting bathroom door. Seizing this chance for escape, the silver kitten streaked between my legs and jumped into the empty bathtub where, of course, he was trapped. The tub was too deep for him to jump back out.

I walked up to the bathtub to rescue him, but he let out such a large hiss that he scared me and I hurriedly backed off. He stared up at me with wide green eyes and a worried expression.

'Can you help me?' I yelled to Ryan.

'What's up?' he said, walking into the bathroom.

'The kitten's stuck in the bath and I can't get him out.'

'Well, this as good a time as any to try and hold the little guy. He needs to get used to being handled if we're ever going to re-home him.'

Ryan moved slowly with a bath towel around his hands for protection.

Suddenly, he swooped down and picked up the kitten, which emitted another enormous hiss. Despite Ryan's best efforts to soothe and calm the angry and scared little fellow, the kitten would not relax in his arms.

In fact, despite our ping pong games and our determined perseverance, the kitten remained stand-offish with us for another week. Finally, a fortnight after being rescued, fed, sheltered, and played with, he decided that we might be acceptable companions whom he was willing to allow to pet and eventually hold him.

With this success, Ryan and I decided it was time to introduce him to the rest of the apartment and his two other roommates. Their first formal meeting was, of course, stressful. There was a lot of hissing and hiding by all three. Fortunately, Iko and Niko quickly figured out that if the kitten was around that usually meant food (the bribe Ryan and I kept using to ingratiate ourselves with the tiny feline). Appetite defeated suspicion and fear. The sisters were no longer so quick to hide away whenever they saw the kitten.

The truth was, Iko and Niko just didn't know what to do with this interloper. The sisters had always got along well together, and they were older. The kitten should have been trying to curry their favour. Instead, he ignored the feline pecking order and shoved the other cats out the way when dinner was served, thinking he should eat before his supposed superiors.

Most adult cats would have swatted and hissed at him to teach him his place. But Iko and Niko were gentle souls, which only grew the kitten's confidence faster and stronger.

In just a few days, he was charging full speed at the other cats. It didn't matter that he was a quarter their size and weight and considerably younger. When he saw them, he turned into a bully – or maybe he just thought he was playing. Whatever the case, he *charged*. Iko was the most frequent target of the kitten's attacks, which surprised me, because she was the largest of the two sisters. Perhaps it was the old masculine cliché of attacking the biggest or meanest guy in town, or the fastest draw, to assert his dominance. Whatever the reason, the kitten ambushed Iko regularly. For him, playtime was never over.

Of course, I did feel sorry for the two older cats being plagued by this tiny dynamo. After a bad start in life, they had found safety, food, and love in this apartment. And then Ryan and I had brought this villainous silver invader into their home, and he was taking over.

When it came to this little boy, the Japanese had it right with their adjective *kawaii* for cute – with a very pink nose, tongue, and matching pink paws, those piercing green eyes, the M on his forehead, and his silver fur, this kitten was the definition of cute. He was also *kowaii*, which means scary. This kitten was definitely a split personality.

During the day, he was a Ninja Attack Kitten waging war on anything near him. Tiny and stealthy, he seemed to have the ability to become invisible, too. He'd spring up out of nowhere, or literally fly through the air, to wage battle on his victims. I watched Iko and Niko scurry away. They knew they didn't stand a chance.

The mischievousness of this kitten knew no bounds. One moment he could be found swinging from the curtains – which were soon in shreds – if in a rebellious mood. A few minutes later, I'd hear the pitter-patter of tiny paws behind me before catching a sudden glimpse of a silver furred missile flying past my head and then literally bouncing off the walls like an electric current.

'Bad kitten!' I said sternly as the green-eyed assassin hurtled toward me with his tail raised upright and ears pricked. But nothing stopped his angry onslaught. He climbed up the double podium cat tree and began performing cat calisthenics, narrowly missing Ryan's and my heads. I picked him up and dropped him on the floor to try and calm him. Fat chance. He simply sashayed off with his tail in the air.

Finally, Ryan and I hit on the only strategy that worked when the kitten was becoming too violent: water. Whenever he was charging Iko or Niko or launching himself at us, we'd squirt him with a water gun and he would scurry off in retreat to lick himself dry and think of another attack plan.

I couldn't believe how such a small innocent animal could change so suddenly and become such a monster. He was like one of those shape-shifting creatures famous in Japanese folklore. It was so hard to believe that this demon kitten was the same one who would sing for his milk before supper, his elfin angular features quivering at first sight of his silver dish. Purring loudly, he would gently rub against my leg before bedtime. In the morning though, he was Ninja Attack Kitten again.

I'd had kittens before, but none with such a destructive nature. Finally, I decided it was time to take him to the vets and get some advice. Maybe there was something physically wrong with him that was causing this outlandish behaviour, or maybe the vet could help with advice on how to change such a war-mongering attitude.

To my astonishment, when I took him to the vets, the kitten switched personalities again. He was completely well-behaved during his first consultation and exam, and with a complete stranger, too.

'*Amerika no short hair desu ka?*' the vet asked as he picked him up to examine him.

I shook my head. *Kawaii*, he most certainly was, but an American shorthair he most definitely was not.

Still, it was true that he did look more exotic than the traditional Japanese bobtail, which has a stocky build with brown patches and a short tail. The kitten's pricked over-sized ears, extremely long back legs, and triangular face gave him an alien-like appearance (something we both had in common).

I described the kitten's aggressive behaviour.

Dr. Iguchi, the vet, nodded. 'Hai-tenshon. Violento kitten desu yo.'

'Yes, very bad,' I said showing him some scratches on my hand.

'*Sou desu ka?*' (Is that so?) He said with a smile.

It turned out that the kitten had nothing physically wrong with him. The aggression was in his nature. Dr. Iguchi gave him a full bill of health and we were sent home with the singularly unhelpful recommendation to feed him a more nutritious brand of cat food.

When we got home, I let the kitten out of his carrier and we regarded each other. 'What am I going to do with you?' I asked.

He looked at me as if to say, 'Why should you do anything with me? I'm perfect the way I am.'

He had the most personality I'd ever encountered in a cat. This small silver tabby could express more emotion and more comments with his black-rimmed green eyes than many people could with words. He was a human in a cat suit: a soul who had once had the ability to speak with words and now could only communicate with eyes, body, and tail.

And express himself he did. When not engaged in battle, he always held himself with a superior air: an emperor in kitten's clothing, noble in appearance and attitude.

Ryan and I had posted flyers trying to find the kitten's original owners, but no one had responded. We couldn't keep calling him 'the kitten' and 'hellcat.' He needed a name. Because of his skillful ping pong ball work, we considered the names *Beckham* and *Pele*, but they seemed too obvious. Later we thought of Hirohito, because of his establishment of his imperial reign. But nothing felt right for this charming little terror.

Then one day, quite by chance, the peaceful chords of a cello filled our sparsely decorated apartment. Ryan and I were watching the Japanese television network NHK, which was airing a documentary about the work of famed German composer Johannes Sebastian Bach. To my amazement, the lovely music had an almost instant impact on the kitten. His high-octane nature reversed itself, his usually tense body relaxed, and his green eyes slid half shut.

That music could have such a dramatic impact on the kitten led Ryan and I to discuss all sorts of musician, singer, and composer names for him. We finally settled on Gershwin, 'G' for short.

And now, besides a name, we also had a new strategy to calm him down whenever his energy or aggression were dialed up too high. We tuned the radio to the classical music station, to be turned on when needed.

'This is only a temporary solution,' Ryan warned, and I agreed. It didn't matter that it was the idea of living with cats that had helped lure me back to Japan in the first place. It didn't matter that I was crazy in love with Gershwin and Ryan loved him, too. The apartment was meant to be a two-cat household, not a three-cat household. The responsible thing to do was to find Gershwin a permanent home, preferably as a single cat.

After a couple of weeks, when no one responded to the flyers we'd posted for the Ninja Kitten, Ryan and I approached our friends, co-workers, and acquaintances. But no one wanted a rambunctious cat.

So, I turned to the Internet and, after an exhaustive search, I found just *one* Japanese animal charity run by a British woman. But it was far away in Osaka. So, I emailed her to see if she knew of any cat animal shelters, humane societies, or sanctuaries in Gifu. Sadly, to her knowledge, there were none.

'What do the Japanese do when they find strays and they don't have an RSPCA or animal welfare group to help them?' I demanded of Ryan.

'They probably try to rehome them through friends or leave them on the streets, or in a forest,' he said sadly.

If there was an animal shelter out there, I couldn't find it. The Osaka charity kindly offered to put a photo of Gershwin on their website, and suggested that I try advertising with vets and in the local newspaper. I took her advice but, again, we had no response.

'Try not to worry too much,' Ryan said reassuringly that evening. 'We'll find Gershwin a home. Maybe one of the vet adverts will work.'

On the following morning, I was rudely awakened by a sharp pulsating pain in my abdomen. I cursed and opened my eyes to be met by a piercing pair of unblinking green eyes. Gershwin placed his paws atop my full bladder and began to knead it. He was already developing ways to manipulate humans. In the morning, every morning, he wanted his breakfast, which meant he needed me to get up.

This feline routine had been happening with greater regularity. Ryan called it 'the bladder stomp.'

I had never been known for my love of mornings. With such a determined furry alarm clock, though, it was becoming impossible to lie in and be lazy and avoid the day. Gershwin's new morning ritual was breaking me from a bad habit I'd spent far too long indulging.

On this particular morning, however, he was unusually persistent, even for him. Then all three cats began running around the bedroom agitatedly, meowing incessantly. I pulled the covers over my head, turned on my side to protect my bladder, and tried my best to ignore them.

But their meows grew more ferocious. The three of them were making sounds I had never heard out of a cat before and Gershwin, who had got back on the bed, was digging his claws even deeper into my easily-pierced flesh.

Reluctantly, I crawled out of bed to see what in hell had turned my cats into psycho-kitties. No sooner had I pulled on my dressing gown, than the old clinic windows began rattling loudly, sending the cats scurrying for cover under the bed. I had no idea what was happening until I heard the city's warning sirens.

Earthquake!

I was home alone and I didn't know where to go or what to do. Panicked, I crawled under the bedroom table like I'd seen people in movies do and huddled there waiting (and praying) for the tremors to pass. I wrapped my dressing gown tightly around my body as everything in the apartment shook. Books flew off shelves. Chairs hopped across the floor. The windowpane shook so violently, I was sure it would break. The very floor I clung to pulsated.

In the midst of my fear, I realised that Iko, Niko, and Gershwin's harassment this morning had been their desperate attempts to warn me that an earthquake was coming. They had known long before the humans' seismographic sensors had known what was coming. In the midst of my fear, I felt my love for that feline trio triple.

Thankfully, the earthquake passed in a few minutes. I cuddled the cats to reassure them (and me), and thank them for their early warning.

Though it had scared me to death, the earthquake really hadn't been terribly strong by Japanese standards. No buildings had been levelled and my home was relatively undamaged. The country's propensity for earthquakes was something Ryan and I had *not* considered when deciding to come back to work in Japan.

According to Japanese mythology, the *Namazu*, or giant catfish, lives under the islands of Japan. Whenever it moves, the ground shakes. Being a fish, it moves a lot. I told myself to learn much more about earthquake safety procedures, should the *Namazu* decide to make itself known again, and to pay much more attention to the cats' warnings of changes in atmospheric pressure.

On the evening after the earthquake, I gazed fondly over at Iko, Niko, and Gershwin, who were eating their dinners contentedly while Ryan and I prepared our own meal. With no response to our flyers, Ryan and I had decided to put the idea of re-homing Gershwin on a back burner. We truly had done all we could to find him a new home. It seemed – to our secret joy – that he was meant to be a permanent member of our temporary Japanese family.

Because of these three cats, I was learning truly, deeply, and for the first time in my life the importance of trust and companionship, commitment and caring. Because of them, I was shedding a lifetime of loneliness and rejection.

And yet . . . Ryan and I had never intended to stay more than a year in Japan. When our contract at the school was up, we would leave. We would leave Iko, Niko, and Gershwin and then, even with Ryan, my life would be lonely again.

Chapter 4: Like a Cat Playing with a Walnut

猫が胡桃を回すよう / Neko Ga Kurumi Wo Mawasu You

Shinto, which means both spirit path and the way of the gods, is the indigenous religion of Japan, originating around 300 BCE. In 1882, it actually became the state religion. Shinto has a reverence for balance, harmony, purity, Nature, family and ancestors, physical well-being, and subordinating the individual to the group. That reverence was so imbedded into society over the centuries that it became the foundation for Japanese culture. Today, close to eighty percent of Japanese espouse belief in Shinto tenets.

Shinto focuses on *Kami* or spirit, found throughout Nature in trees, mountains, rocks, rivers, animals, and even people. In Shinto, spirit and human beings are one. I never knew about Shintoism until I lived in Takayama, but it quickly spoke to something deep within me. I was particularly drawn to the Shinto reverence for Nature and how God and Nature are viewed as one of the same.

The religion celebrates many different things and has many different festivals, which is how I was first introduced to Shinto. One night, at Bagus bar, Tamotsu, the owner said to me:

'Come see my penis.'

I was stunned. Tamotsu was happily married. Surely he was not making a lewd advance?

No, he wasn't. He and his friend were carving a phallus effigy for *Kanamara Matsuri*, the Shinto festival of fertility held in Spring. With its love of balance, Shinto also has the *Hime-No-Miya* (Grand Vagina Festival), which celebrates, you've guessed it, vaginas. Both very popular 1,500-year-old fertility festivals are designed to further a good harvest and generate more babies. Unlike so many Western cultures, Japan has never been ashamed of sex.

While my prudish British upbringing kept me from running around a mountain-top half-naked with a giant phallus, there were other Shinto festivals with which I was fully on board.

Festivals are held throughout the country. Takayama puts on its own spectacular display, called the Hida Takayama Festival. (It also has an autumn Hida Festival.)

Shinto in origin, Takayama's Hida Festival dates back to the seventeenth century. It is renowned throughout Japan for its beauty, and particularly for twelve spectacular floats accompanied by sacred flute and percussion music and participants who are dressed in traditional Edo costumes. When I heard the word *yatai*, which means floats, my mind instantly conjured the plywood, chicken wire, and *papier maché* floats found in many Western parades. Takayama blew up my expectations like a firecracker under a balloon.

I could feel excitement for the coming festival bubbling up under the parks and streets and buildings, infecting everyone. The locals who were going to actually participate in the festival took their responsibilities very *very* seriously. Wherever I walked through the town, at any time of day, I would see men, women, and children practicing lion dancing and drum and flute playing. Other Takayamans were busy cleaning the town, literally scrubbing everything in sight.

Colourful two and three metre-long paper lanterns, flags, and streamers hung from streetlights and doorways, swaying gently in the breeze. Imitation pink cherry blossoms poked out of shop windows and streetlights, and purple plastic flowers decorated traditional paper umbrellas hung high above street level. Even our school had been decorated with bright pink plastic cherry blossoms and covered the walls with posters of the magnificent floats.

Even though I wasn't keen on the prospect of packed streets and raucous spectators on the actual day of the festival, I was happy to get involved and the school gave me the perfect outlet.

First, I encouraged many of my adult students to practise their English in class by telling the history of the festival. Some were more successful than others. Nevertheless, thanks to their lessons, I soon had a good grasp of what was happening throughout Takayama and why.

On the morning of the big day, Ryan and I walked to the top of Honmachi Street to join the crowds. We were sucked instantly into the festival excitement. *Hundreds of thousands* of people had come together for this festival in our usually quiet mountain town. It was a convivial mix of eager foreign tourists, mostly Chinese, happy Japanese tourists, and good-natured kimono-clad locals. Children, from babies to teens, wore perfectly customised blue and grey kimonos, the girls had their hair pulled up into geisha-style buns. All of the kids and adolescents carried themselves like grown up royalty.

Amidst the press of people and the warm sunlight, the gentle mountain breeze was cool and delicious. Silent anticipation dominated the crowd as tourists fiddled with their cameras in preparation for the parade and children strained to be the first to see the floats. Little ones were lifted onto their parents' shoulders. Aside from the odd muttering in Mandarin from the Chinese tourists, the only sound came from the banners flapping in the breeze.

Ryan and I carefully maneuvered our way through the crowd. We finally positioned ourselves to the left of the glistening red Nakabashi Bridge, which would give us a clear view of the floats as they were pulled onto Honmachi Street. To my surprise and enormous relief, I found there wasn't any of the pushing or shoving or irritated complaints that you might find in a Western crowd of this size. Everyone was happy and polite, even welcoming as Ryan and I settled in and waited eagerly for our first sight of the famed *yatai*.

Each of the twelve Festival floats had originally been sponsored by a rich merchant in a specific neighbourhood who had hired local artisans to build an extravagant confection that celebrated not only the merchant's wealth, but also his neighbourhood, the arts, and the gods. Children got to ride on the floats from their respective neighbourhoods while costumed men from their neighbourhoods pulled the floats through the streets.

Suddenly, we heard a huge roar go up from the crowd and traditional Japanese music began playing from street loudspeakers. The first float was on its way. My heart beat fast in my chest and I grabbed Ryan's arm in my excitement. 'I can't wait to see the float with the marionettes. I've heard so much about it.'

'Me, too,' he said.

From behind the throng of the backs of people's heads and their raised cameras, I saw a procession of men dressed in dark grey robes with giant rice paddy hats on their heads. '*Wow*,' I said when I saw the first float. 'It's huge!'

It was *Kagura-Tai*, 'The Way Opener.' A pair of gold metal upraised wings glistened in the sunlight. They rested upon a gold and black metal disk which, in turn, was supported by a mini-temple: glossy black and orange with red doors on each side. Intricate carvings decorated the two-tier base of the temple. The big wheels were black and gold. Ryan and I had to tilt our heads back to see everything. The *Kagura-Tai* float was being pulled down the street by six men dressed in white, while four flute players in brown robes walking with it played the loveliest airy spring music.

Ryan (snapping photos non-stop) and I cheered and applauded loudly along with the crowd around us.

I gasped again when I saw what followed: a golden *mikoshi* (portable shrine) in which stood the statue of a Shinto deity taking a brief tour of the town, pulled by men dressed all in white.

The *mikoshi* was followed by an elaborately carved black and red and gold lacquered shrine *two storeys tall* riding on giant metal and wood wheels and pulled by Japanese men in gorgeous blue and white kimonos, white gloves on their hands, saucer-shaped metal hats on their heads.

'This is just stunning,' I said in wonder.

'There's something otherworldly about it,' Ryan said, snapping more photos as the *yatai* passed us by.

Next, heralded by the thumping sound of drums and bamboo flutes played by street musicians, came the four-hundred-year-old *Kinzoujishi*, the acrobatic Lion Dance, performed by the older children and teenagers from the town, each of whom wore a ferocious-looking lion's head (made from orange fabric) and a green patterned kimono.

The dance re-enacts the true story of Kinzou and Okame, two sweethearts who, individually and together, battled a wild lion that had been terrorising the town and destroying farm land. When they were finally victorious, saving Takayama from destruction, the citizens honoured Kinzou and Okame by deifying them. Ever since, they have been the town's God and Goddess of abundance and happy family.

Before us, the acrobatic back and forth battle of ferocious lion and determined male and female warriors who leapt onto the lion's back and were thrown off, was a carefully choreographed dance that enthralled me, but frightened a few children in the crowd into tears.

'Do you want to go home yet?' Ryan asked as the Lion Dance passed us by.

'Not yet,' I said, surprising both him and me.

'Let's go over toward the Old Town,' I said. 'Maybe we can get a better view.'

Ryan and I slid – politely – through the crowd to get a closer view of the amazing *Karakuri Ningyo*, mechanical puppets that burst out of three of the floats. They looked like mini-wizards, dressed in black and red capes, with long white beards. They cast spells on all the spectators, and spun around, and even danced to recorded music played over loudspeakers and by human musicians walking with the floats. Their disjointed movements were surreal, because they looked so human, particularly from a distance.

On one float, an old man marionette burst out of a vase and threw cherry blossoms to the crowd. On another, a drummer marionette leaned back at a ninety-degree angle and then jerked upright to strike the gong in front of him again and again and again. Loud applause greeted each new float, the *yatai* creaking and swaying a little as they were pulled down Honmachi Street. Ryan and I clapped just as loud and long as everyone else.

Looking around at the immense enthralled crowds, I suddenly felt the most intense gratitude that I could be one of their number, that I too could witness and drink in this spectacular display found in no other city, no other country.

I was so grateful to be a part of Takayama.

After the parade, Ryan and I glided along with the crowd for a while, moving like a raft down a stream, its gentle current pushing us forward through a steady sea of people. When we reached a side street, we snaked off.

While we had been wandering, I had been salivating. The rich fragrant aromas of the famous *Mitarashi Dango* (skewered sweet rice flour dumplings) had been tantalising and tormenting me. I followed that intoxicating scent to a pavement food stand where a little old lady wearing a pale blue apron, a white scarf covering her head, was calmly and methodically feeding the large crowd of eager people gathered around her.

It took a while, but we finally made it to the front of the line and claimed our prizes. We sat down on a low stone wall and slid the chewy soy-glazed *dangos* into our mouths.

'Oh my God, I'm in love!' I said around a big bite of *dango*. 'These are amazing! Why haven't we tried them before?'

'Because *you* never wanted to,' Ryan said with a wink.

Oh. Right. Note to self: take more chances with Japanese food.

As I chewed my third *dango*, I noticed a young Japanese couple sitting on a patch of grass with a very small tabby kitten on a lead. I cannot resist any cat, particularly kittens, and I was curious about that lead. I'd been thinking about using a lead on the cats for a while. So, I got up, walked over to them, bowed, introduced myself, and leaned down to pet the tabby.

'*Kawaii*. She's so cute,' I said as I touched the tiny blue cotton strap. 'Is this a cat harness? It's so small.'

'No, it's a . . .' The young woman's words trailed off as she tried to think of the translation. '*Rabbito beruto desu,*' She said. The harness had been designed for rabbits.

Hm. Would Iko, Niko and Gershwin submit to wearing a harness? Would they accept a lead? If they did, I would be able to take them outside without arousing my neighbours' ire.

As I had done a week before when I let Iko and Niko outside. It seemed cruel to keep them inside when it was so beautiful outside. They never roamed far and were usually back home within an hour, ready for their mid-morning naps.

One morning, as I was getting ready for work, I heard a knock at the door. I peered through the frosted glass and could just make out the figure of a man. I pulled open the door and there stood the school's owner, Mr. Iwaki, looking significantly less friendly than usual.

'Oh lord,' I said inwardly, 'what's gone wrong now? Has there been a complaint? Was there a drop in student numbers? Did I do something wrong?'

As I stood there in my navy blue dressing gown and blue spotted slippers, completely unprepared for his surprise visit, he said: '*Big puroburemu.*'

40

Big problem? Wonderful. '*Nani?*' (what), I asked. (My Japanese had improved.)

'Katto outosaido.'

'Yes, I know. They're outdoor cats now.' I said proudly.

'Big puroburemu.'

There was an awkward silence. Why was Mr. Iwaki standing on my doorstep telling me my cats were a problem?

'Katto outosaido.'

'Yes, that's what cats do,' I said bewildered. Why was letting my cats outside causing such a fuss?

'*No outosaido toire.*' He pointed to the house opposite and made a squatting gesture.

I am no Sherlock Holmes, but I was still able to figure out that the neighbours across the street must have complained about Iko and Niko. These were the same neighbours who weeks before had informed the rubbish collectors of our failure to recycle properly, which resulted in a yellow label being unceremoniously plastered on our bin bags for all the world to see.

'*Big puroburemu,*' Mr. Iwaki said again.

I was instantly defensive. How dare someone target my cats for doing what Nature dictated? Was it because Iko and Niko lived with *gaijins*? Was the proximity of two Brits too much for our Japanese neighbours to handle?

Then it dawned on me: this was *Japan*. I had inadvertently humiliated Mr. Iwaki by letting the feline sisters urinate outside as Nature intended. It was the cat's choice of *location* for their WC that had prompted this intervention. Whether the sisters had been spotted performing the act or whether the stench of cat urine had reached some sensitive noses, I couldn't be sure. I might not agree with my neighbours' horror, but I could not let Mr. Iwaki suffer.

'I promise to keep them inside . . . for now,' I said.

'Please try,' he said.

I cringed inwardly, but kept a respectful smile on my face.

Still, I must confess to feeling downright gleeful a few days later when I saw a cat, unknown to me, position its bottom at the corner of my neighbour's house, lift its quivering tail, and pee . . . outside. My girls were vindicated.

As T.S Eliot once wrote:

For he will do

As he do do

And there's no doing anything about it!

Watching this tiny kitten sitting happily on a leash in the middle of the crowded streets had given me the sign I'd been looking for. To avoid any further issues with the neighbours I'd do the same with my cats.

Since we lived so close to the city centre, Ryan and I decided we'd go home for a while so we could freshen up before *yomatsuri* – the evening procession.

By the time we walked back to Honmachi Street, the sky was a dark indigo, and excitement permeated the air. The crowds had thinned just enough that, Ryan and I had more room to move around and watch. Suddenly, drums and Japanese flutes announced the evening procession. Camera flashes began sparking through the night.

The *yatai* were now adorned with glowing red and white paper lanterns, which lit up the night, adding a magical glow as men pulled them through the streets and even occasionally sang in deep baritone voices with the music.

Unlike the morning procession where the *yatai* all stayed together in a long line as they paraded through town, the evening floats began to separate, each taking a different street to circle the historic town.

In the dark, the *yatai* looked like they were floating elegantly along gentle rivers through the town, not rolling through streets. Watching them gliding through town, I felt the greatest happiness. And was grateful to Ryan for pushing me to come back to Japan.

Having once sipped the joyous nectar of a Japanese festival, Ryan and I were hungry for more. Much more.

Fortunately, just five days later, our receptionist, Kimiko, invited us to join her for a spring festival in her home town of Furukawa, just a thirty minute drive from Takayama.

Furukawa is a much smaller historic gem of a town in northern Hida surrounded by forests and mountains. Famed for the historically skillful craftsmanship of its carpenters, Furukawa has a beautifully preserved ancient town centre, old houses with wood-slatted windows, narrow commercial streets crowded with two- and three-storey buildings, and a narrow stone and concrete-lined canal in which schools of big orange koi swim past gleaming white storehouses.

After we parked, we strolled along Furukawa's canals and tossed bread to the brightly coloured carp. Furukawa is also famous for its stone-walled Shinto shrines and Buddhist temples, so we visited a few of them.

The temple interior, lit by dozens of candles, had stone floors and a golden central altar where incense burned, tendrils of smoke snaking outside to perfume the night air. The crowd around us threw coins into a hole in the ground beside an incense table to bring themselves good fortune.

I was quite moved that so many families – children, parents, grandparents – visited the temples together. It was a community gathering and a spiritual gathering all in one.

As the sunlight faded and the evening grew colder, we could feel the burgeoning anticipation in the air, which quickly infected us, for we had come to see what is called the 'Naked Festival,' which had been celebrated in Furukawa for 1,200 years.

As we drew near the town centre, Ryan's and I saw to our amazement that the streets were swarming with men who, despite the cold, wore only a small piece of cloth that covered nothing but their nether region (and not even that particularly well).

'I've never seen so many men wearing nappies before,' Ryan said, which made us laugh.

Kimiko shook her head at us with a smile. 'Those nappies are actually loincloths and they're called *fundoshi*.'

'*Fundoshi*. Right. Sorry,' Ryan said with a wry smile.

'I didn't realise there were so many people in Furukawa,' I said.

'There's not,' Kimiko said. 'Most of these men either study or work in Tokyo and come back especially for this festival.'

The official procession began with beautiful lantern-lit floats, similar to those we had seen in Takayama. They alone were worth the trip and the cold. Then the deep bass sound of a huge drum being beaten reverberated up and down the street, and up and down my spine.

Throngs of people now lined the streets, often three or four people deep. Children were perched on their parents' shoulders and foreigners stood on tiptoe to watch the spectacle. In the houses all around us, people sat in the windows and even on the roofs.

As I peered over the shoulder of the man standing directly in front of me, I saw a sea of bare bottoms moving faster and faster toward an *Okoshi Daiko*, a massive drum perched on top of a tower that was being carried through the streets by hundreds of *fundoshi*-wearing men. Two men sat on either side of the drum and beat it one at a time, the deep basso boom rumbling in my belly.

The bare bottomed men converging on the drum tower were representatives of twelve neighbourhood groups. Each group had its own *Tsuke Daiko*, a staff about three metres long that was attached to a small drum. Their goal, Kimiko told us, was to get their *Tsuke Daiko* as close to the huge *Okoshi Daiko* as possible, because the closer they got, the more prestige they earned.

Of course, each of the neighbourhood groups was trying to get closest to the huge drum tower which led, inevitably, to a running battle. Blood was not drawn, but a good deal of pushing and rough shoving ensued, sometimes catching up the innocent spectators in their midst. It was hard to believe these people were Japan's normally quiet, socially conforming, polite salarymen. The atmosphere was verging on the scenes you see after a premiership football match. It was fuelled by just as much alcohol – in this case saké – as in England, but it had much more good-natured shoving. Most of the time.

Meanwhile, in the midst of this insanity, other loin-cloth-wearing men balanced daringly atop what looked like thirty-metre-tall poles while large raucous crowds surrounded them and cheered them on.

As a first-time participant in this renowned *matsuri*, it seemed to me that everyone in Furukawa had completely lost their minds. I loved it.

Going from the peace of the temples to this insanity, I was shocked, stunned, that Japanese people would behave in this very raucous un-

Japanese manner.

Ryan laughed himself silly through it all.

'He's taking cultural immersion too far,' Ryan said with a grin, pointing toward the only nappy-wearing foreigner in the crowd. The sagging of his behind suggested he was older than the average *matsuri* participant.

'Look at *him*,' Ryan said, pointing upward.

We turned around and craned our heads in time to see a rather large Japanese man balancing precariously on his stomach on top of a high post, which must have been at least five-metres high.

We stared at him incredulously. 'Someone's going to get hurt,' I said.

'He looks like he might fall,' Ryan agreed.

'I hope he doesn't land on me,' I said as we stared up at the bulky spread-eagled man hovering haphazardly overhead, the crowd cheering him.

The Furukawa festival was everything that Japan usually is not: reckless, loud, and boisterous. I wondered if it acted as a safety valve: allowing people constrained by rigid social rules throughout the year to really let off steam from night to morning without having to worry about the consequences.

It was wonderfully entertaining, but I confess to feeling a little relieved when Kimiko suggested it was time to join her mother for dinner. The crowd was getting a bit too intense for me. Besides, I was starving.

Fortunately, her family home was just a few blocks away on one of the main streets, so we made our way through the crowd, passing under the eyes of hundreds of people perched high up on the surrounding rooftops to get a better view of the festival.

Kimiko's family home was an historic dark wood three-storey townhouse with a wood slat roof and dark wood shutters. It was bordered on either side by equally historic townhouses, leaving no room for even a single potted plant.

Kimiko opened the black lacquered front door and there was her mother, waiting to greet us. Kimiko provided the formal introductions, and Ryan and I bowed to her mother, who was short with greying hair. She wore the usual pinafore, a collarless sleeveless dress worn over her clothes that all the Japanese housewives seem to wear when they are cleaning or cooking.

I forced myself to smile at the introductions to hide my unease. I was panicking about making a major *faux pas* at the dinner table, like eating the last bit of food from a dish, as I'd done previously, and had consequently been labelled as 'unreserved' (a terrible charge) and about as far away from *enryo* as one could get.

Enryo (having self-restraint) is central to Japan's culture. The people work daily to prevent conflict through their own self-control which, I had learned in my first months in Takayama, I was still some way from achieving.

Kimiko's mother led us into the sparse dining room: white walls, tatami mats on the floor, and a window that looked out onto the street. Ryan and I sat down awkwardly at the low traditional dining table.

Kimiko's mother had lovingly prepared traditional food, which she presented one by one in brown and black lacquered bowls. There was, of course rice, fish, and mountains of vegetables. As usual for Japanese meals, each of the dishes was cold.

'*itadakimasu*,' said Kimiko's mother.

She and Kimiko clasped their hands together and bowed their heads at the same time. Ryan and I quickly joined them.

'*Ikki daki masu* means "I humbly receive,"' Kimiko explained to us as bowls and platters were passed around the table. 'It is similar to "*Bon appetite*" in French, or a little like saying grace. In Buddhism and Japanese culture, we are saying thanks, not just to the cook, but to Nature, to the animals and plants who sustain us as well.'

The Japanese, I had learned, were appreciative of most things, including the things I usually took for granted. Their endless use of the word '*sugoi*,' which means great or amazing, over simple everyday things constantly surprised me. How could they be so enthusiastic over the sight of a cake or another person's holiday photos that they had seen a trillion times before?

Sitting at that table filled with delicious food and good company,

I realised that I *was* surprised . . . by my blatant indifference. I couldn't believe how wrong I had been.

In England, I had been obsessed with material things, ignoring the beauty and many basic pleasures that were in my world. In Japan, I realised, I had not only started enjoying the simple things – good health, drinking green tea, going for walks – I had *absorbed* that enjoyment rather than simply noting it and forgetting it. I had also stopped obsessing so much about the things that were absent from my life, like parents, connection with my extended family, and financial solvency.

This was a gift indeed. Maybe, just maybe, I wouldn't always feel like something was missing in my life. Maybe this new Japanese perspective would help me to see my world with new eyes and finally help fill the holes within me.

Without realising it, in these last months I had been falling in love with the Japanese way of life that was so very different from my Anglo-Saxon upbringing. I admired the Japanese respect for family and the elderly. I appreciated the culture of politeness.

Surrounded in Takayama by the grand beauty of Nature, I was breathing differently, seeing differently, thinking differently. It was propelling me forward. I was finally leaving my past where it belonged: in the past.

Sitting at that table with Ryan beside me and Kimiko and her mother opposite us, it felt like Japan was an opportunity to reboot myself. It was a chance to rebrand and present a new me to the world. It was up to me to stop harrying myself with thoughts of the past and to stop sabotaging my own happiness. It was up to me to claim the peace, the joy, and the love I wanted.

In a few short months, I had come to think of our worn-out apartment, the cats, and Takayama as home. They *felt* like home as my previous flats never really had. *Sugoi.*

Chapter 5: A Long Bath from a Cat's Tongue

猫舌の長風呂入り / Nekojita No Nagaburoiri

The shimmering golden light that seeped through our bedroom window seemed more magical than usual this morning. Something was different . . . I just couldn't put my finger on what.

Ryan had already left for the kindergarten. That was normal on a Tuesday. The cats were awake and padding noisily up and down the long corridor *encouraging* me to feed them. That was normal, too. A little frustrated that I couldn't identify the difference in the morning, I got up, dished out the cat kibble, and got ready for work.

It was as I was cycling along my usual route, starting from behind the Red Cross Hospital and then crisscrossing between rice paddies, that the Something Different finally hit me. Today was significantly hotter than yesterday around 26°C or 78.8°F, augmented by a humid breeze that swept in a desultory fashion across the city.

It was like someone had flicked a switch overnight and suddenly *Natsu*, summer, had leapt forth. The unmistakable blaring hum of the cicadas broadcasting their familiar summer love anthem to attract mates escorted me through the rice paddies and then the streets.

I passed a group of schoolchildren who looked startlingly different. No longer hidden from the world in their heavy winter uniforms, they had all changed *en masse* into lightweight summer uniforms, with the girls sporting even higher hemlines.

The Japanese workers I passed had also changed their attire. The women now wore pastel shades, and some of them, whom I recognised, were sporting noticeably shorter haircuts. As for the men, instead of jackets and trousers, they were now wearing short-sleeved shirts, no jackets and (perhaps the greatest shock of the morning) no ties.

Obviously, Takayama, and perhaps all of Japan, had strict guidelines on when to acknowledge summer and how to dress for it, but no one had bothered to tell me. I felt a little foolish and out of place cycling along in my black trousers, camel cardigan, and black boots, visually clinging to spring while summer rioted around me.

I was wholly unprepared for the season. In fact, I hadn't really been aware that it was approaching. Unlike England and Australia, Japan doesn't have Daylight Savings Time (DST), so summer had managed to sneak up on me. Mind you, I was grateful not to have to endure the hour-long sleep deprivation of DST, but I felt a little discombobulated not to have it. I also felt odd realising that I associated the changing of the season with the changing of the clock, rather than with the changing of the leaves on the trees, or the higher temperature and humidity, or the frenzied activities of insects and animals alike. The Japanese, I decided, had it right.

When I arrived at school, I asked Kimiko, why everyone suddenly looked different today.

'Oh. It's *Koromogae,* changing of the wardrobe day,' she said. 'It's officially summer now.'

'Everyone knows to change into summer clothes on this particular day?' I said, unable to believe that people could be so regimented.

'Yes. It is Japanese custom. The first of June is when summer officially starts.'

'I'd better go to UNIQLO [a popular store] and stock up on shorts, then,' I said a little sarcastically.

She smiled as if to suggest I should.

Humbled, I walked into my classroom filled with summer clothes-wearing students.

At break time, I decided to get a cup of tea from the vending machine downstairs. But my usual choice was not available. The light that announced tea was ready and waiting for me was not lit. I put in my money, pressed my usual button, and nothing happened. I pressed the red button again. Nothing.

'*Nani?*' (what?) I said to myself and tried again.

Still nothing.

I tried again, but the vending machine lights stubbornly only lit up for cold drinks. Apparently, the hot beverages had been switched off! Now, anyone knows that the English enjoy a cup of hot tea no matter what the weather, but in Japan it seemed that not only fashions, but drinks, too, were changed at this time of year.

I went back upstairs to grumble.

'Kimiko, do you know why the hot drinks aren't working in the vending machine? Don't tell me,' I said, holding up my hand. 'It's *Koromogae.*'

'Yes, of course.'

'But what if I want a hot coffee or tea, what then?'

She smiled at me a little strangely, clearly wondering why I would want to have a hot drink in summer, and why I was making such a big fuss over it.

That smile made me finally realise that *I* was the weird one for over-thinking a centuries-old custom. I did some quick mental and internal reshuffling. Away from home, hot drinks, from vending machines, at least, would have to wait until autumn.

Summer might have closed the door on vending machine tea for me, but it was about to open another door: the city's only public swimming pool near the kindergarten where I taught was scheduled to open on the first of July . . . even though it was already hot in June . . . and it would remain open for exactly two months. Even though it would still be hot in September and even October, the pool would close at the end of August and go back to its ten-month-long hibernation.

I was so excited at the prospect of having somewhere to relax outside and cool down in the hot summer that, while Ryan was trapped in a classroom with kindergartners, I made sure to get to the pool early in the morning on the First of July for its official opening.

Set in a quiet neighbourhood adjacent to a large wilderness area on the opposite side of town from our apartment, the Junior Olympic pool was surrounded by shade trees, with a children's pool on one side and a large lap pool for adults on the other. The facilities may have been a little worn, but the place had character and it was clean and well organised. I was so happy, I was practically humming as I pulled on my swimsuit in the changing room.

I wasn't the only one who had got to the pool early on its first day. Ten or so people, mostly mothers and their children plus a few slender looking middle-aged men stretching with such purpose it seemed as if they were about to enter a swimming competition, were as eager as I to enjoy the pool's opening.

I set my things on a lounge, then sat by the water enjoying the sun's warmth on my face. When I finally got in the pool, I swam slowly for about ten lengths, luxuriating in the coldness of the water on an already hot morning.

The poolside lounge I had picked gave me a perfect view of the entire pool area so I could people watch to my heart's content. I dried myself off and set myself up for a day of lounging in the sun.

Just as I opened my book – Salman Rushdie's *Midnight Children* – eager to lose myself in his colourful language, I heard the pitter-patter of piano music spill out from speakers around the pool. To my amazement, everyone stopped what he or she was doing and rushed out of the pool. As if they had been rehearsing for weeks, they got into horizontal lines on each side of the pool. '*What is going on?*' I wondered.

I looked around and that was when I became painfully aware that I was the lone hold-out. Afraid that the *gaijin* was committing some huge public solecism, I scrambled off my lounge and got into the line nearest me behind one of the men who had been stretching earlier with such determination.

With perfect precision, everyone, including the children, stood to attention and, on the count of ichi, proceeded to perform the famous rajio taiso – warm-up calisthenics – in time to the rajio taiso music coming out of the speakers, courtesy of the NHK radio broadcasting company.

I'd seen this carefully choreographed routine performed by children at Kindergarten, but not outdoors in a public place where anyone and everyone joined in. I wasn't convinced my strength, stamina, and flexibility were good enough for public display, but I was in Japan and when in Japan, I joined in.

This nearly century-old cultural institution is said to promote 'health among the population' by getting the population to stretch in unison. I liked the way everyone at the pool participated. It felt inclusive and fun, even if I did feel a little odd and self-conscious learning the routine.

After the six-minute-long calisthenics ended, I was well and truly warmed up. I settled back down to enjoy my book, with interruptions every hour for another round of *rajio taiso*. At this rate, I was going to be the fittest *gaijin* in Takayama.

Having sampled the pleasures of a public swimming pool, I was more willing to listen to my friend Sayuri, who had been trying for months to get me to join her at a bathhouse.

We had clicked immediately when Ryan introduced us at school. She was his student and was planning to go to London and study English.

Sayuri was not your average self-effacing twenty-something Japanese woman. Largely unmotivated by money or designer brands, she was an aromatherapist by day and a fun-loving free spirit at night. From the moment we met we regularly got together for gentle interrogations about each other's lives.

Still, it made no sense to me to go somewhere very hot on an already hot day. Where was the relaxation in that? But Sayuri persisted and, before the summer temperatures soared even higher, I finally accepted her invitation.

The ritual of bathing is serious business in Japan. It gets its power from both its connection to Shinto purification practises – the idea that bathing creates not only a clean body, but also a clean mind and spirit – and from its emphasis on community.

You don't bathe alone in Japan.

The idea of sitting in a pool of boiling hot water with a bunch of naked women wasn't my idea of fun. Exposing my body to a bunch of strangers who would probably gorp at me, not only because I was naked, but because I was naked and foreign, would make me feel more than just a tad self-conscious.

But Sayuri steadily eroded my resistance.

'*Dai joubu* (It's no problem),' she said. 'Nobody will look at you. Too much thinking. Just enjoy.'

I wasn't looking forward to baring my bouche in public, let alone my breasts, which were significantly larger than the Japanese norm, because that, no matter what Sayuri said, might mean staring. But after several weeks of her gentle persuasion, I managed to pluck up enough courage to parade my pubes in public. If Sayuri didn't care if her wobbly bits were on display, why should I be embarrassed?

We decided to meet at a small and less busy bathhouse in a quiet residential district on the outskirts of the north side of town for my initiation into the traditional Japanese spa bath (*onsen*). Because this *onsen* was new, and most of the locals hadn't discovered it yet, I wouldn't have hordes staring at me.

The bathhouse exterior looked like a normal brick building with no distinguishing features. The foyer was a different story. It was painted a shade of pastel pink you might see in a nursery, and had stacks of carefully folded and organised white towels in a corner. Lift music filled the air.

As Sayuri and I entered the *onsen* changing rooms, I caught my first glance of a nipple, then another . . . then another . . . and another. There were literally more nipples in front of me than in a maternity ward. All of them were attached to a wide variety of young, middle-aged, and old breasts.

In the past, I'd heard rumours that a common feature among Japanese women was the unruly bouche, and I'd heard some male *gaijins* make unsavoury remarks about the size of Japanese women's bouches. Up until now I had thought it was just culture clash mixed with the harsh words of bitter lovers. In this changing room, however, I was confronted with more pubic hair than I'd ever seen in my life.

Caught unaware, I realised *I* was the one who was staring, more out of self-interest than anything else. I loathed wasting my hard-earned money on waxing, it went against my feminist principles, and it bloody well hurt. So this Japanese freedom of the bouche was liberating. It got me rethinking Western society's obsession with the bottlebrush, the landing strip, and the hedge cut.

I shuffled over to a shower cubicle to get some welcome privacy, being particularly careful as I maneuvered through the other women not to drop my crotch towel (which was literally the size of my crotch).

As I shuffled, I became aware that all eyes were on the *gaijin* (foreigner), and I don't think it was merely curiosity. I racked my brain to make sure I was doing everything in the correct order, which in Japan can often be a minefield.

The problem was, Sayuri seemed to think I automatically knew what to do and had disappeared into a white cloud of steam. Desperate, I sat alone in a corner and surreptitiously observed the other women performing the correct order of the *onsen*.

53

Fortunately, it seemed I had stumbled into the right section. Even better, above my shower cubicle was a sign demonstrating to the ignorant (and barbaric) *gaijin* how to bathe. Rather than feel disparaged by the patronising verbiage, I studied the four images indicating what the *gaijin* could do wrong in this situation, and I had to agree they made sense.

For the Japanese, standing while taking a shower before using the spa is a major *faux pas*, as is shaving or using soap in the *onsen*. To outsiders, these rules might seem strange, but they made sense within the culture I now lived.

To avoid causing an uproar, I followed the rules carefully. I sat down on the little white stool in my shower cubicle, taking care not to stand when I reached for my shampoo bottle. I began washing my hair and then got myself into an entirely different lather.

While shampooing, I caught a glimpse of a woman's reflection in a nearby mirror. She seemed completely comfortable with her nakedness. The stark contrast between her casual ease and my continuing unease, along with the hypercritical attitudes among many Westerners, particularly Brits and Americans, toward nudity was startling and mind-opening. We're usually the first to strip and flaunt our attributes on a summer vacation at the beach or by a pool, but stripping in this more cultured setting seemed to freak us out. Why was it so difficult to bare all in a public bath?

Doing my best to shed cultural hypocrisy, I rinsed off and carefully let go of my crotch towel, like a child leaving their security blanket at home for the first time. Not sure what to do with it, I looked around and then placed it on my head like everyone else. Taking a deep breath, I walked with feigned nonchalance to the in-ground pool and dipped my toes in the sulphurous water. I dared a little more. Feeling the hot smooth water ripple against my legs, and trying my very best to avoid eye contact with the other women in the pool, I immersed myself.

It was glorious. The hot sulphorous water held me lovingly, soothing me, and relaxing every muscle I had.

Once I was acclimatised, I made my way awkwardly over to Sayuri, who was sandwiched between two *obaasans* (grandmother types). I sat opposite her, wanting to speak. But, like the unwritten law in the London underground, speaking is forbidden in an *onsen*.

I found the silence rather nice after awhile. The sensation of the soothing mineral water rippling against my skin felt both hot and healing. I allowed myself to lean back and luxuriate while keeping my eyes closed to avoid the quizzical glances I may, or may not, have been getting.

In an attempt to avert Japanese or self judgement, I decided to put my worries on a fluffy cloud and concentrate instead on the meditational powers of the water. My breathing became slower as I relaxed into the bubbling bliss. My thoughts were carried away with the steam, fading like condensation on the *onsen* walls. The shoji screens that separated the *onsen* from a small courtyard garden turned the rays of light into shadowy patterns on their delicate panels.

The bathhouse was creating space in my mind, slowing my usually cluttered and frenetic thoughts.

The Japanese, I decided, were definitely on to something. As I sat in this public oasis of peace, I finally understood author Kathy Lette's assertion that 'It's scientifically proven no woman ever shot her husband while she was having a soak.'

Now I understood why. I think that if the United Nations held all of its meetings in one giant *onsen*, we'd have world peace faster than you can say 'Bob's your uncle.'

I lingered in the hot mineral water and resisted getting out from enjoyment rather than embarrassment. Every inch of my body and brain felt intensely revitalised, more than I'd ever experienced before. The sensation was instantly addictive, and a far healthier pick-me-up than several rounds of Hennessy at the local pub.

After one dip, I was hooked. I remembered the famous Japanese woodblock prints by artists such as Kuniyoshi Utagawa, who anthropomorphised cats at the local bathhouse, and I wondered if Gershwin might like to join me on my next visit.

Chapter 6: A Cat's Craving for Cold

猫の寒乞い / Neko No Kangoi

With summer in full swing, I finally had the opportunity to hike up and explore Mount Norikura (aka Mount Norikuradake), the 3,025-metre (9,926-foot) high mountain that loomed over Takayama.

Norikura means 'riding saddle,' because that's what the third highest volcanic mountain in Japan looks like: a Japanese samurai saddle, sort of a cross between an English saddle and an American western saddle with a high pommel and back and a lower seat. Even in the depths of summer heat and humidity, glittering white snow covered the northeastern face of the mountain, attracting hikers, sending welcome cool breezes over the people trekking ever upward, and freshening the twelve crater lakes found all over the mountain.

Perhaps because of all the grey skies and rain in England, I had been primarily an indoor person during adulthood. In Takayama, however, I was discovering more and more that I got a tremendous amount of pleasure from walking around town, enjoying the gardens and the koi ponds, and the traditional Japanese architecture and cute bridges. I particularly enjoyed the freedom of being able to walk in a relatively quiet and uncongested city.

I figured that walking at a higher altitude would be more comfortable than enduring the sweltering heat of Takayama that was reaching 30°C/86°F on some days, and Mt. Norikura seemed like a great way to escape the city for awhile and enjoy some physical activity with my always active boyfriend.

So, early one Sunday morning in July, Ryan and I got ready, put on flipflops (which were free from cat fur), but I'd later regret wearing, drove to a bus stop, caught a little white shuttle bus, and rode higher and higher up the winding mountain road. Private cars are prohibited on Mount Norikura and this road. Aside from walking every metre of the 3,000-metre tall volcano, taking a shuttle is the only way you can get onto the mountain.

At the Norikura Bus Terminal, about 2,700-metres above sea level (which saved us a lot of work), we stepped out of our shuttle and entered a little gift shop that was almost deserted, save for an elderly couple deliberating over the purchase of some unidentifiable vacuum-packed delicacy. Avoiding temptation, we paid the small entrance fee and walked outside to our starting point: a gravel service road that was already being trod by a steady stream of hikers, which surprised me. I had thought Ryan and I were early birds.

On the thirty minute hike up the service road to a mountain hut that served as a sort of way station, I quickly became acutely aware of how unsuitably attired I was for this walk. I wore short white shorts, a Billabong tee shirt, and flip flops. Compared to everyone else, I looked like I should be on Bondi Beach, not a mountain. The gravel kept getting wedged between my flip flops, the bottom of my feet and between my toes, which slowed our progress, because I had to keep stopping to remove them.

We walked past a group of six white-haired warmly-dressed *obaasans* who were walking back down the mountain path. They looked at me strangely and said '*Samukunai desu ka?*' (Aren't you cold?). I wasn't yet but, judging by their clothes, I would be soon.

Four middle-aged hikers passed us, each of whom was wrapped up in several layers of clothing. It seemed that everyone but us had come appropriately dressed in fashionable windproof jackets, sensible walking shoes, and hats. I cursed myself for not being better prepared.

I looked at Ryan. 'It must be really cold up there.'

'Do you want to turn back and try this another time?' he asked. (He was wearing jeans and a navy tee shirt and seemed unperturbed about how out of place we were.)

I shook my head. 'I came to hike the mountain and see the views. I'm not going to let beach clothes stop me.'

A very nimble group of *obaasans* passed us, briskly tackling the steep slope without stopping for a breather, making the hike upward look ridiculously easy. Appearances were deceiving.

Just a third of the way to the top, I had to stop at the mountain hut to regroup. I faced at least another full hour of hiking if I was going to reach Kengamine Peak and I was already tiring. I sat gratefully on a wooden bench, drank water I had brought with me, ate some fortifying trail mix, squared my shoulders and told Ryan I was ready.

We left the gravel service road to start up the steep mountain trail. I tried to ignore my physical discomfort by focusing on the beauty all around me: the green plains rimmed by pine and deciduous trees; the different green hues of grass, leaves, shrubs, and lichen; the rough bulging dark grey rock outcroppings; the small dark blue crater lakes to which an occasional bird came to drink; some fine patches of snow that refused to budge, like a stubborn old lady in a comfortable chair; and the wide blue sky above us dappled with a few small white clouds.

'This is why I'm doing this,' I thought. 'This is what makes it all worthwhile. No concrete, no cars, no overhead telephone and utility wires. Just the rich beauties of Nature.'

Half way up the mountain trail, we stopped to rest again. An older Australian couple about twice our age appeared on the trail behind us. Thankfully, they were also wearing shorts, but *they* had the sense to wear walking shoes and sweaters.

'G'day!' they said enthusiastically and in unison, although out of breath.

How lovely to hear familiar accents. (And how nice not to be the only one struggling with the mountain trail.)

'G'day,' Ryan said with a smirk.

'Hello.' I said.

The couple stepped off the trail beside us for a mini rest stop.

'Great weather for it!' the husband said.

'Yeah, great,' Ryan and I said in unison.

'It's so clear up here,' the wife added.

'Wonderful,' I agreed. Part of me wanted to pepper the Aussie couple with questions about their time in Japan but I was enjoying the mountain silence too much to say anything more.

Fortified by the break and the brief conversation, I glanced at Ryan to let him know I was ready, we said adieu to the Aussies, and then continued with the hike.

Soon, though, I was again struggling with the rocky pathway. The big stones kept getting caught in my flip flops. I cursed myself again and again for not thinking about any of the practicalities of a mountain hike. I started to lag behind, growing even more tired as I witnessed the effortless trek upward of all the people who passed me.

Ryan, who had always been more physically active than me, moved ahead at my urging and I fell further back, growing ever more agitated with myself. I began tallying up the number of footsteps I'd taken, how many minutes I'd been hiking already, and how many *hours* it would take me to reach the top.

I thought about giving in and suggesting to Ryan, who had rejoined me, that we go home and try another time when I was better equipped for the physical challenges of the hike. Then I saw on the trail ahead of us a one-and-a-half-metre-tall vision in fuchsia. She couldn't have been more than five or six years old. With bright blonde hair, pink check pants, and black sunglasses, this kid just kept going and going, nothing was stopping her.

Ryan and I were only able to catch up to her and her parents when they stopped to take photos.

'This must be like climbing Everest for her,' I said with a smile and nod at the little girl.

'No, actually,' her blonde and very fit mother said in German-accented English. 'She's quite used to it.'

Of course she was. These Germans were sturdy fleet-footed mountain goat. I was more of a beribboned miniature poodle.

The fuschia vision was still posing for pictures as Ryan and I walked on again. Up ahead, we saw the older Australian couple, who were taking another breather, with the wife taking photos of everything in view.

'Hello,' the husband said with a grin. 'Another hill.'

I found mountain etiquette both charming and a little odd, like when you go to the countryside and everyone you see suddenly starts bidding you 'good morning.' I knew we'd see the older Aussie couple several more times during this hike, as my level of fitness seemed on par with theirs. But how many times should we address each other before it became awkward or, worse, annoying?

Despite my flip flops, and unsuitable clothing, and lack of hiking fitness, I finally made it to the look-out at the top of Kengamine Peak. This was a real triumph and I felt it keenly. Despite everything, including my self-doubts and physical discomfort, I had persevered.

As if to demonstrate how high Ryan and I were, a grey-green Japanese Self-Defence Forces military helicopter flew past and *below* us. The determined grumble of its engine and the whipping of its rotors through the pristine air seemed to bellow all around us, marring the peace and beauty of this gracious mountain.

I grimaced at Ryan. 'Silence is even broken up here.'

'It can be broken anywhere,' he said, like a Cockney Deepak Chopra.

Still, the views *were* spectacular.

Fragmented clouds hung loosely in the sky, seeming so close to the mountain peak and us that we could reach out and touch them. We could see other, lower peaks, poking through a layer of clouds spread between them, while the sun emerged from behind the higher clouds like a celebratory sign for us having made it to the top.

The determined beauty and sheer power of Nature in the hills and peaks all around us was breath-taking. I felt at once small and insignificant and, on a deeper level, connected in every molecule to this mountain in all of its different aspects. I had never before felt this union with earth, sky, and planet. It was exhilarating.

Shivering as I stood at Ryan's side (the *obaasans* had been right: it was very cold), I looked out over mountain tops and valleys and thought about the little German girl and the old Japanese ladies who had seemed so effortless in their ascent. What, I wondered, was their approach to life when things got hard? Were they, like me, worrying all the time about their clothing, footwear, and ability to reach the top? Or were they quite happy to keep going and see where their steps took them?

I suspected I knew the answer. Would I ever become more like them?

Ryan and I took some pictures of the views, and each other, and took some more photos as we made our way back down the mountain . . . *much* easier going.

On the final slope, my feet throbbing and my hair blowing in all directions in the breeze, I saw the Australian couple sitting down beside the trail and looking rather worse for wear. Ryan and I had no words left. The Aussie husband, also unsure of what to say, simply lifted his thumb and motioned the universal sign for hitchhiking. We all laughed.

By the time Ryan and I got home, the low-land weather had brought us firmly back to earth. Despite the four or so hours we had been gone, the city's temperature had scarcely dipped. We were engulfed by the still, stuffy, airless heat that I knew, no matter how long I lived in Japan, I would never get used to and, judging by the number of *'atsui desu ne's'* (hot, isn't it?) I heard daily, neither would the Japanese.

Gershwin was also struggling with the heat and was more than usually pleased to see us when we walked back into the apartment. I opened the door so he could go out onto the balcony and stretch and roll on the ground outside. But it wasn't enough.

Back inside, his usual antics weren't on display. He ignored Iko and Niko and even his food bowl. In fact, he looked almost drowsy.

'I think he's suffering from *natsubate* [heat fatigue],' Ryan said with a worried frown.

Seriously concerned by Gershwin's lethargy, I picked him up and carried him to the kitchen sink. I turned on the cold water and let it stream onto his silvery fur. He didn't struggle as any wet cat worth its salt would do. Instead, he let out a grateful meow as the water ran down his back.

'I think we'd better start leaving the air conditioner on during the day for the cats when we're not here,' Ryan said as he helped me towel-dry Gershwin. 'The electric bill be damned.'

'Agreed,' I said as, revived, the adolescent cat sprang to the floor and went to get a drink of water from his bowl. 'I had no idea the heat was building up so much in here.'

That evening after dinner, to prove his full recovery, Gershwin launched several sneak attacks on Iko and Niko, who were not impressed.

The next day at work, every muscle in my body ached and I had painful blisters on my feet, but I was pleased with myself. Yes, I had been more than a little stupid in making my preparations for the hike, but the important aspect of my mountain experience was the fact that I'd kept going and hadn't given up. This was new. In the past, when things got tough, I got going in the opposite direction. If, however, I could apply my Mount Norikura experience to my life, what else might I achieve?

My classroom (like the city) was insufferably hot, even though it was filled with fans, and it looked like all of my students were suffering. So, I used the subject of how to cope with the intense heat of summer as a way for everyone to practise their English . . . and maybe I'd learn a new strategy or two. That's when one of my students told me that today was 'Fish Day.'

For this traditional one-day summer event, people don't eat any cooked meat. Japan is at its hottest from mid-July to the beginning of August, so, to deal with the heat, the Japanese believe that eating raw food is best. This made sense to me. Maybe, I thought, it was the summer heat that had driven inventive Japanese chefs centuries ago to invent sushi and sashimi.

On the way home, I decided to stop off at a little hole in the wall store I liked and buy a pile of sushi. I was keen to see if eating raw food in summer could make a difference in how my body responded to the heat.

Sitting on our small balcony that hot evening, Ryan and laid out cucumber and avocado sushi for me, and prawns for himself, poured cold *karupisu* (a popular fermented milk and sugar drink), into tall glasses, and sat down to eat. Suddenly, I heard a low dangerous growl from under the table.

'What's that?' I asked in alarm.

'Look,' Ryan said with a grin.

Gershwin had hunched himself into a contorted angry ball of fur a few centimetres from my feet. He had something small and pink in his mouth, a prawn that had fallen to the floor, his growls warning us and the other cats that he wasn't giving it up without a fight. Suddenly, he hot-footed it over to a corner with his prey, challenging anyone who came near him with his uncharacteristic snarl.

'I think we've just discovered what his favourite food is,' Ryan said.

We both laughed as Gershwin gulped his treat down, thoroughly licked prawn juice from his paws and whiskers, and then stretched out in the sun, satiated and contented after devouring his *ebi*.

'He's as crazy for prawns as Koizumi [a former Japanese prime minister] is for karaoke,' Ryan said.

'Prawns. Who knew?' I said.

From that day on, our pescetarian puss would wrinkle his nose in disgust if presented with anything other than *ebi*.

It was only later that I discovered that the idea behind Fish Day had been somewhat lost in translation. It is actually about *unagi* (eel). That was what we should have been eating on that special day. According to the Japanese, the eating of raw eels is an historical remedy that helps to rejuvenate the body and overcome the summer heat. While we had not eaten traditionally, we had certainly learned the value of raw food in summer. Both Ryan and I felt better after our sushi feast. Until the temperature cooled, we'd be eating more uncooked food.

Chapter 7: Better to Enclose a Cat Than to Scold It

猫叱るより猫を囲え / Neko Shikaru Yori Neko Wo Kakoe

Clothes shops kept irregular hours in Takayama. Three different days, at three different hours, we tried to visit a local vintage store, and each time we found it closed.

It was refreshing to see that a country that had appeared, at first, such a stickler for rules, actually had a whole community that seemed to do the opposite of what was expected.

'It is *ikigai*,' explained James, the bald Kiwi ALT whom we had called *Jēmusu* (the Japanese word for James) as a joke.

'What is *ikigai*?' I asked. 'A fish?'

'No,' he said with a grin. '*Ikigai* means finding your purpose, your meaning in life, and combining it with your profession, your work. It is the balance of doing what you love while making a living and letting neither path control your life.'

I didn't really understand *ikigai* until one spring day I actually found the vintage clothing shop open and went inside to explore as I'd longed to do for over a month. The owner, G-Kun, a snowboarder in his early thirties who wore his long black hair tied back in a ponytail, was busy checking orders on his computer.

Ryan was looking at skateboard tee shirts while I browsed some different-coloured beanies made from hemp that I loved and would probably never wear.

'I'm so glad I finally got to come in,' I said to G-Kun.

'Why has your store been closed so often? Were you ill?'

'Not at all,' he replied with a friendly smile. 'I have just been concentrating on something else.'

'Like what?'

'My music career.'

I stared at him.

'I travelled in Europe some years back and became friendly with some European DJs,' he continued. 'I ended up co-producing some dance tracks with them.'

He had my rapt attention. To my very British mind, this was an entirely new concept. I had been told as a child to forget working with horses and get a job in a bank, because in England I was supposed to be a responsible adult with a steady good-paying job doing something I loathed rather than something I loved.

But in Takayama . . . Was what G-Kun telling me real? Could an avocation and a job actually be combined? And if they could, did I have my own *ikigai*, something that would bring deep satisfaction to my life?

Once I understood *ikigai*, I saw it all around me. In Takayama, many people had turned their passions into businesses from which they earned an actual living wage. Of course, that's not to say all Japanese follow *ikigai* but it seemed widely practiced here. And then there was Keisuke, who worked in a brewery and wanted to start his own *saké* company someday.

Twenty-something Keisuke was not particularly well educated or rich, but he seemed more contented than anyone I'd met in a long time. In fact, he was so happy and so passionate about his job that I never saw him in anything other than his cream-coloured brewery overalls.

One night in Keisuke 's apartment, he proudly poured me his employer's clear rice wine into a tiny white and blue ceramic cup, beaming with something more than pride.

Ryan took the first sip and beamed back at him. 'This is good stuff! You've got the *saké* magic, Keisuke-san. Like Harry Potter.'

'So, so, so,' Keisuke said and paused for a moment to think. 'You know what, I am not Harry Potter. But I am . . . the *Saké* Potter.'

And from that day on, that's exactly what we called him.

A few nights later, while out for dinner with some friends, we came across a stray cat that was to begin my search for *ikigai*.

'*Kawaisō*, it's such a shame,' Sayuri said. 'There's so many *noranekos* [stray cats] in Takayama. It's sad.'

I leaned down to pat the bedraggled kitten and he tapped me with his paw, as if begging for more. 'Poor baby,' I said. 'He must hang around the restaurant in the hope of getting food scraps,' I said.

'The staff probably feed him,' Ryan said as he joined us, the kitten instantly turning to him for attention.

'What should I do?' I asked.

'Why do you have *do* anything?' Mike said, joining us.

Takako, our friendly waitress was standing at the door and confirmed our suspicions about the kitten. '*Hai. Nora-neko desu.*' (Yes. It is a stray.)

'Come on, you can't save them all,' said Dominic as he marched off down the pavement.

Reluctantly, I followed him, along with the others. But, as we wandered tipsily back to our apartment, the kitten tried to follow us. He looked unwell. Snot was dribbling down his scrawny face. Everyone picked up their pace.

I forced myself not to turn around as we walked back home. If I had, I'd have scooped that kitten up and to hell with the consequences. Actually, that would have saved me time and trouble, because when we got back to the apartment, all I could think about was the abandoned kitten with the big affectionate personality struggling to survive outside all by himself.

Our friends stood in the kitchen noisily making plans about how to get to the next party, oblivious to the kitten's plight. I was unable to even smile, let alone participate. 'I'm sorry. I'm not going to make it to any more parties or bars tonight. I've got a headache, so I'm going to stay here,' I said.

After the noisy crowd, including Ryan, had left, I tried going to bed, but I couldn't sleep. I was unable to purge the image of the friendly little feline from my mind. Finally, fuelled by *Chu-Hai* and cheese sticks, I got dressed, crept outside, grabbed my bike, and cycled along the fluorescent-lit pathway armed with dry cat biscuits and a cat carrier.

Sure enough, with no other place to go, the kitten was still at *Murasaki* begging for food and attention. He didn't struggle one bit as I lifted him into the cat carrier and set it in the front basket of my bicycle. Apparently, taking his chances with the kindly stranger and her weird contraption was better than spending another dangerous night on the street.

I knew that Ryan would not be impressed with my philanthropy, and less than thrilled about this new addition to our household, but I also knew that this little boy didn't stand much chance of survival if we left him on the streets. I also felt I could relate to the kitten's predicament of abandonment. After all, I'd faced similar emotions myself as a child. Displeased boyfriend versus dead kitten? It was no contest.

Still, when I carried the cat carrier into the apartment, the enormity of what I had done hit me. Just as a matter of practicality, we couldn't take on another kitten. We already had three cats we would have to re-home before we returned to England in December. Plus, this little guy was clearly sick. His eyes looked rheumy and painful. His nose was dripping. He might infect Iko, Niko, and Gershwin. I'd have to keep them apart. Into the laundry room he went with food, water, a litter box, and bedding. Fortunately, he had no interest in hiding under the washing machine.

Ryan got back the next morning looking a bit worse for wear, possibly hungover, and definitely sleep-deprived. Perfect. This was the right time to tell him what I'd done, while he was in a weakened state.

'Don't get angry,' I said. 'But there's someone you might want to meet in the laundry room.'

Ryan looked at me with bloodshot green eyes. 'Oh no! You didn't. Did you?'

'I couldn't leave him there. Anyway you've been gone nearly all night,' I said, trying to shift the focus onto his fictional misdeeds.

'Have you introduced him to the other cats yet?'

'No, I'm waiting until I've taken him to the vets.'

'Good idea,' Ryan said wearily. He gave me a kiss and crawled into bed, leaving me to keep the cats separate as best I could, which was difficult, because Gershwin was eager to meet our houseguest.

It was at this moment that I realised I had found the start of my own *ikigai*. I wanted to incorporate my love of animals into my life's work, but in order to do that, in the future I would need to find a healthier way to do so. So my other cats didn't get hurt.

I went to the vets that morning, surprising Dr. Iguchi when a bedraggled tabby kitten strode confidently out of the carrier, rather than

67

Gershwin. Surprise turned immediately to concern as the kitten sat on the exam table, smiled at both of us, then sneezed violently, sending lots of yellow discharge all over the vet's pristine white smock.

The prognosis was not good. 'He could have feline flu,' Dr. Iguchi announced. 'Very contagious. Very bad. It could be much worse. He might have FIV virus.'

My stomach clenched. The dreaded and deadly cat AIDS.

'There is a vaccine for your other cats,' he continued. 'For now, you must quarantine this kitten until we get his test results back.'

'I think Gershwin has had the vaccination already,' I said hopefully, 'but I'm not sure about Iko and Niko.'

'So, so, so. Gershkun had the vaccinations before, not the sisters. But you must keep *all* the cats away from the kitten for now.'

There was no alternative. If I didn't want a house full of sick cats, and I didn't, this was the only way. I just had to pray that the others hadn't already been infected. I told myself they were strong, *genki* [healthy] animals and I was blithely certain they could fight off any infection, not realising in my ignorance how contagious and potentially deadly feline flu really was.

I drove home and put the kitten back in the laundry room, praying that he didn't have anything that could kill him, or the other cats.

It wasn't long before Gershwin wanted to go in and carouse with the kitten. He knew something was wrong straight away. He was always good at reading situations. So, he sat by the door and started meowing to be let in. When I came to see what was bothering him, he stared at me with every ounce of his feline superiority and demanded to see his potential Best Friend Forever. He uttered a particularly piercing *nyan* [meow] in protest at my having exiled the kitten to the laundry room.

'You mustn't go near him for a while,' I said.

Gershwin rubbed his soft furry body against my even furrier legs and looked me straight in the eyes as if to say 'Think again.'

When I wouldn't give in to his demands, he started playing angrily, jumping onto the bookshelf, hurling himself off the top, somersaulting in mid-air, and landing unceremoniously a few centimetres from my feet.

'Right, that's it,' I said as I picked him up, carried him to the bedroom, and shut the door.

It was always the same with Gershwin. Despite being a Ninja Attack Kitten, he had a delicate soul. Whenever he was reprimanded, he would become so hurt by the scolding that he'd disappear for hours (and once for days) at the shock of being chastised. Then, it could be days before he would actually forgive us. He could out-sit our most ardent lures to be returned to his good graces. If I tried to tempt him with his favourite treats, he would sniff them with disdain, turn his back, and walk off scornfully. I was always the first to give in and let him have his way.

This time, Gershwin didn't know best. He was banned from the laundry room. Iko and Niko took one look at the closed laundry room door, sniffed the scent of an unfamiliar feline, and avoided that part of the apartment just as they tried to avoid Gershwin when he came over all Ninja Kitten.

That night, I lay awake in bed worrying about what the test results would be. What if, in bringing this stray kitten home, I had inadvertently infected the other cats with the FIV virus? I felt deeply guilty at potentially jeopardising their wellbeing, even their lives. In trying to do the right thing by the sick kitten, I may have done an incredibly wrong thing by Iko, Niko, and Gershwin. If anything happened to them, it would be entirely my fault.

For the next week, while we waited for the test results, the poor kitten, whom I named Takashi after a jovial Bagus bartender, suffered from inflamed and discharging eyes and a badly running nose. I had never seen a cat in this condition before. His tatty coat needed some love and his sore eyes needed constant care. The vet had told me to wash them twice daily with saltwater, which helped them tremendously. He had also given me a medicinal orange powder that I was supposed to mix into his food. Cats being cats, he could smell the concoction a mile off and he was having none of it. I ended up mixing the powder with butter and rubbing it around his face so he was forced to lick it off.

I agonised all that week. Ryan was equally concerned for the poor little guy. 'When are you going back to the vets?' he asked me daily. 'You're sure the other cats won't get it?' I dared not answer.

Finally, the dreaded, long anticipated morning arrived. A week after I had confined Takashi to the laundry room, I plopped him back into a cat carrier and drove off to see the vet and get the test results.

By now, I had become a regular and familiar face at the animal hospital. I was the only pet-owning *gaijin* in the vicinity, as far as I was aware, which meant I was a bit of a novelty in the waiting room. People stared at me and some smiled, a few of the braver ones even made conversation, which helped distract me from the potentially dreadful news I might be getting today.

Finally, Takashi's name was called and, cat carrier in hand, I was ushered into an exam room. I waited nervously as the vet found the kitten's file.

'No *Katto Eizu*,' he said.

Oh, thank God. Takashi didn't have the FIV virus!

Before I could celebrate, he continued. 'But Takashi-kun is very sick,' Dr. Iguchi said in a somber tone. 'He has cat flu.'

The tone of his voice was my first clue that feline flu was a far more serious disease than I had believed.

'Very contagious,' he continued. 'Other cats should be immunised against the virus immediately, and Takashi-kun should be isolated from them for another week, maybe more. Keep giving him the medicine and bathing his eyes.'

My enormous relief that Takashi didn't have a death sentence, and my fears for Iko, Niko, and Gershwin, warred within me all the way home.

Chapter 8: All Cats Are Grey in The Dark

暗闇では猫は全て灰色 / Kurayami De Wa Neko Wa Subete Haiiro

Thankfully, none of the other cats had contracted feline flu and Takashi was well on the road to recovery. Getting up every day no longer meant that I would have to wipe orange medicine caked in butter across his mouth. Still, get up I must. Three very healthy cats were charging up and down the hallway like freight trains, demanding their breakfasts. If I didn't get up now, they would start running their freight trains over *me*.

I also had something to look forward to.

Mie – a beautician and one of my former adult English language students to whom I had given private lessons and whom I had befriended over tea and talks on our favourite subject, travel – had invited me to her house to be dressed by her like a geisha for an afternoon. Mie was another example of *ikigai*. She enjoyed her work, and would now be combining her skills with her love of travelling by dressing up the foreign girl. I wondered if it would be possible for me to combine my love of animals and travel to find my own version of *ikigai*.

While wearing kimono is a tradition that predates Versace by millennia, it involves just as much brilliant colour. Unlike some famous female European fashion traditions – powdered wigs and the bustle come to mind – the Japanese kimono has maintained its importance in the twenty-first century and with it the people's connection to their past, their traditions, and their culture.

Wearing kimono, I thought, would be a good way to learn about and appreciate Japanese culture from a female perspective. By walking in the shoes of Japanese women (or, in this case, walking in *geta*, their traditional footwear – a cross between flip-flops and clogs), I hoped I would be better able to understand what makes Japanese women the way they are. So far, all I'd really learnt was that Japanese women were more often than not painfully polite, took great care of their appearance, and rarely pruned their *bushes*.

'You must come,' Mie had insisted. 'You'll look beautiful!'

How could I refuse?

Mie lived not far from the Kajibashi Bridge, which had a curious bronze statue of a folklore character: an old man with unusually long arms pointed skywards. He sat half naked in a meditative position with an angry expression that perplexed passing tourists and locals alike. I had asked around, but no one knew who or what he was supposed to represent.

I cycled over to Mie's small single-storey home and knocked on the front sliding doors.

She greeted me joyfully. 'Hi, CJ-san! Please come in.'

I followed her into a dark narrow hallway that opened into the lounge where she introduced me to a man sitting and reading a newspaper: her husband, Erikku, an older gentleman with gold teeth and a good head of hair. Then, before I had even finished saying hello, she disappeared behind a white plastic curtain that hid her beauty salon.

Appalled at being left on my own in a strange house with a complete stranger, I heard Mie rummaging around and opening boxes as I waited nervously, attempting to make polite conversation with her husband, who was monosyllabic.

Suddenly, he smiled. His gold teeth gleamed. 'Drink?' he asked as he stood up, walked into the kitchen – which was in a corner of the room – and switched on the kettle. We waited in silence for it to boil, not quite looking at each other.

Just as I was about to take my first sip of green tea, Mie reappeared as suddenly as she had disappeared. In her arms she held a long red silk kimono embroidered with pink and white flowers. 'Come! Try it on,' she said eagerly.

I jumped to my feet with the greatest relief, which was quickly supplanted with dismay as she led me, not into a bedroom with a door, but behind the plastic curtain. With her husband seated just a few metres away, I reluctantly pulled off my clothes and stood at attention in my underwear, like a mannequin, as Mie carefully draped the heavy red kimono over me. Weight is how kimonos are valued. The heavier they are, the greater their worth. If a kimono is too light, people will think you bought it from a Japanese version of K-Mart.

I must have been wearing a fortune.

Mie relentlessly tugged and pulled the kimono into place on me, explaining that she had bought it years ago when she had worked as a model.

'*Sugoi. Kirei,*' Mie said as she stood back to admire me. She thought I looked beautiful, but I wasn't so convinced.

She wrapped around me a cream-coloured *obe* – a kind of cummerbund used to accentuate a women's waist – cutting off about half my lung capacity. To distract myself from my growing discomfort, I imagined myself as a geisha getting ready to perform for her guests. But all I could think was how uncomfortable they must have been, because this kimono was constricting my un-Japanese body, which was perspiring heavily from both the summer heat and the heaviness of the kimono. Then I saw my footwear.

Traditional white Japanese socks have a separate section just for the big toe, because *getas* have a strap, like a thong on a sandal or flip-flop, that separates the big toe from the rest of the toes. The *getas* Mie had chosen for me looked like wooden clogs with a five-centimetre base and a black fabric strap to keep them attached to my feet.

This, I thought, must be what aristocrats feel like when they're being dressed for the evening as Mie knelt on the floor and squeezed my large Western feet into the petite and painful footwear.

Next, she led me over to a chair and pointed to the seat. 'Let's start on your hair now.' Moving carefully, I sat down gingerly on the chair. Then, she went to work on my hair, painstakingly spraying each blonde strand and pulling it tight into an up-do at the back.

'Japanese men consider the nape of the neck very sensual, so the hair must be worn up,' she said. 'That is also why the cut of the kimono shows off the nape.'

Half an hour later, Mie stood back, beamed at me with pride, and announced: '*Sugoi.*'

I looked at myself for the first time in the full-length mirror. It was a shock. I felt anything but great. My face was flushed from the summer heat. The scalp-stretching up-do she had given my blonde hair revealed my dark roots. The *obe* didn't accentuate the positives of my body shape. It made my breasts even more prominent *and* unattractive because of the unflattering way the kimono's heavy material fell over them. The kimono also made the rest of me look wide and heavy. The problem was that the kimono was designed for slender Japanese women, not big-boned Brits.

The colour of my hair conflicted with the scarlet kimono. Red looks good with dark, not light, shades. Even the makeup was wrong. The Japanese for some reason admire white skin (hence the skin-whitening adverts in every airport and train station). The makeup Mie had used was too white against my skin tone. I was about as far away from the elegant women described in *Memoirs of a Geisha* by Arthur Golden, as anyone could be.

I knew Japanese and Western perspectives of beauty were different, but this was ridiculous. I felt like an imposter. My tall body, big breasts, blonde hair, and rouged cheeks looked completely out of place with the scarlet kimono. In short, I felt silly.

'*Sugoi*,' I said with forced enthusiasm, because it was vital that I do nothing to diminish Mie's happiness. I was being very Japanese. In this country, everything seemed to be hidden under politeness. I had to toe the cultural line. 'I love this braid you created in the front.'

'Thank you.' Then, to my horror, Mie shouted: 'Erikku, come look at CJ-san.'

Her husband promptly walked in with a huge grin on his face. It was difficult to tell if he was amused by my appearance, or proud of his wife's handiwork. Whatever it was, that grin did nothing to allay how graceless and unbeautiful I felt.

Things quickly went from bad to worse. Despite my protests, Mie insisted we go outside – *in public* – so she could take some photos. Ignoring all of my arguments about why we should *not* be doing this, she led me down her street to a large wooden temple, which was closed. There, she had me strike several poses like those of geishas and Japanese models I had seen in books.

To my enormous embarrassment, I quickly became a tourist attraction. People taking their daily constitutionals, or returning from work, or out and about on their errands, or getting out of school stopped and stared *at me*. Maybe they thought I was a visiting actress from overseas. I don't know. I only knew how much I did *not* love the unwanted attention. They even asked to photograph me, the blonde *gaijin* in the red kimono.

At first, I wanted to crawl under a rock and stay there for a decade or two. But slowly I began to register the smiles on kids' faces and the enthusiasm from the passersby. They were not laughing at me. They did not think I looked ridiculous. Their honest appreciation finally made me forget my image in Mie's mirror. I even joined in with the kids. We struck a silly jumping pose, like in a Toyota ad, for the benefit of all the people whipping out their cameras. Of course, I also raised my hand, my fingers making a V, the international peace sign the Japanese always displayed in their photos.

Finally, we went back to Mie's house where she served me some tea and cake and we talked about the tradition of wearing kimono and the kind of entertainment geishas provided, particularly the music, some of it played on a *shamisen*, somewhat like a long-necked banjo, which Mie played. That got her to talking about the instrument, including the fact that it was made from cat skins. (I had to hide my revulsion – Iko, Niko, Gershwin, and Takashi carved up for *shamisens*? It was the stuff of nightmares.)

Sitting or standing, walking or sipping tea, all I felt in the beautiful kimono, elaborate hairstyle, and *getas* was restricted. This gave me my first real insight into Japanese women. The heaviness and long cut of the kimono made it difficult to walk, which was worsened by the elevated and clunky *getas*. All I could think was that, if ever presented by danger, a kimono-wearing Japanese woman would be trapped, because she wouldn't be able to run away.

Those thoughts, and the continuing physical sensation of restriction, brought my mother and grandmother into my thoughts. They had struggled with their own restrictions. Their society, their culture, had shunted them into the role of housewives. Unlike me, they had not been free to follow their dreams. Was this why my grandmother had become so perpetually angry and my mother had struggled with mental health problems throughout her adulthood?

My time with both Mie had provided me with an important insight. Firstly, before I could fully concentrate on finding my life's purpose; marrying cats with work and travel, I'd need to figure out a way of dealing with my own family issues.

I had to hide from Mie my enormous relief when she finally helped me take off the kimono. I could breathe normally again. I took my hair down from its painfully tight hairdo, but kept the braid she'd done at the front, because I actually did think it looked cool.

This experience had given me a new respect for all the Japanese women who wear kimono so elegantly. The blonde *gaijin* had looked like a sack of sweaty potatoes, while they always managed to look both demure and sophisticated.

Fortunately, most Japanese women no longer had the physical constraints of the kimono. They could wear whatever they wanted and most of them wanted the most current Western fashions and kept the kimono for special occasions.

Taking off the kimono wasn't the end of this interesting episode in my Japanese life. You know all of those Public Service Announcements warning people, particularly teenagers, about the dangers of the pictures and words they post on the Internet? What goes on the Internet lives forever. About three weeks later, someone at Let's English somehow got their hands on copies of the photos Mie had taken and splashed them across the town for everyone to see as adverts in newspapers to come study with CJ at Let's English.

At first I was horrified, then I laughed. In Japan, it just didn't matter what I looked like or how I acted. I was what I had always been to the locals: the crazy *gaijin*.

Chapter 9: When a Cat Washes Its Face, a Guest Will Arrive

ねこがかおをあらうときゃくがくる / Neko Ga Kao Wo Arau To Kyaku Ga Kuru

Ryan and I were invited to dinner by one of Ryan's friends and student, Ryo, a thirty-year-old salaryman. Even though Ryo lived on the other side of town from our apartment, we decided to walk. We still had some trouble finding the house, because it was tucked down an unlit side street on a block of modern homes with traditional Japanese-style roofs and stone walled gardens.

When we finally found the house number, we were greeted at the door by Ryo, who wore a loose white tee shirt and jeans, his black hair swept to one side. He gave us some house slippers and promptly thrust small porcelain cups of *sake* into our hands. I felt my face flush after just a few sips. There's an old Japanese saying: 'A cold area produces good *sake*.' Clearly, the mountains of Takayama were the best place to brew *it*.

Ryo introduced us to his wife, Hitomi, a nurse in her mid-thirties whose hair was pulled back in a sensible bun. She seemed friendly, but she spoke little at first, either because she was shy or because she was uncertain of her English language skills.

The dinner she had prepared for us featured fried chicken and rice. I couldn't tell her I was a vegetarian, so I pretended to eat to avoid insulting our hostess. Fortunately, there was also a dessert of melon and yoghurt that we ate with tiny child-like spoons. We sat at a small plastic dinner table on small plastic chairs talking mostly about the foods we liked.

After dinner, we sat in the lounge sipping *sake* and the couple brought out some of their family photo albums to share with us, which amazed me. I was not used to people who liked to talk about their families, let alone show them off.

Some pictures dated back to the 1950s and 1960s. They were in black and white and featured relatives wearing smart Western clothes. Other pictures were newer and in colour. I was amazed that Ryo and Hitomi knew all of the stories of these relatives and their histories going back for generations. I knew so little about my own family.

After the boys went outside to smoke some cigarettes, I joined Hitomi on the sofa. She pointed to the picture of a slim, unsmiling, middle-aged man wearing a polo shirt and glasses who was seated on an armchair. 'That is my father.' Her face revealed a deep grief. Her eyes welled with tears. 'He died five years ago. I miss him so much.' She fell silent.

'My mother died,' I blurted out. 'My father is still alive, but I don't see him much.' I needed to say something, anything, to let Hitomi know I understood her pain, even though I didn't miss my parents the way Hitmoi missed her father.

'When did your mother die?' Hitomi asked as she pulled herself back into the polite hostess role.

'About twelve years ago. Who's that?' I asked, pointing at one of the other pictures to distract her from her sadness and any further questions she might have asked about my family.

It worked. Holding one photo album partially on her lap and partially on mine, Hitomi continued flipping through the pages of photos, explaining who the various relatives and friends in the pictures were, most of whom were posed rather formally, and telling me brief stories about a relative or an event formalised in the pictures.

Then she pointed at a typical tourist shot of a young man in typical gear: sneakers, jeans, and a plain tee shirt. He was short, and very happy, his smile huge as he held his fingers in a V-sign.

'That's my brother,' Hitomi said sadly. 'He lives in the U.S., in Ohio, now. I don't see him much anymore.' She went quiet.

Her grief was palpable. 'Will you visit him some day?' I asked tentatively.

'I hope so, but it's complicated.'

I smiled at her encouragingly. I was sure she wanted to talk, and I'll admit I was curious about the sad story behind the happy young man in the photo.

'You see, my mother doesn't speak to my brother anymore. She doesn't agree with my brother's lifestyle – he's gay – and my mother doesn't like my brother's partner or any of his other choices.'

'Well, I know that rural areas and rural people in Japan are much more conservative than in the cities.'

'It's not just that. They could have accepted him if he had married and stayed in the closet. But my brother would not live a lie. He chose freedom in America through a university exchange program and then he just stayed. In Nebraska, you see, the Americans see him as just another Asian and he relishes that anonymity.'

'I know exactly how he feels,' I said with a smile. 'I'm just another *gaijin* in Japan.'

'Yes,' Hitomi said with an answering smile. 'In the end, my mother accepted my brother's participation in the university exchange, because she just has to tell neighbours and friends that he is studying in the U.S. and no one asks any questions.'

Sitting there, looking at those old pictures, seeing how much Hitomi still grieved the loss of her father and how close she was to her brother, sadness welled within me. I had never known what she and her brother shared. I had no siblings. There was pain, too. Here was Hitomi, a virtual stranger, telling intimate stories about her family history, while I had no contact with my relatives. My father hadn't even been bothered to tell me twelve years earlier that he had a new wife. Two years ago, when he had divorced my Stepmother, I was one of the last people to know. At that moment, I had no idea where he was living, and I knew very little about my other relatives on his side of the family.

After the boys rejoined us and we enjoyed several more rounds of *sake*, Ryan and I finally thanked our generous hosts for a wonderful evening and left, walking back home slightly worse for wear.

Fast on the heels of our dinner with Hitomi and Ryo and my unexpected immersion in family came *Obon*, the three-day Japanese Buddhist festival of the dead, considered by many to be the most important of the Japanese holy days. It is celebrated in mid-August in most parts of the country that adhere to the solar calendar, and in mid-July for areas that base their holy days on the lunar calendar. The Gifu Prefecture celebrates *Obon* in August.

Essentially, *Obon*, which has been observed in Japan for more than 500 years, honours one's ancestors. The Japanese believe that during *Obon* their ancestors return for a sort of annual reunion with their families. So, people clean their homes (as anyone does when relatives are coming to visit) and hang lanterns in front of their houses to guide their ancestors home. Many people even travel to their hometowns during *Obon* to welcome back centuries of their relatives (which gives people an even more urgent reason to clean their houses).

During the festival, people also visit and clean their ancestors' graves and leave offerings for them at Buddhist temples. They put *chochin* lanterns (a bamboo spiral covered in silk or paper) and flower arrangements around their *butsudan* (altars) at home, leave food offerings on their altars to welcome their ancestors, fill their homes with *senko* incense, and of course pray for their relatives' spirits.

On the first day of the three-day festival, *chochin* lanterns are lit inside houses and everyone goes to their family's graves to summon their ancestors' spirits. *Chochin* lanterns and sometimes small fires called *mukae-bi* are also lit at the front doors of their houses to guide the spirits back home.

Unlike my own family history, for most people in Japan the *Obon* family reunion is a joyous time, and they celebrate accordingly. Some towns even have carnivals, complete with amusement park rides, games, and lots of summer foods.

Each town, sometimes each neighbourhood or district, erects a *yagura*, a high wooden tower with a stage for musicians and singers. On each of the three nights, the residents dance the *Bon-Odori*, a folk dance unique to each region, even to each town, to welcome and celebrate their ancestors' spirits. The *Bon-Odori* is danced in a circle around the tower and anyone can join in – strangers, tourists, *gaijin* – as long as you follow the dance steps of everyone else.

The songs can be spiritual, or folk songs, or songs relating the history of the town or region, or a combination of all of them. Even *enka* (popular Japanese music with a traditional style), pop songs, and kid songs can be played, as long as they have the *ondo* beat – a two/two swing style.

The Gifu Prefecture is famous for its all-night dancing on each of the three nights of *Obon*.

Because the festival is all about family, all of our friends were with their families and Ryan and I were on our own. On the first night, we ambled through the town, carried along by the music of drums, flutes, and *shamisen* that floated out from the different neighbourhoods. Thousands of lights hung from posts along all of the roads. The streets and pavements were crowded with people, but not as much as at the Hida Festival, because tourists generally did not come to *Obon*. Most of the townspeople were wearing *yukata*, light cotton kimonos in bright colours. Remember: This honouring of the dead is done in the boiling hot days of summer and dancing works up a sweat.

In the centre of town, we came upon a group of women in blue and white *yukata* dancing reverently and in unison to shamisen music.

'You could join in,' Ryan suggested.

I shook my head. 'This is a sacred festival that has tremendous meaning to those women dancing. I'm just a Brit on the outside looking in. I understand all of this, but I don't *feel* the meaning of *Obon* or this dance the way that those women do. Besides, the last thing I want is to be the town's idiot *gaijin* again.'

The second night we stayed home, because we were outsiders. We played with the cats and watched TV, as families do.

In the evening of the third and final day of *Obon*, people painted *chochin* with their family crests and hung them on their ancestors graves to guide the spirits back to their resting places. Then, thousands of people sent candle-lit lanterns floating down the Miyagawa River, their flickering lights reflected on the dark water, to guide the spirits of their ancestors back to their own world.

The sight was beautiful, magical, almost mystical. My first thought, however, was *'Isn't this bad for the environment?'*

Whenever I want to block my feelings, my head always obliges. And, thanks to *Obon*, I had a lot of feelings to block. I failed, of course.

First came the big picture worries: Where are we all headed? Where am *I* headed? What does life mean?

Then came the more religious worries: Where have all the people who have died ended up? Is there a Heaven? Where did my mother and grandmother end up?

Walking home with Ryan through the beautiful streets of Takayama, the intense celebration of *family* all around me on the last night of the festival, grief suddenly welled up within me for my own lack of family, which surprised me. It had never happened before. I tried to push it away, make it a non-issue. I didn't want to suddenly *care*. But I did. I always had.

Immersed in *Obon*, I finally allowed myself to feel the depth of my loss, not only my mother's death, but the lack of family connection in my childhood and adolescence. I had grown up alone. Generations on both sides of my family had never been keen on any iteration of family beyond the nuclear, and from my parents' divorce to my mother's hospitalisations and my father's disappearing act, I had not even had that.

I found myself also grieving my relationship with my beloved Aunt Cora, my mother's sister, which had diminished to an exchange of Christmas and birthday cards. Once my sanctuary, the progenitor of my love for horses, all animals, and writing, she had married when I was twelve, moved away, and had three children who had been born when I was going to university and working in London.

To my surprise, a longing to connect with my Dad's side of the family welled within me, along with frustration at my inability to do so for the simple reason that I just didn't know *how*. I had no idea where they were living, or how to find them, let alone reach out to them.

In fact, I knew surprisingly little about either side of my family. Hitomi, with all of her photo albums, knew her family tree going back decades, even centuries. I, however, had never really known my Aunt Lydia (my father's sister-in-law), her husband, or her two children (my cousins), because they had settled in the U.S. when I was young.

Hearing only negative stories about that side of my family, I hadn't wanted to meet them. Now, in Japan, with the power of *Obon* all around me, I suddenly felt eager to connect with them. No, it was more than that. I was desperate to know if I truly was alone or if they had experienced the strangeness of our family in the same way that I had.

The fragmentation of my family was expressed in different forms, most particularly in secrecy and walls of silence. My Great-Grandmother on my father's side had become a Jehovah's Witness as did most of her children and grandchildren. This did not go down well with other family members, so they all stopped speaking.

Worst of all, for generations the different sides of my family had walled themselves off from each other. My Aunt Cora had disappeared after her marriage. I had seen my Aunt Lydia only a few times until the age of ten.

Secrets. Walls. Silence.

Yet my childhood cats knew all our family secrets and it didn't seem to matter to them much. I became acutely aware of how extremely grateful I was to the cats at that moment because they had been there for me to share my emotions when I needed it most.

How hard it had been for me as a child and teenager to talk, really talk, to anyone in my family about anything important. I saw now how careful I had been not to show my emotions when I was with my family, where the words 'I love you' were rarely spoken.

Now, here in Takayama, seeing the importance of family and the many different kinds of families all around me, I realised that my Aunt Lydia and cousins in America were not at fault for their silence. They were just acting out the family dysfunction in a way that was usual in my family.

This was a profound moment for me. I suddenly felt lighter. Looking around at all of the *Obon* celebrants, I realised that releasing blame at long last opened me up to other much more positive possibilities, because now I did not have to carry it around with me all the time.

Under the influence of Japan and its people, I had been trying in fits and starts to become more Zen in my life. I was reading books like Eckhart Tolle's *The Power of Now* that encouraged me to live more in the present and also accept the past. I started telling myself 'Stop' whenever I caught myself dwelling on negative thoughts or memories. I even re-read the Old Testament to check if I'd missed anything important the first time around. I read the Dalai Lama's *The Art of Happiness* where I first heard about Viktor Frankl, a Holocaust survivor whose theories were heavily influenced by his suffering in the concentration camps during WW2. Frankl was the founder of logotherapy, similar to *ikigai*, this theory focuses on the importance of finding meaning in life through having a purpose.

All these books helped me look deep inside myself and begin to question the way I had been feeling for most of my life. I could see that I did in fact have a choice: I could either keep dwelling on the past or set it aside and start looking at things differently. Looking at *me* differently.

The knowledge I had gleaned from these and other books I'd read in Takayama had been gestating deep within me and had begun to emerge naturally into my life. Sitting in the kitchen the next morning and looking out the sliding glass doors at the beautiful day, I realised that I could have reacted negatively to *Obon* and Hitomi's stories as I dwelt on my absentee and uncommunicative parents.

But I hadn't. Instead, I had chosen to start releasing past grievances, pain, and fear.

Free from the constant reminders of my past that London always threw at me, I was able to put some distance between me and my past and to start letting go, which meant I was freer to start changing my thoughts, my feelings, my present, and my future.

Instead of overthinking things, I began trying to see unpleasant situations and challenges as part of my life's path, and an opportunity to shine a light on the good parts of my life.

Being away from family and friends and England was also enabling me to see the world with eyes uncoloured by others' expectations and prejudices. Here, in this mountain city, I could feel a seismic shift taking place. I was *consciously* focusing on what made *me* happy, rather than on what made other people happy.

Suddenly, Gershwin jumped up onto my lap and stabbed a claw in my thigh, as a sign of affection, and began to purr. Home, I was starting to learn, doesn't mean where you come from, but where you find yourself right now, in this moment.

Chapter 10: To Change Like a Cat's Eye

猫の目のように変わる / Neko no me no you ni kawaru

The yellow leaves that blanketed the tiny shrine at the end of our road were disappearing, blown away by an increasingly cold breeze. It seemed like colour was being drained from the city as winter approached.

The leaves began their life cycle as verdant green and these rich colours were fading fast, just as fast in fact as our work contracts were due to expire.

I watched as the vermillion and lemon yellow coloured leaves were swept away by cold October winds, and I noticed how this seasonal foliage delighted the local cats, who appeared mesmerised by the slightest gust of wind propelling themselves forward in an attempt to catch the leaf litter, tails perpendicular they chased their tasteless prey away.

Despite my monthly deposits, Ryan and I had only made a small dent in our debts back home. The exchange rate was very much against us, and our Takayama expenses were more than we had anticipated. I had originally thought we'd pay our student loans off in nine months, return to London, and I'd start working on a Master degree, but it was becoming painfully clear that this was as much a dream as us returning to Australia.

'We need better paying jobs if we're to have any hope of being debt-free when we return home,' Ryan said one night as we sat at the kitchen table once again hashing out our financial situation. 'If we stay in Japan and work in a school in a bigger city, we might possibly earn a couple of hundred pounds more a month.'

'But a bigger city means bigger living expenses,' I said.

'True,' he said.

'Besides, I love Takayama, and I love the cats.'

'Me, too. But we have to be practical. We can't make a go of it here. We still have a few months remaining on our contract. There are other schools needing English language teachers, schools that might pay more. It couldn't hurt to have a look at what's out there, could it?'

'I suppose not,' I said with an unhappy sigh.

I hated reality, but I knew how to face it. Even though Ryan and I loved Takayama and our four cats, even though my confidence as a teacher had grown, even though we had forged many wonderful friendships, we couldn't stay. If we were going to fulfill our main goal of returning to England debt-free, we had to find better-paying jobs. We had to leave. With more experience and a better skill set, we stood a good chance of making more money somewhere else. This also meant that any further investigations into *ikigai* or attempts at family reconnection would be put on the backburner while we figured out our next move.

'Whatever job we find, we're at least taking Gershwin with us,' I insisted. I loved all of the cats, but Gershwin was special and Ryan had rescued him, which made him dearest to Ryan's heart and mine. I couldn't, I just couldn't leave him in Takayama.

'There's no need to worry just yet. Let's see what happens,' Ryan said.

With the fate of Gershwin and the other cats on hold, Ryan and I looked for better paying jobs in Japan. Ryan had discovered a website called '*GaijianPot*' that specialised in job vacancies for ex-pats. He trolled the site daily looking for positions that would best suit us.

'CJ! I found it!' he yelled one evening from the bedroom.

Curious, I padded down the noticeably colder hallway from the kitchen and poked my head through the bedroom doorway. 'Found what?'

'The perfect job!'

'There's no such thing,' I assured him as I sat beside him on the big bed.

'The school is called British Hills,' Ryan said, pushing the laptop computer toward me. 'It's sort of a language school set in an English Disneyland™. Take a look.'

Sure enough, located high on a mountaintop, the school was a replica of a Tudor English village, complete with red bricks and black beams, a village green, a sandstone castle with turrets on either side, a chapel whose stone masonry and stained glass windows had actually been shipped over from a church in Scotland, and green lawns around all the buildings. British Hills even had a croquet lawn and a traditional pub.

All the teachers came from the Commonwealth. The lessons included drinking tea with students (something I was already expert in), baking scones (I was an expert at eating), and playing cricket (well, two out of three wasn't bad). Still . . .

'It sounds great, but it looks like they want "real" teachers,' I said as I perused the long list of requirements for applicants.

'But, we both have experience now and we are both British,' Ryan said. 'Let's just apply. It can't hurt, can it?'

Ryan is a laid back guy, but he was practically vibrating with excitement beside me. Suppressing a sigh – I was not as motivated to move as he was – I read through the posting again.

British Hills was close to a ski ground, which ticked Ryan's requirement, and it had a staff swimming pool, which ticked one of my boxes. Staff housing was provided with a significant subsidy. We'd only be paying two hundred pounds a month, a significant savings compared to what we were paying in Takayama. British Hills was not in a big expensive, noisy city, but in another remote rural area of Japan surrounded by forests just made for hiking, which ticked both of our requirements. Best of all, it would give us a twenty-five percent pay increase.

We had spent a year wrapped in the Japanese culture, so different from our own, which was what we had wanted. Now, it was time to be practical, earn some money, and finally pay off our debts.

'We have to apply,' Ryan said.

Internally, I was still torn about leaving the known for the unknown, but rationally I couldn't deny that Ryan really seemed to have found the perfect jobs. 'Absolutely,' I said.

'Right now,' Ryan insisted, 'before someone else gets these jobs.'

'My CV is ready.'

We applied that evening, emailing in our updated CVs and our photos. Image is an important factor in securing a job in Japan. No references were required.

We were quickly contacted via email and scheduled for an interview to be conducted in Tokyo in just two weeks.

I squashed my usual dread about confronting a major metropolis and instead looked on the trip, the city, and the job interview as an adventure. I was becoming Zen, dammit, and I was going to prove it by not freaking out about the city or the interview.

The interview was scheduled during a long three-day holiday weekend, so we didn't need to take much time off work. To my enormous relief, Sayuri agreed to look after the cats. Gershwin, that All Seeing Eye, spotted our packed bags by the door long before any of the other cats. He knew something was up, something he probably wouldn't like. He jumped down from his favourite spot on top of the bookshelf and zoomed down the hallway, tail aloft, and meowing loudly in that haunting noise he made when things weren't to his liking.

'We won't be gone long,' I said as I patted him reassuringly. 'This is necessary so we can make more money and take you home with us next year.'

He blinked his green eyes at me, a feline sign of affection, and then stalked off in a sulk.

Oh, how I wanted to stay! But reality pushed me out the door with Ryan just after ten in the morning. We put our bags in the car, got in, and drove to the Takayama train station through quiet streets, the last quiet I expected to enjoy that weekend.

We stood on the platform and waited anxiously for the JR train, the Hida Express, to arrive.

'Tell me why we're doing this?' I demanded.

'You know why. We need to the money to pay off our student loans.'

Grumbling, partly because I couldn't argue that one down, I settled into unhappy silence.

'After the interview, we can look at the shops and have a nice dinner,' Ryan added.

I had to (silently) concede that his plan had its merits.

Now familiar with Japanese protocol, we became part of an orderly line that boarded the train, found seats in the front car, and settled down for the journey.

The long train trundled out of Takayama station and wound its way through the mountains and the steep forested inclines as it rattled south, ever south. Mountains became foothills and foothills became naked rice paddy fields and small villages. The JR Train was called an express, because it made very few stops. It was, in fact, maddeningly slow. Ryan and I had plenty of time on our hands during the two-hour thirty-minute train ride to the city of Nagoya, where we would be changing trains.

As we journeyed further south, the landscape became more and more built-up with towns. As we neared Gifu City, the landscape was completely transformed. Gone were the lush wild forests, alpine scenery, and paddy fields of mountains and outlying farmland. Everything green looked like it had been pulled back, pruned, and tamed to reflect the efficiency of the city residents and workers. Anything that had dared to poke its head up had been immediately cut back down.

After Gifu City, we passed unending suburbs separated only by a few waterways, until we reached the grey, densely-packed city centre of Nagoya.

Once the train pulled into the station, we found the platform for the *shinkansen,* Japan's renowned bullet train. I was more excited to ride on the high-speed railway, the envy of most of the world with its brilliant engineering and renowned punctuality, than I was about the coming job interview.

Since the 1960s when the train was invented, no passenger had ever been injured or killed in a *shinkansen* train accident. Not bad for a country prone to typhoons and earthquakes. This naturally made me wonder about those four words that Londoners dread to hear: 'leaves on the track.' That always meant often lengthy delays in train travel . . . but not in Japan.

The interior of the train was, of course, spotless. The seats had perfectly positioned white cloth-covered headrests that I suspected were changed prior to each journey. It looked like we had boarded a luxury airliner rather than a train. We sat in the unreserved section near the front of the train and waited for the usual announcements to finish.

I had heard stories of train drivers in Japan being put on extra training if their trains were ever late (just management's little nudge toward punctuality). There was no need to censure the driver today. We pulled out of the station spot on time. Farmland, suburbs, and cities rushed by my window in a blur.

A cute dimpled girl wearing a green apron pushed a trolley heavily laden with sandwiches, snacks, and even beer up the aisle toward me. The *shinkansen* treats its passengers like adults, which is rare on public transport in most Western countries, where you must refrain from practically everything, even talking.

No rubbish was left anywhere. Nothing was dropped unmindfully to the floor; nothing was spilt on the tables. The passengers treated themselves, their fellow travellers, and the train with respect. Oh, how I wished Londoners would demonstrate even a tenth of that consciousness and consideration on buses and the underground.

Just after three o'clock that afternoon, the bullet train pulled to a smooth stop into Tokyo. The station was, as I had feared, mobbed with people coming and going at urban speed, not the peaceful rural pace I had lived in for nearly a year.

The cluttered station walls and video screens had a mixture of adverts vying for the attention of the bustling passersby. The small cafes located in the centre of the platforms were full to capacity with salarymen slurping noodles and lost-looking tourists clutching subway maps. We boarded the crowded train to Shibuya.

Well-trained by now, Ryan and I stood on the left side of the escalator as everyone else did as we rode upward to the main floor of the station and the city beyond. Endless streams of people were pouring from every orifice of the city. With the sun waning in the sky, every building was lit up. Neon signs blanketed the skyline, along with ginormous video screens streaming an endless array of commercials.

I pulled Ryan to a stop before the famous statue of Hachikō, the dog who used to wait outside the station every day for his owner to escort him home from his commute, until one day his owner did not return. He had died in an accident. But Hachiko went back to the same spot day in day out in hope his master would return. The Japanese treasure this true story as a perfect lesson in loyalty.

Our job interview was at five-thirty, so we didn't have time to go to our hotel, drop our bags, and clean up. Instead, we headed straight for Tokyu, a DIY store in the heart of town. Our interview would be conducted in a café on the seventh floor.

It has become something of a cliché, but Tokyo really is like a 1980s

Blade Runner version of the future. Its towering buildings and glaring adverts made me feel as distant from my small mountain home as if I had flown to another planet. Halloween – one of the two Western holidays the Japanese adore – was nearing and orange was everywhere. Ugly-faced witches peered at me unnervingly through shop windows. There was so much to see and do, all I wanted was to shake off my pre-interview nerves and go explore.

'Look at all this amazing stuff,' I said eagerly as we maneuvered our way through the throngs.

'I know. I wish we were shopping instead of interviewing,' Ryan agreed. .

When we stepped off the escalator, I hurriedly switched gears, because there, seated at a table by a window with expansive views of Tokyo, was Mr. Maki, who was in charge of teacher recruitment for British Hills. I recognised him from pictures on the school's website, and he recognised us from the pictures we had submitted. He stood up to greet us and I was a little taken aback. He wore glasses, which had been missing from his picture, and he was less well groomed than I had anticipated. His suit was a little crumpled and he was unshaven.

Then he smiled warmly, greeted us casually in flawless English, and urged us to take a seat and order something. He was the most laid-back Japanese man I'd ever met. Some of my anxiety evaporated into the store's filtered air.

'It's nice to finally meet you,' Mr. Maki said. 'You both look younger in person.'

Fortunately, that didn't seem to be a bad thing in his book.

'It's great to meet you, too,' I said.

While Mr. Maki sipped on his green tea, I splurged on tea and a slice of orange Halloween cake from one of the circulating trolleys, and Ryan asked for a simple cup of coffee.

'So, CJ, can you tell me about your teaching experience in the UK?' Mr.Maki said.

'I have over two years' experience working with students of all ages from different countries, especially Europe. I've also worked with students who have learning disabilities.'

'She has a teaching qualification,' Ryan added.

This pleased Mr. Maki. 'You have the requisite visas to continue working in Japan?'

'Yes, we do,' Ryan replied. (I was too busy salivating over my luscious slice of cake to answer.)

'That's good. Then we can simply extend them if you come and work for us.' Maki said.

I was keen to immerse myself in my cake, but Mr. Maki had other ideas. This was a job interview, after all, and he actually had questions he wanted to ask and answers he wanted to hear.

'What's your background, Ryan?'

'Before I came to Japan, I worked for a press agency in Australia. I have a Fine Arts degree from university.'

'Good,' said Mr. Maki. 'Because you have a creative background, you might be interested in some of our artistic classes.'

He had Ryan's rabid attention.

'We like to teach our students through immersion and activity,' Mr. Maki continued. 'A photography course lends itself to that process. How do you find teaching?'

'I enjoy it,' Ryan lied. 'I like meeting lots of different people.'

The questions continued until finally, Mr. Maki leaned back in his chair to spin a tempting web of incentives to accept the posts he was offering. While he expounded on the glories of British Hills, I could finally dive into my cake. I had to suppress a moan of pleasure. Velvet with a zesty orange kick melted on my tongue.

'In addition to standard English-language classes, you will be teaching things like British sports, scone-making classes, and aromatherapy. Your normal work days will be Monday through Friday, but there will be special occasions when you will also be asked to work six or seven days a week. In recompense, you will have a six-week paid holiday in the summer.'

This sounded too good to be true.

'Because you are a couple, you won't be expected to live in the staff house with everyone else. You will be given your own separate living quarters in a villa further down the mountain and you will have a car to get to work. Will that be okay?'

I could barely disguise my excitement.

'That would suit us very well,' I said eagerly.

'When do you need us to start?' he asked.

'Well, that's the thing,' Mr. Maki replied with a cautious smile. 'We really need teachers who are able to start at Christmas. We have people leaving and we need replacements urgently.'

I glanced at Ryan. He met my eyes. Once again, we would be starting a new job during the Christmas season without a holiday for just us, the cats, and our friends first.

'Can you start on Boxing Day?' Mr. Maki asked.

I wasn't sure I wanted to leave Takayama so close to Christmas. I loved the town during the holidays. Then there were the cats to worry about. We hadn't found homes for Iko, Niko, and Takashi . . . and we hadn't told Mr. Maki that Gershwin was part of our package. This was October and we hadn't even thought about packing, let alone moving. This potential new job was suddenly too real. Everything was happening way too fast. The heat rose in my face.

'Sure,' Ryan said. 'We're ready to start then.'

I promptly kicked him under table and rolled my eyes. He maintained his bland smile.

'Excellent,' said Mr. Maki. 'Then let me officially welcome you to British Hills. I will be sending you additional information about all of the arrangements to get you set up properly.'

He stood up. Ryan and I quickly stood up. He shook our hands and walked off.

The interview was over. The move was on.

'Shouldn't we have discussed this first?' I demanded when Mr. Maki was out of earshot.

'I thought we had.' Ryan said.

'How are we going to re-home three cats?'

'They're lovely cats. Someone will want to give them a home, I promise.'

We rode the escalator down to the ground floor, navigated our way through the throng of shoppers, and finally stepped outside into the hustle of the streets teeming with people.

After living the best part of a year in a rundown rectal clinic in a rural mountain town, I had wanted a taste of luxury, so we had booked ourselves into a European-style hotel on Odaiba. The hotel had shops, restaurants, a swimming pool, yoga classes, and an *onsen*. We walked into our room on the twenty-second floor and just stared at the spectacular view of the bay and the city beyond.

This was luxury with a vengeance.

I threw myself onto the huge bed, glad to be off my feet, away from the madding crowds for a while. Part of me wanted to mentally dissect the momentous decision Ryan and I had just made, but I was too weary, too hungry, and too interested in enjoying my brief time in Tokyo with Ryan to bother.

We only had two days in Tokyo and we wanted to see as much of it as possible. So, I tried as much as I could to fend off worrying thoughts of re-homing three out of four cats.

The next morning, we took the computerised train, similar to London's Dockland's Light Railway, back over Tokyo Bay, the water glistening in the sunlight and reflecting the forest of tall buildings that surrounded it. Back in the city centre, we got off the train, switched into full tourist mode, we tried to go to the Imperial Palace, but had arrived to find we had missed the tour.

'Let's head to the nearest cat café,' I said brightly.

Ryan rolled his eyes, but he was smiling. He wasn't as keen as I was to go to one of the city's famed cat cafés, but he was perfectly willing to humour me.

We had waterproof rain jackets and so, undaunted by the wet, we made a dash for the main street and started walking in the general direction of where my guidebook said we would find a cat café.

Our path led us through the Ginza district where the streets were less busy, because they were lined by high-end shops that only the wealthy could afford. We also walked past interesting nooks that held *yakitori* (ramen) eateries whose entrances were decorated with coloured posters of old shogun movies. My nose was assailed by the aromas of fermented soy sauce wafting out the open doorways.

We stopped at a tiny Shinto shrine tucked under a train bridge that seemed to be dedicated to some sort of animal. At first glance, I thought it was either a cat or a dog. When I got closer, I realised it was a fox. A pair of foxes, actually: beautiful stone fox sculptures stood on either side of the little shrine with a red and white rope dangled perfectly in the centre over the doorway. People had left offerings, even *Maneki-Nekos,* the white beckoning cat, and other good luck charms.

The fox plays an important role in the Shinto faith. It is the messenger of Inari, a major Shinto goddess who is the deity of rice. Inari is literally the goddess of the nation's sustenance. Honouring the animal at the shrine made me question how a fox could be so revered in Japan, yet vilified in England as a pest worthy of being hunted down by packs of ravenous hounds.

Ryan could have stayed at the shrine for an hour snapping photos, but I was determined to visit a cat café. With my improved Japanese skills, I asked a few people for directions but, as usual in Japan, no one seemed to know where the cat café was. So, Ryan and I jumped into a black saloon-style taxi, hoping the driver would know the way to the feline-petting establishment.

'*Wakaranai*,' (I don't understand) the taxi driver said, shaking his head at the address. He started driving down a side street. I swung my head back and forth like I was watching a tennis match as I looked for kitty signage.

I was growing increasingly disheartened by the lack of anything feline-related when Ryan said suddenly: 'That's it! Over there.'

He'd spotted a large poster of a white mother cat with ginger ears and four white and ginger kittens on a billboard beside a building, which also had a wooden sign, a hand drawn poster of other cats, and an arrow pointing at the door.

The taxi driver had understood the address after all. We paid him gratefully and got out of the taxi.

We dashed through the front door of the cat café to avoid the rain and were brought up short by a matronly-looking Japanese woman dressed in an over-sized sweater and green apron. We dutifully paid our cover charge, placed our backpacks in a locker, washed our hands, removed our shoes, and put on the usual brown slippers provided in public establishments. Finally, we were allowed to climb a flight of stairs to the first floor taken up entirely by the café. We walked excitedly into the large main room to meet the kitties.

The café had a linoleum floor with lots of mats for cats to scratch, along with lots of cat trees and cubes, and shelves with cat beds. Long windows on the back wall let in lots of sunlight in which many of the cats were napping. Five low lounges with low coffee tables and armchairs around the perimeter were presumably for human visitors, but of course several cats had claimed some of them. A few brightly-coloured cat-themed knick-knacks were displayed on shelves and counters, along with for-sale items like tea in cat-shaped packages, cat-shaped clothes pegs, and designer cat-shaped handbags.

Unlike almost every other Tokyo establishment, the café was not crowded. In fact, it was nearly empty, probably because it did not serve food, only tea. This was a place for people to come and pet and play with cats and then leave.

A rather large ginger Scottish fold swaggered past us, keeping an eye on the Japanese customers sipping tea, talking, and petting whatever cat was to hand. I spied a pretty ginger and white cat sitting in a regal faux leopard-skin chair, its eyes half closed and mouth slightly open.

I was in heaven.

We sat down at a low wooden table. 'Look at this,' Ryan said, opening a photo album that rested on the table. It had pictures, descriptions, and profiles of all *twenty-three* cats living at the café.

Our efficient waitress had appeared at our table before I could read even the first profile. Ryan ordered a coffee to warm himself up, I ordered green tea, and then I settled in to read aloud to Ryan every single one of the twenty-three cat profiles.

'This is wonderful,' I said happily.

'This one looks like Garfield,' Ryan said pointing at a rotund ginger tabby with a self-satisfied expression.

Having gone through the entire album, Ryan picked up a cat wand with something feathered at the end and became instantly engrossed in playing with a tabby that resembled Takashi.

After our waitress brought our drinks, I settled back in my chair to people and cat watch. A middle-aged Japanese couple sat happily in one corner with an eager black kitten batting at and scampering after the feathered toy they dangled in front of it. A mother looked on with a smile as her seven-year-old daughter squealed in delight at a young male tabby, an exact Takashi lookalike, batting at the feather at the end of the wand she held. The tabby clearly loved the attention they were lavishing on him.

A pair of American tourists in their twenties walked into the café and promptly sat down on the floor, dangling a string for a pure white female cat that delighted in jumping in and out of wicker baskets on the floor in determined pursuit of that string.

What amazed me was not the diversity of the cats, but the diversity of the customers, all of whom had come together because of one thing: their love of cats. I felt a little overwhelmed with happiness at finding other people who loved cats as much as I did, and also the fact that it was another sign of *ikigai* was at work.

It took some doing, but after almost an hour, Ryan finally pried me out of the cat café. 'I want to see the more traditional side of Tokyo,' he insisted, so we made our way via subway to the historic *Asakusa* entertainment district, which is famous for its enormous Buddhist temple, *Sensō-ji*, built in the seventh century, destroyed in World War II air raids, and rebuilt after the war.

Stretching over two hundred and fifty metres from Thunder Gate is *Nakamise-dori*, a narrow shopping street originally built in the early eighteenth century. It is lined with nearly ninety different shops and stalls, some of them over two hundred years old. Each one of them was packed with tourists from all over the world buying up souvenirs. We were not immune. We inched our way along the crowded pedestrian path, stopping at various shops on the way.

Among the tourist souvenir stalls were some wonderful finds. One shop had brightly-coloured folding fans, another sold Japanese chopsticks, one shop displayed dozens of different Japanese masks, ranging from animals like cats to cheerful peasants and fierce demons. One shop actually specialised in pet clothes, so I bought Gershwin a red *matsuri* (festival) kimono.

Ryan couldn't hide his amusement. 'Do you actually expect to convince Gershwin to let you put that on him?'

'Yes, of course! You know how much he loves attention.' (Not only did I get the kimono on Gershwin and he accepted it, I often had him dressed up.)

Walking out of the retail world of *Nakamise-dori*, we came to the scarlet Hozomon (Treasure) Gate, which is the entrance to the complex's inner grounds and buildings.

When we walked through the Gate we saw, immediately on our left, the famed Five Storey Pagoda (*Guju-No-To*), which symbolises the five elements: earth, water, fire, wind, and sky.

The Five Storey Pagoda is particularly important, because it is said to contain some of the Buddha's ashes, along with thousands of memorial tablets. Which meant, to my enormous disappointment, that it is closed to the public.

So, we walked on with the throng of visitors and came to an enormous incense cauldron. Taking our cue from the many Japanese visitors, we rubbed the incense smoke into our clothes and bodies, we later learned it brings good health. (The incense stayed in my hair for days.)

Next came *Omizusha* (water hut), a purification fountain from which water pours from eight dragon statues. We saw people briefly washing their hands and mouths with the streaming water in a specific order, so we did the same.

On either side of the path leading to the actual temple are small stalls and buildings. One of these was particularly popular: it had *omikuji* (paper fortunes). I'm not normally superstitious, but I thought I could use some direction. 'We have to go in,' I said.

'Why?' Ryan asked.

'Because we are about to make a major change in our lives and I, at least, feel the need for some guidance, and direction with what to do with my life.'

'I'm in,' he said.

So, we walked inside, which was a little difficult because of all the other people who had also come for a little guidance. On either side of the small building were rows of wooden drawers. I put a one hundred yen coin in a slot, chose a silver canister from a group of canisters next to the drawers, and shook it carefully. Out came a stick, which had a number in *kanji* on it. That number told me which wooden drawer to open. I replaced the stick and the canister and hunted for the right drawer. When I found it, I opened it and found neatly folded pieces of paper. I took one.

On this paper could be a great blessing, a middle blessing, small blessing, blessing, a future blessing, or (gulp!) a curse.

'Don't worry,' Ryan said. 'If it's bad news, you just have to tie the paper to that rack over there. That's where bad luck *omikuji* are put. Then you can try again for a good fortune.' Ryan knew this from watching what the other tourists were doing.

Biting my lower lip – I could not believe I was so nervous – I slowly unfolded the strip of paper and read my fate. It was *dai-kichi*, the luckiest one! 'This is incredible. I'm never usually lucky. I never win anything.'

'What does it say?' Ryan demanded.

I read it carefully to myself and then, grinning, read it aloud to him. 'It says that if I am more honest with myself, I will have more good luck and that, if I set my desires aside, if I spend more time helping others, I will be happy.'

'Sounds like teaching to me.'

'Me, too,' I said with relief.

'Do you think helping *others* means cats too?' I asked.

'I don't see why not,' Ryan said.

Reassured that our decision to come to Tokyo and take the new job at British Hills was the right one, I walked happily out of the temple and headed for the ferry back to Odaiba.

The late afternoon was cool and dry when we got off the ferry and began to walk to our hotel, joining throngs of shoppers and tourists strolling along and enjoying a day away from Tokyo's dense crowds.

The next morning we got up early and, under a clear blue sky, went for a walk before breakfast around Tokyo Bay. The sun was out, but it was still chilly. There was a keen bunch of middle-aged Japanese walkers who exercised around the bay each morning.

Closer to the marina, which was packed with people waiting for the ferry, we watched hip-looking men with their trendy canine counterparts kitted out in similar clothing. I was going to miss the sights of Tokyo.

'We really need to visit more often,' I said.

'Absolutely,' Ryan agreed.

Later that morning, as we checked out of our mock European hotel, I said a sad farewell to our room.

As hard as it was to leave all of that luxury, I had cats waiting for me and I was eager to cuddle with them again. So, Ryan and I bundled our cases into a taxi, which delivered us right on time to the crowded train station.

I was going home to what would soon not be my home. A momentous decision had been made on this brief holiday and I wondered again and again how the new home and the new school and the new town would impact not only our lives, but four cats. Somehow, we had to find good homes for Iko, Niko, and Takashi and, based on our previous efforts to re-home Gershwin, that seemed like a nigh on impossible task.

And then there was Gershwin himself. Ryan and I had carefully not said a word to Mr. Maki about the feline roommate we would be bringing with us to Fukushima. We both knew better than to ask permission from him, as it would result in a big fat 'No.' We'd have to make our own (secret) arrangements to smuggle him from Takayama to our new home. Keeping him secret, however, would be difficult, because Gershwin could be piercingly vocal when placed in the cat carrier.

Still, whatever it took, Gershwin was coming with us.

Chapter 11: No Cat Was Seen on The Street

通りには猫の子一匹もいなかった / Tohri Niwa Neko No Ko
Ippiki Mo Inakatta

The crisp autumn leaves that once covered the grounds of the small lacquered wood shrine at the end of our street were gone. Snow was coming, much to the consternation of the elderly caretaker, whose job it was to keep the shrine in an impeccable state. The old man had spent the last few months diligently fending off the yellowing leaves, badgering away at all hours. Soon, though, he would be putting his broom down and picking up a shovel to wage his winter battle against snow and ice.

As the strength of the sunlight faded and the evenings came earlier and grew darker, smoke fires perfumed the chilly air.

I had realised since we'd come back from Tokyo how much this old rundown apartment felt like home . . . just as we were about to leave it forever. I'd had fun seeing the cat café and the temple in Tokyo, but I was so much happier to be home with our cats, enjoying the peace and simplicity of life in Takayama.

As the weeks passed and the temperature dropped, the TV weather presenters, who always greeted their viewers with a formal bow, had swapped their smiley summer icons on their weather maps for less friendly looking white blizzard icons. Any day now, the Japanese Alps – and Takayma – were about to get seriously dumped on. This extreme change in seasons heralded a similarly extreme change in our lives. October had passed, November was nearly through. At the end of December, Ryan and I (and Gershwin) would embark on our new lives.

Doubts continued to plague me. I reminded myself that the opportunity was too good to miss. Earning a higher salary meant that we could afford to finally pay off our debts *and* pay for one cat's flight ticket back to Europe with us when our new year-long contract ended.

Still, I could hear those old negative voices in my head start to chatter. Whenever I grew anxious, I used the Zen proverb 'move and the way will open' as my daily, sometimes hourly, mantra, hoping it was true, hoping the way would open enough for me to believe Ryan and I had made the right decision.

Back at the apartment, belief was hindered by four pairs of feline eyes watching every move I made as I began packing for British Hills. My heart broke every time my gaze met theirs. Each moment I spent with them now seem tarnished by our looming exit from the city that had been so good to us and our final goodbyes to three of the four cats watching me.

New homes needed to be found for three wonderful, loving cats. Well, two, actually. Sayuri had made a deep connection with Takashi and, although she hadn't said anything yet, I felt sure she would offer to keep him. That left finding a new home for Iko and Niko. The school was uncertain if it would keep this apartment for its teachers. They couldn't stay here. Much more importantly, I had promised our Canadian predecessors, Kath and Jake, that I would find Iko and Niko a good home. Ryan and I decided that the sisters should first be advertised in the local newspapers to see if we could find them a new home together.

So Kimiko, our school receptionist, placed adverts in the local paper. We had no response. I put up signs at my local vets, where I was now a familiar face. I felt confident that the doctor and his staff would put in a good word for my kitties with their clients. Above all, I was determined that Iko and Niko would be re-homed together. Then disaster struck.

One night in November, heavy snow blanketed the city as I was preparing dinner for the cats, I called out to them but only three appeared. Iko was missing, which was unusual because she loved her food. I searched her usual hideouts, but she was just simply not in the apartment. Iko must be outside. We'd started letting the two sisters outside now and then, because it was just too unfair to keep them inside all the time. They always came back, particularly for food, so where on earth had Iko got to? Surely she couldn't have gone far in this blizzard.

I opened the kitchen's sliding door and called to Iko again and again, but she remained stubbornly absent.

With the early and very dark evenings had come a dramatic drop in temperature. I was frantic with worry. The empty pink cat basket haunted me. Iko, a cat so used to creature comforts, would not survive long in the severe cold. Ryan and I bundled up and went outside, circling the apartment building and walking up and down the street calling for her.

'CJ, it's late. We're freezing. We have to go home,' Ryan said finally.

'She can't have gone far in this weather. She'll be back soon. Maybe someone thought she was a stray and took her in from the cold.'

I didn't believe him. I knew he was just trying to ease my anxiety.

Iko was gone.

I wanted to knock on every door and ask if anyone had seen Iko, but because of the language barrier, and because the cats were not supposed to be let outside in the first place, I couldn't.

Iko was gone.

Walking back into the apartment, my eyes filled with thick unshed tears as I made myself accept that she might be lost. I made myself carry on with our usual evening routine. I went to bed with Ryan, but I tossed and turned and couldn't sleep. I'd been entrusted with Iko's care and I had failed her.

I got up early the next morning and hurried to check on the cat dishes I'd left outside. The biscuits were gone and there were paw prints in the thick snow. But I couldn't be sure if Iko had eaten the food or if one of the numerous stray cats who lived in the area had stopped by for a plate of food. Nevertheless, the sight gave me some hope that she might be okay.

As soon as I could, I hurried over to Sayuri's house. I'd called her the night before and she had kindly offered to design some Lost Cat posters in Japanese. It was surprising that, despite the large numbers of pets in Japan, animals never seemed to get lost, if posters were anything to go by. I hadn't seen one the whole time I'd been in the country. That changed that morning with a vengeance. We plastered Sayuri's posters all around the neighbourhood.

But all day long, not one person called to say they'd found Iko.

Iko's disappearance couldn't have come at a worse time. Not only did I need to re-home her – which meant showing her off to prospective new owners – but if she magically reappeared a few weeks later, she would come home to an empty apartment. We would have left for Fukushima, and Let's English was still leaning toward not using the apartment for its teachers. No shelter, no food, no sister, no one to care for her.

This past spring, summer, and autumn, Iko had taken to racing after our bikes when Ryan and I cycled to work each morning. What if she had taken that familiar route and gone too far and couldn't find her way back? Or perhaps she had sensed our impending departure and had run away in protest.

'I think I saw some paw prints in the snow outside when I came in,' Ryan said. 'Maybe she came back while we were at work.'

I waited late into that night, but she didn't come home. Her sister Niko was distraught, pacing up-and-down the hall and in and out of rooms. I tried to tell her that everything would be okay, but she just meowed plaintively and went off to search the house again. Struggling against a fresh bout of tears, I left some more cat food outside the kitchen door in case Iko came back and, reluctantly, went to bed.

Two whole freezing cold nights passed and Iko was still missing. I felt horrible. Why had I let the sisters outside in the first place? I should have listened to Mr. Iwaki (and our neighbours).The sisters should have remained indoor cats. They should have been safe inside the apartment. If Iko ever returned, I vowed that inside was exactly where she would stay from now on.

I spent the next day imagining all kind of horrible scenarios: what if she was trapped somewhere and couldn't get out and was slowly starving and freezing to death? What if she'd been run over by a car and was injured and couldn't walk home? What if she'd been run over and killed?

Once again, I walked along the ice-covered streets of my neighbourhood calling and searching for Iko, my heart leaping at every shadow that might be her . . . and wasn't. Later that night, the third night she'd gone missing, I put out yet more cat biscuits and a few blankets. The weather forecast was for more snow and even colder temperatures.

A fourth night passed. And a fifth. And a sixth. I finally lost hope of ever seeing my sweet Iko again. Even Niko had given up calling for her.

I awoke the next morning to a quiet house and the heavy depression that had beset me the moment I had realised Iko had disappeared. Feeling sluggish, I got up and put on the kettle. The house was freezing. Even blasting the heater couldn't warm the kitchen up. I sat at the table shivering as I sipped my tea.

Suddenly, I saw something moving outside the sliding kitchen doors' frosted glass.

I didn't leap to my feet and rush to the door, because I didn't want to scare away whatever it was outside. Instead, I tiptoed over to the door and gently slid it back. Cold air rushed over me as I stared down at a miracle.

Iko, a slightly thinner version of her former bulky self, stood uncertainly by the door. Her small pink tongue emerged from her mouth as she hesitated to come in, like an unwelcome guest. Then, before I could say a word, she streaked past me and headed straight for the food bowl.

'Where on earth have you been? We've been so worried about you!' I cried as relief swamped me, tinged with a little anger at the hell she had put me and Ryan through. Relief and gratitude won out. As she gobbled her food, I crooned welcome and love to her as I petted her. Through cold, damp grey fur I could feel her spine and her ribs.

I rushed through the apartment searching for Niko so I could show her that Iko had returned. But, when I carried her into the kitchen, to my surprise, Niko took one sniff of her sister, let out an uncharacteristic hiss, and ran off. I could not believe my eyes. These two cats had been inseparable their entire lives and now, after a horrible ordeal, her sister had turned on Iko! Instead of welcoming her, instead of comforting her, Niko treated her sister like a stranger – and therefore a danger – because Iko had lived on the streets for six long nights and she smelled different. Therefore, as far as a cat was concerned, she *was* different.

'Well, *I'm* glad you're home,' I crooned to Iko as I picked her up and cuddled her against my chest, her heavy purr reverberating against my ribs. Nearly limp with relief that she had finally come home, and was uninjured, I gave her an extra big portion of tuna. While she devoured her second course, I made a bed just for her under the *kotatsu*.

Gershwin and Takashi seemed unfazed by Iko's different scent. They glided over to her, smelled her at both ends, and then became distracted by the empty tuna can on the kitchen counter. As far as they were concerned, Iko was now officially old news.

While Iko cleaned herself under the *kotatsu*, I called Ryan, Sayuri, and everyone else who had helped in the search for Iko to let them know of her safe return.

When he got home that night, Ryan tried to keep a good English stiff upper lip, but I could see that he was overjoyed at her return. In the next days, he kept giving her extra pats and treats during our afternoon breaks and every time we got back from work at night. She, of course, lapped up all the attention . . . and food.

Ever since Iko had disappeared, I had started to wonder if taking Gershwin with us, first to British Hills and then England, was the right thing to do. After all, he was a Takayama city cat. Perhaps he'd be better off with a nice family in the home town he loved rather than enduring a long journey to the other side of Japan and then the eventual international flight to a foreign country. Was I being selfish expecting this cat to want to travel with us to a country that wasn't his own, that had very different odors and sounds and people?

'Cats love England,' Ryan assured me. 'There are thousands of picture books showing happy felines lounging in lush English back gardens, sprawled on rugs in front of electric fires, and sleeping on the backs of over-stuffed chairs.' He considered a moment. 'I wonder if Gershwin will get a Cockney meow if we move to the East End.'

While I worried myself silly over moving Gershwin, Sayuri had been working on our behalf. The day after Iko returned home, she called me. 'I have found someone who might want to take one of the sisters!' she said announced.

'What? Who? How?' I exclaimed.

'She is a lady I know who works in a *ryokan* [an inn] and she wants a personal companion. But CJ, she only wants one cat, not two.'

My happy bubble burst.

'She would like to come see the sisters today as soon as she can get time off from work,' Sayuri continued. 'Will that be okay?'

'What?' I said, my breaking heart trying to listen to my head reminding it that Iko and Niko were no longer bonded. 'Oh! Yes. Yes, of course! Send her round.'

As soon as I hung up the phone, I turned into an English version of a whirling dervish. I cleaned the apartment from top to bottom, hampered by the many boxes Ryan and I had started to pack. (It is amazing how many things you can acquire, on a budget, during a single year in Japan.) Then I rushed out to shop for the best green tea I could find for the occasion.

Rather than mirroring my frazzled energy, Ryan was less emotional when the doorbell rang. He opened the door and politely greeted Maika, a conservative-looking woman in her mid-twenties with neatly cut hair and a quiet disposition. In short, the polar opposite of Sayuri in every way who followed her into the apartment to both provide formal introductions and act as our interpreter.

When I led everyone into the lounge to drink my specially procured green tea and to chat, Gershwin pushed himself to the front of the other cats (all of them curious about the stranger) to put on a heart-stopping show for our guests. He jumped up on top of the glass case holding a Samurai statuette we had inherited with the apartment, then vaulted up to the ceiling beams, and perched on a ledge to watch us.

'The sisters are just over there,' I said, a little embarrassed by Gershwin's bad manners.

'This is for you,' Maika said, handing me a small pink box which held, I soon discovered, the most delicious tiny cream cakes and macaroons I'd ever seen. I was deeply touched. Maika was taking care of me in this vital meeting, not the other way round. It was a good sign. Whichever cat she chose, the sister would clearly have a loving new owner to care for her.

She put down her cat carrier and went over to meet the sisters. Niko, of course, was acting shy. Iko walked right up to Maika and Maika began to gravitate toward our little runaway. As she gently pet both sisters, I told her about their history, their characters, and what made each of them unique, while Sayuri translated for me.

'I think Niko might be . . . easier to manage,' I said. Iko's recent disappearance would not be a recommendation to this woman, nor did Iko's robust personality seem like a good fit.

So Maika picked up Niko in her arms, and Niko began to purr. They bonded instantly. My relief was vast as Maika smiled. Niko was going to have a happy life when she left this apartment.

Finally sitting down to tea and the amazing little tea cakes and macaroons (I had two), and with Sayuri translating, Maika explained that she worked and lived at the *ryokan* in Hida-Ichinomiya, a small village about twenty minutes south of Takayama, where she was feeling both isolated and lonely. She had grown up with pets and she missed having a furry companion. Niko would have all the attention and care from Maika that she could crave plus attention from the *ryokan*'s guests. Niko was going to a cat paradise and I could finally stop worrying about her future.

After tea, Maika put Niko put in the cat basket with relative ease. I gave my sweet little koala cat a final pet and, tears filling my eyes, said goodbye. Then Maika carried Niko down to her car, Sayuri joining her because she had to go back to work. With that, Niko was gone. I would never see her again.

The house seemed extraordinarily quiet when they'd gone. I reminded myself there were still three other cats who needed my attention, and tried as best as I could to talk myself out of the sadness I felt separating the sisters.

But when Ryan and I got up the next morning, the kitchen felt empty with one less cat. I packed Niko's yellow cat bed away with a heavy heart. She had a new bed now in her new house.

Ryan gave me a long hug. 'Look, you've done the best you could under the circumstances. Remember how Iko and Niko were found. They are lucky cats, really.'

I told myself to listen to his words and stop beating myself up for not keeping the sisters together. Iko helped. Unlike Niko's reaction when Iko had disappeared into that blizzard, Iko did not go hunting for her sister through the apartment. She seemed, in fact, remarkably unperturbed by Niko's absence and Gershwin and Takashi were downright nonchalant.

If the cats could take Niko's absence in their stride, I could, too.

Chapter 12: Like a Cat Burying Poop

猫の手も借りたい / Neko No Te Mo Karitai

A few days later, I was busy making breakfast when I caught a glimpse of Gershwin doing something quite out of character. He squatted on top of a green shopping bag on the kitchen floor and proceeded to pee unabashedly in front of me.

'What are you *doing*?' I demanded in horror.

He looked at me with his big greens eyes, completely unconcerned by my outrage, and then ran off, leaving a yellow puddle of piddle behind him.

'Is that his comment about our sending Niko away?' I demanded of Ryan.

He shook his head with a smile. 'I think it's something else entirely. We're going to have to get him done before we leave,' he said. 'It won't be fair to Sayuri for us to hand Gershwin over to her when he's behaving like this.'

Sayuri had agreed to take care of him, Takashi, and Iko if necessary, while Ryan and I moved everything to British Hills and got the lay of the land. Once we were settled, we'd come back to take Gershwin to our new home.

As I already knew, countries like England require that any travelling animal have a pet passport and that animal must also be spayed or neutered. Without the procedure, Gershwin couldn't get an entry permit and return with us to England in a year. Nor, as a more immediate concern, could I let him pee all over Sayuri's apartment while she cat-sat for us.

There was no choice. Gershwin's nuts were toast.

'You're right,' I said with a weary sigh. 'I know you're right.' Great. Another job in the midst of packing for our move.

I booked Gershwin that day for an appointment at the vets. I did not need him peeing all over the apartment and our things when we were trying to pack everything up. De-sexing was the right thing to do, even though I felt a bit guilty about doing the procedure in the midst of moving, which was already proving stressful for the cats.

I took Gershwin through the main doors of the clinic the next day and waited nervously until his name was called. To my surprise, Dr. Iguchi himself walked into the waiting room with the same warm smile I'd come to know so well over the last year. This Japanese vet had helped me so kindly through all of my feline misadventures despite neither of us speaking much of each other's language.

'Gershwin-sama,' he said, stretching out his hand.

This was it. I handed the cat carrier over and told myself that this was the next stage of our journey together.

'Come get Gersh-kun tomorrow,' Dr. Iguchi said.

I nodded in agreement and that was that.

I went back home and, despite all the moving boxes, the apartment felt empty. Only one cat greeted me when I walked through the door. Sayuri had visited us nearly every day and every time she had walked into the apartment, Takashi made a beeline to her, she would pick him up and pet him, and he would purr like a lion on steroids. The pair had become nearly inseparable over the last few weeks. One day, she looked into his yellow eyes and said: 'Takashi-kun, would you like to stay with me?' He rubbed his head under her chin in agreement. Her happiness was equal to my relief. Takashi had found his home.

With Takashi living with Sayuri, Niko settling into her new home at the *ryokan*, and Gershwin at the vets, I only had Iko to greet me at the door when I came home from work. She was noticeably less pushy to go outside these days and much more affectionate after her misadventure. She ran up to me now, emitted a loud 'meow!' and performed a giant ankle rub. I picked her up, cuddled her for a long moment, and set her down reluctantly.

Then, with a sigh, I got back to packing up more belongings to ship via Japanese Post to our new lodgings, wondering all the time if I had made the right decision. Deep down, I wanted to hide away in the Japanese Alps forever, but I knew that wasn't Ryan's dream. Teaching had become fairly enjoyable for both of us, but our hearts wanted something else. We needed to figure out what we wanted to do with our lives and staying stuck in one place wouldn't help.

The next morning, I went back to the vets to collect Gershwin. An assistant ushered me into an exam room. The next moment, the vet walked in carrying a drowsy Gershwin. He lifted his head and blinked his green eyes twice at me. I could sense he was as eager to leave as I was eager to get him back home.

'The surgery went well,' Dr. Iguchi announced. 'Gersh-kun is fine. He must get lots of rest.'

'Right. Thank you so much, Dr. Iguchi,' I said as we loaded Gershwin into his carrier. I turned to thank the vet again and found a white tissue thrust in my face. 'What's that?'

'You want to keep?'

I peeled back the tissue to find Gershwin's tiny balls. Trying desperately not to turn green as images of sushi filled my mind, I shook my head. 'No! I mean, thank you, but no. I don't want them.'

The vet nodded in his kindly fashion, I said a hurried goodbye, and then scurried out of the clinic, Gershwin (a little lighter now) in tow.

Iko and Gershwin had never been the best of friends, but to my surprise, when I carried Gershwin back into the apartment, there was none of the drama Niko had enacted when Iko had returned home. Iko merely sniffed Gershwin cautiously, inspected his refurbished nether region, and then walked off in search of food. Since her own return home, she seemed calmer. With two of the cats re-homed, the apartment was quieter and so were Gershwin and Iko.

Fortunately, Gershwin healed very quickly, stopped peeing in the apartment, and didn't show any signs of resentment at losing his manhood. But he most definitely resented our coming departure. I frequently caught him staring in contempt at the packed boxes strewn around the apartment. Of course, he didn't know he would eventually be coming, too, though I did try to explain it to him.

I was very close to freaking out, not only from the stress of the move, but from the added stress of not yet finding a new home for Iko. Sayuri had very kindly agreed to look after both Gershwin and Iko while Ryan and I settled into British Hills, but after that . . . Iko's future was uncertain.

But I had to keep packing. Ryan and I also gave away and recycled

111

many of our belongings as the day of our departure grew closer. Finally, in addition to the boxes we had already sent to British Hills, we squeezed everything else that mattered to us into two backpacks and a Vari-Kennel. All that remained in the apartment was the bedraggled furniture it had come with and two cats, who would be relocating soon. Looking at all that emptiness, I finally accepted that our life in Takayama was over for good.

Fortunately, Ryan and I didn't have to devote precious time to training our successors as Kath and Jake had trained us. Our replacements had been stationed at the Let's English headquarters in Kani for the past year, and they were already adequately trained, so no hand-over get-togethers or even introductions were necessary. They would reach Takayama a few days after Ryan and I left for Fukushima.

Our students reacted to our coming departure according to their ages. The younger kids didn't really understand what was happening. The teenagers were relatively indifferent. The older women were sad because our tea-time conversations were coming to an end.

To mark our coming departure, the students and staff set about organising bowling events for the children and dinners with the adults, who added to our ever-burgeoning boxes and backpacks with different farewell gifts, trinkets of Takayama, personal letters, and photographs. The children gave us cute handmade cards that made me well up each time I opened one. Even Ryan got a little misty-eyed.

All of our friends insisted that we could not leave without first having a *sayonara* party and one last get together with everyone who had made our time so special in Takayama. Of course, there was only one possible place for our party: our favourite reggae bar, Bagus, where we had spent so many wonderful nights in the last year.

As Ryan and I got ready for our party in an apartment that now felt barren and foreign on our last night in Takayama, I thought about all of the people who had made our time here so memorable. From our students to the shopkeepers, from Dr. Iguchi to the waiters and waitresses at our favourite restaurants and bars, I was already missing all of them and the community they had given me. The people of Takayama always seemed to have time for each other, and they had gone out of their way to make us feel welcome and a part of their community.

I had learned much from them, and their city. I had learnt the importance of community and connection and vowed never to isolate myself again. I had been taught the vital lesson that work needn't be something that had to be endured. I had witnessed the power of *ikigai* every day of the past year in the local businesses I loved, from the vintage clothes store to Bagus and the saké brewery. I finally believed that I could turn my passion into something profitable and, more importantly, something that gave me a joyous reason to get up in the morning . . . once I figured out what my passion was.

Most importantly, Takayama had given me a growing appreciation of the natural world. I no longer took for granted the sound of water rippling down a river, or the warm breeze blowing against my cheek and through the pine needles on a sunny afternoon, or the pristine majesty of a snow-covered mountain. That lesson will stay with me forever, no matter where I roam.

Ryan nudged me. 'No dawdling! We have revellry and drunken friends waiting for us.'

We chose to walk to Bagus, despite the cold, because we knew we would be drinking a lot and we had no designated driver. The night was black, moonless, and bitterly cold as we climbed the black spiral staircase up to Bagus just after eight o'clock, taking care not to slip on the ice that caked the metal steps.

'Looks like we're expected,' Ryan said with a smile, pointing at the many familiar faces in the crowded room. We were *kampaied* (cheered) and applauded by all of the enthusiastic locals and consumers of alcoholic libations seated at the tables and bar stools.

'Good to know we're in the right place,' I said with an answering smile.

The *sayonara* revellries were in full swing. We were blasted with reggae anthems, courtesy of the DJ, the heavy baseline vibrating through the room and shaking the interior. Ryan's best friends Ken and Chiyo (an acquaintance who looked like a famous Japanese wrestler) raised their glasses. Someone thrust Hennessys loaded with ice in tall *Kirin* beer glasses into our hands. Taka the barman yelled to us over the music, '*Meri Kurisumasu*!' Then stepped from behind the bar to give us each a big hug that surprised us both.

The open affection and riotous good cheer chased away all my melancholy. The narrow timber bar was festooned with a combination of all things Christmas and all things Jamaican. Bob Marley pictures, images of the Lion of Zion, and a Santa Winnie the Pooh decorated the walls. Shiny Christmas ornaments dangled above the counter where the chef worked.

By mutual unspoken agreement, Ryan and I sat at the bar. Before we could order anything, Tamotsu dished up our favourite veggie ramen and poured what was left of my Hennessy into a very tall tumbler with lots of ice. We sat at the bar talking with Taka, and Yoshiko (decked out in one her colourful hand-made scarves), and a steady stream of well-wishers.

The Bagus doors swung open. Sayuri, wearing a stylish black beanie on her head, walked into the bar carrying Takashi in her arms. 'Surprise!' she said beaming.

This tabby, an adventurous puss, was becoming a bit more dog every day. He was not scared in the slightest of being in a noisy crowded bar with dozens of strangers. In fact, he loved the attention he got from the staff. Everyone made a big fuss over him. He even took place of honour in many of the photos the celebrants took that night, including several with me and Ryan.

This was one of the things I loved most about Takayama – the little things people did for each other. Where else would a cat attend a farewell party? Only in this mountain town!

When Sayuri and I had a moment alone together, I asked her for probably the thousandth time: 'Are you sure about looking after Gershwin and Iko while we move? With Takashi, you'll have three cats in your apartment until we find a forever home for Iko and take Gershwin to Fukushima.'

'*Daijoubu* [no problem]. Together life is no problem for us,' she said with her reassuring warm smile.

Ryan was hanging close to the bar, because he loved Tamotsu and he wanted to get as much time with him as possible.

As the night continued, more and more people crowded into Bagus, many of them bearing gifts to help Ryan and me remember them and their beautiful city. I knew it was not the custom in Japan to unwrap gifts in front of people, but by this point I was too emotional and too tipsy to obey the rules. One of my favourite gifts came from a guy we barely knew, Chiyo, the one who looked like a famous Japanese wrestler. We'd only met him a handful of times in the bar. Nevertheless, he had given us a red bottle in the shape of Sarubobo, the city's mascot. The bottle was filled with sake from a local brewery.

'It's perfect,' I told him mistily, and it was, because it captured everything I loved about Takayama: a symbol of Japan, a reflection of things unique to the region that reflected *ikigai*, like the local brewery, rather than impersonal things imported from China, and the contrast of filling what had once been a child's toy with alcohol.

'That's so kind of you,' Ryan said to one of his bar buddies, getting a little misty himself as green gift paper fell to the floor. He had unwrapped a very nice package of *mocha* (Japanese rice cake).

Around eleven-thirty that night, the DJ turned the music down to a murmur. Taka, who was now wearing a red Santa's hat, took the mic and said, 'Good luck in Fukushima, Ryan-san and CJ-san. I'll miss you.' He lifted his glass to the room and shouted '*Kampai!*' which was echoed around the room as everyone drank with him.

In broken, and sometimes incomprehensible, English, people began making actual speeches. Of course, the Japanese are very conservative and don't show emotion in public, so the speeches were all pretty similar, which just drove home all of the love beaming at us.

'I will always remember the good times we've had together,' G-Kun said. 'Ryan DJing in the bar and snowboarding and throwing tricks like a champ.' He passed the mic to Ryan's good friend Ken.

'I want to thank you both for the friendships we've made, and good times we've had during your stay,' Ken said. 'Remember, I'm coming to visit you in London!'

Several other people made speeches in our honour, some funny, some sweet, all of them greeted by cheers (and occasional heckling) from the other guests. Then Tamotsu, the bar's manager and cook, stepped forward. 'CJ-san and Ryan-san.' He paused for a moment to collect himself and his English. 'We have been friends for one year now. Everyone in Bagus here tonight will miss you very much. You have become part of our Bagus family. Please don't forget us and please come back to Takayama! We'll be waiting for you.' He raised his glass and shouted '*Kampai*!'

I broke every English (and Japanese) taboo as warm tears slid down my cheeks. There was a lump so big in my throat, I could barely breathe. Ryan didn't shed actual tears, but his head was down as he stared sadly into his *Asahi* (beer).

Finally, Tamotsu called for me and Ryan to say something nice about everyone else. I was too overcome with emotion to speak, and my legs were too wobbly to stand, so I pushed Ryan to his feet. He walked to the centre of the room and took the mic from Tamotsu.

He had to clear his throat. 'I just want to say thank you so much to everyone for making our time in Takayama so special. We've really enjoyed your company, and friendships . . . and drinking with you! [Cheers from the crowd.] Come snowboarding in Fukushima! [More cheers.] *Kampai*!'

'*Kampai*!' everyone shouted, downing their drinks.

It was at this moment that Sayuri leaned into me and said, 'You know this is a special moment for us. In Japanese, we call it *ichigo ichie*, I don't know how to say in English but it means that nothing in life happens again, this party tonight, this time together is unique and precious.'

I could feel myself get teary because I knew it was true. I may return to Takayama one day, but who knew when, and it would be another time, under totally different circumstances. This night, right here, all together was important because life moves on so quickly, things happen, people change, and nothing, I was starting to realise, is permanent. I was experiencing so many changes, so quickly; it felt like I was in need of Dr Who's blue Tardis.

When Ryan and I finally said our goodbyes and walked out of Bagus, it was a humble, grateful, CJ who walked at Ryan's side.

We returned to a frigid apartment – the temperature had dropped precipitously – to find Gershwin and Iko huddled together under the *kotatsu*. Ryan and I huddled together beneath our electric blankets in our huge bed as we watched snow begin to fall outside our bedroom window. It seemed appropriate that the scenery would be the same as when we had arrived a year earlier. I will forever associate snow with Takayama.

The next morning, Ryan and I were definitely the worse for wear after that huge *sayonara* party. But we were on a schedule, so we dragged ourselves out of bed, fed the cats, ate our own breakfast, and got dressed just before Sayuri arrived promptly at eight-thirty to take us to the train station. Gershwin and Iko, of course, decided to play Hide and Seek, so it took longer than we had planned to corral them and get them into their cat carriers.

'You're going to be fine,' I kept telling the newly-neutered Gershwin, who was actually acting rather unconcerned. 'You'll be with your friends Sayuri, Iko, and Takashi until we can take you to our new home.'

We bundled up (which did little to fend off the biting cold), and then piled the cats and our belongings into the car. I turned to Sayuri: 'Are you *sure* this is okay?' I asked.

'Together life, no problem for us,' she said again with a warm smile.

I nearly burst into tears right then.

Ryan got into the passenger seat, I got into the back seat with the cats, and Sayuri put the car in gear. We were leaving. Leaving our home. Leaving Takayama. Forever.

She carefully eased the car down the snow-packed and icy road and passed the little Shinto shrine on our road for the last time. We stopped briefly at Sayuri's apartment building. Ryan and I said our final goodbyes to Iko – whose future was still uncertain – and a temporary goodbye to Gershwin. Then Sayuri took the cats up to her flat as I choked back tears.

Sayuri came back quickly and drove us away. She parked her car on a street across from the train station and followed us as Ryan and I carried our luggage to the train platform. There were only a few other passengers brave (or foolhardy) enough to travel on this frigid morning, except . . .

'Isn't that Ken?' I said to Ryan, pointing surreptitiously to Takayama's Japanese George Clooney, who was bundled up against the cold.

'Yeah, I think it is,' Ryan said. 'What's he doing here?'

Then onto the train platform walked Taka and Tamotsu from Bagus. Quickly joining them were Ryo and Hitomi and other Takayama friends who had been a part of our lives for the last year.

'It's a bon voyage party!' Ryan said in amazement.

I couldn't speak. I was getting teary again. I'm not sure which surprised me more, the fact that Sayuri had organised this wonderful surprise farewell at the station for us, or the fact that these friends cared enough to show up on such a bitterly cold morning.

Ryan nudged me and gave me a warm smile. 'They must like us.'

'Yeah,' I said, fighting back my tears. I wanted to blub like a baby. Instead, I laughed and Ryan quickly joined me as more and more friends joined us.

'Take care of yourself, and I hope you're always happy.' Tamotsu said, hugging us one last time.

'I'll see you in Fukushima,' Ryan insisted. 'We have a lot of snowboarding to do.'

Our other friends came up and offered their own final farewells, some hugging us, some fighting tears, some trying to joke their way out of sadness.

The other passengers must have thought we were some sort of minor celebrities to be drawing this kind of crowd. By the time the train pulled into the station, there must have been at least fifteen people on the platform all waving and calling their farewells.

I hadn't had even half this many people see me off when I had left London the first time, yet here were these people, who had been strangers just a year ago, braving snow and ice and a frigid breeze to shower us with love and kindness.

I looked at Sayuri and could see that she had tears in her eyes, too.

'I'll see you again in a couple of months,' I promised, hugging her tightly through all of her layers of winter clothing.

She hurriedly pulled out a tissue as the public address system sprang to life, announcing that all passengers had to board.

Overwhelmed at having to say a final goodbye, tears slid down my cheeks as I hugged my best friend one last time. Then Ryan and I boarded the train. We heard the final call for the train to depart. The doors banged shut. As the train slowly pulled away from the Takayama station and our friends, I looked out the train doorway at the happy affectionate faces of people of whom I'd grown deeply fond, knowing deep down that, with one vital exception, I was never going to see them again.

'I'll see you soon!' I shouted to Sayuri.

'*Sou da ne*!' (That's right!) she called back to me.

Chapter 13: Not Even a Kitten Around

猫の子一匹いない / Neko No Ko Ippiki Inai

It was just eight-thirty in the morning on the day before Christmas Eve when we left the Gifu Prefecture and Japanese Alps in central western Honshu. Once again, we took the JR train from Takayama, and then transferred to the bullet train, which took us east to Tokyo. There, we changed to a different shinkansen. This one took us north into Fukushima Prefecture in northeastern Honshu. As I gazed out the window, I wondered how Gershwin would find this journey when he would be joining us in March.

The new prefecture we'd be living in stretches from the Pacific Ocean to the mountains of the Aizu region. Our second bullet train was taking us into the southern mountains and the ancient town of Shirakawa.

More than 1,500 years ago, Shirakawa was the most northern outpost of 'civilised' Japan. It was connected to the country's seat of government, Kyoto, by the Ōshū Kaidō, one of just five major roads used by government officials to keep tabs on their provinces. And that was a problem, because the Ōshū Kaidō was also the best route for the 'barbarians' of the north to invade.

So, around 400 C.E., the military constructed the Shirakawa Barrier, essentially a large and heavily fortified checkpoint, Fukushima's version of Hadrian's Wall, but with much less wall, because the densely forested mountains surrounding it effectively stopped raiders in their tracks. If the northern heathens wanted to invade, they'd first have to get through the Shirakawa Barrier and the army guarding it.

From about 900 C.E. on, when the threat of northern invasion had been neutralised by the (not entirely successful) assimilation of the northern 'savages' under the Japanese government, the Barrier was used to monitor trade between north and south. By around 1200 C.E., the Barrier fell into disuse, eroded, and eventually disappeared, but not from memory. It became a part of the country's poetic mythology.

One of the most famous of Japan's classical works, Matsuo Bashō's *The Narrow Road to the Deep North*, written in 1689, turned the Shirakawa Barrier into almost a site of pilgrimage for other poets and travellers, then and now.

The Barrier has long been associated in Japanese literature with both spring and particularly autumn. Nōin (998-1050 C.E.), a Buddhist monk and waka poet wrote '*I left the capital with the spring haze, but at the barrier of Shirakawa the autumn wind blows.*' Other poets have focussed on the Shirakawa Barrier as a metaphor for remoteness, isolation, loneliness, and separation.

Staring out the window of the bullet train as it sped through a vast white world of snow-draped forested mountains, I felt that isolation keenly. I only hoped that we would not spend the coming year living in loneliness and separation from the cats, the rest of the country and our friends. This remote landscape made me feel like I was being transported to a different country . . . a different world.

For half an hour, Ryan and I sat in silence on the Tōhoku Main Line, staring out the train window as the unfamiliar landscape flashed past us.

Relief poured out of every pore he had when we finally disembarked from the *shinkansen* at the Shirakawa train station just after one o'clock in the afternoon. Ryan immediately forgot about what had been, for him, the interminable journey when the icy winds from Siberia blasted us across the train platform. We were both shivering violently when we finally entered the shelter of the station. Mr. Maki's smiling face warmed us right up. The bitter cold had reddened his face. A black wool scarf tucked inside a tired-looking coat seemed ineffective at fending off the frigid wind.

'Oh, I'm glad you've made it,' he said happily. 'Is it cold enough for you?'

'A little more than enough,' Ryan assured him.

'Let me get you into my SUV and warm you up,' Mr. Maki said.

Unfortunately, we had to brave the Arctic conditions outside once again to get to Mr. Maki's SUV parked near a children's empty playground. Our breath creating a thick fog around us in the frigid air, we hurriedly loaded our belongings into the back of his four-by-four, and jumped inside, Ryan riding shotgun as usual, while I was able to spread out in the back seat. Every window fogged up immediately from the sudden exposure to our body heat.

The sky was so heavy and overcast that, even though it was early afternoon, we might have been travelling at night. With the defroster running at full blast, Mr. Maki drove us out of Shirakawa Station.

'Thank you for starting over Christmas,' Mr. Maki said as we circled around Shirakawa, a city of low-rise and mid-rise buildings and 60,000 people. 'It's actually a very busy time for us, because many Western staff like to go on holiday at this time of year. So, the other instructors have to pick up the slack.'

'It's fine,' Ryan. 'We're glad to help.'

All too soon, the city was behind us. We were driving past large farmhouses standing in front of huge snow-covered rice paddy fields with rolling, pine-forested mountains behind them. Then, we began climbing into the mountains.

Mr. Maki had been chain smoking from the moment we had left the train station, quickly filling the SUV with smoke, which made it a little difficult to see the landscape we were sweeping past.

As we got higher up the mountain, Mr. Maki pointed out the nearby ski slope, which of course led them into comparisons of different ski mountains in Japan.

We had another few kilometres to drive northeast, all of it uphill. As we climbed the Hatoriko Highlands, it felt and looked so cold outside the SUV, I was certain the brakes would seize up on the icy road.

Every kilometre we covered drove home more and more just how remote we were from anything resembling civilisation. I had wanted to live in a rural area, but was this too much of a good thing?

I saw no other cars on the road. The snow on either side of us was piled up about double the height of Mr. Maki's SUV. Watching him carefully navigate the treacherous road, I began to think I'd never see another human outpost. Just then, however, woodland cabins and large, expensive vacation homes sitting on considerable acreage began to appear on either side of the road.

'The Regina Forest Resort is just down that side road,' Mr. Maki said, indicating a signpost. 'It is more of a summer resort. It has a lake for fishing in the summer, a bathhouse, and chalets for guests. My niece holidays there with her dog.'

The road became more vertical. 'That's Villa Fuji,' Mr. Maki said, pointing to our left. I saw a green sign and then a very large house with very big windows. 'That is the owners' house. They mostly use it on weekends. The car park is for them, you, and the teachers, another couple, are in the neighbouring chalet.'

Owners? Teachers? Out of nowhere, we had suddenly emerged into the outskirts of British Hills. I began to perk up.

The owners of our accommodation had a white timber holiday house with large windows. Behind it were two smaller houses. 'That will be your house,' Mr. Maki said, pointing to a Swiss-chalet style building painted (ironically) white with a very large tennis court (also white for now) next to it.

Our house. I was looking at Ryan's and my new home. Not another apartment, but an actual *house*.

Mr. Maki kept driving. 'Over there, under all that snow, is a golf club that a lot of people come up from Tokyo to use,' he said, pointing to a vast expanse of white.

Suddenly, the winding road reached the top of the snow-bound mountain and there before us were the tall open wrought iron gates of British Hills. An ancient forest surrounded the campus, emphasising its isolation.

I looked out of the nicotine filled car in growing amazement as the SUV inched up the long driveway. On our left was an authentic-looking English tearoom, the Ascot, a white building with a red tile roof and a perfect red telephone box outside. Beside it were two big Tudor houses (the student accommodation), that looked rather like barns. On our right were four mock Tudor two-storey buildings – dark wood beams against white facades and steeply slanted roofs – that I learned later were used for the cooking and English conversation classes.

Across the narrow street from them were three more Tudor-style buildings – Henry II, Bentley and Wren – which provided different kinds of housing, from dormitories to luxury suites.

The attention to detail in this faux English village was marvellous, from its traditional English signage to its slim black Victorian lampposts. When the Japanese do something, they do it properly. Clearly, no expense had been spared in building British Hills. (I later learned that many of the school's construction materials and decorative features had been shipped out from Britain to ensure authenticity.)

To our right, I caught a glimpse of an old English pub, the Falstaff, its black and white Tudor beams peeping out from the snow. Through the leaded windows, I could see inviting lights beckoning us with the promise of warmth and merriment. Sadly, Mr. Maki did not stop and buy us a mulled wine or British ale.

'Can we watch football in the pub?' Ryan asked. I knew this would be a deal breaker for him, because one of the things he missed most about being away from home was not being able to watch his beloved team, Liverpool.

'Yes,' Mr. Maki said, 'I'm pretty sure they play most major sporting events there.'

'Sweet!' Ryan said, barely able to contain his excitement.

Just beyond the pub and adjacent to the Manor House dominating the hillside was Ye Olde Shoppe, a red brick souvenir shop with white trim that sold, according to the display window and signs, teddy bears, fudge, and shortbread biscuits imported from the UK.

Just as I was thinking that I'd seen everything, we drove between a pair of white stone-carved British lions facing each other. Just past them, in the middle of the driveway, was a statue of Shakespeare holding what turned out to be an Australian flag . . . presumably added by an Aussie prankster. I smiled at the joke and felt some of my tension at entering this new world ease up a bit.

Beyond Shakespeare, at the very top of the hill, stood an imposing mock Medieval Manor House overlooking the faux village.

'That is the Manor House and the main reception,' Mr. Maki said. 'It's where all the students and our guests check-in. We have very wealthy people come up from Tokyo to stay for a few nights in the Manor House. We even have weddings here.'

Rather than stopping at the Manor House, Mr. Maki followed the driveway down into a car park on the east side of the Manor which was hidden from view by a row of tall evergreen trees. Beside the car park was a bland off-white concrete block that housed the admin and teacher's offices. Its stark contrast to the Medieval architecture of the Manor House was probably why it was hidden out of sight.

'Your office is in the Admin building,' Mr. Maki said, parking the SUV, 'along with the staff canteen where you'll have your meals.'

This was it. We had arrived at our new jobs. Our new home. I got out of the SUV cautiously, fearful that the concrete covered in thick layers of ice would have me slipping and landing on my butt within five seconds. But it was the strong Siberian wind that nearly toppled me. I hurriedly put my hand on Ryan's shoulder to steady myself. The cold air freezing my lungs, we walked up the treacherous icy hill to the Manor. Mr. Maki (puffing on a cigarette) and Ryan were talking, but I'd completely lost interest in what they were saying. All I cared about was getting into a warm building.

We started walking up the icy front steps to the towering front door of the Manor. Just as I started to think that this introduction to my new school and home was just too hard and cold, something like a bomb *exploded* behind us and I jumped a good five metres into the air.

'What the hell?' Ryan exclaimed.

'What was that?' I demanded, my heart thundering in my chest.

'Oh, that's just to keep bears away,' Mr. Maki said.

'Bears?' I squeaked.

'We *are* surrounded by wilderness,' Ryan said.

'Exactly,' said Mr. Maki. 'And at this time of year, before they go into hibernation, they are looking for food and they know they can find it at British Hills.'

Bears. Bombs. Terrific. I soon learned that the bear deterrent, the explosion, was employed several times a day. The first time I heard it I could have jumped up the nearest tree. I'm sure it scared staff members and students much more than our hungry four-legged neighbours.

We walked into the warmth of the Manor and found ourselves in a grand Victorian entrance hall with a cream-coloured marble floor, an impressive grand staircase to the upper floor, and a chandelier above us hanging from an embossed ceiling. Before us was a big mahogany desk with one female staff member acting as receptionist.

Opposite the reception desk, a fire crackled merrily in a large fireplace with an intricately carved mahogany surround. Two chesterfield chairs faced it. A big Christmas tree (professionally decorated – perhaps someone from Harrod's had come out to do it) was in the right corner at the far side of the hall.

The only sound, other than the crackling fire, was muted Christmas choral music from hidden speakers.

It was all *very* refined.

A group of Japanese high school students scuttled past us in snow-covered black robes, similar to the academic dress you'd find at the University of Oxford, and waved at us enthusiastically. Mr. Maki gave them a nod and then gave us a whirlwind tour to help us get our bearings.

'The swimming pool and sauna are yours to use as often as you like,' Mr. Maki announced. My happiness spiked ten-fold.

Next, Mr. Maki led us up the grand staircase with its lovely stained glass windows to the first floor. The first floor East Wing had a long green carpeted corridor lined by paintings of English dignitaries who had contributed to Japan in some way and two guest bedrooms: the King's Room and the Queen's Room.

Why, you may ask, had a mini-England been constructed on top of a remote Japanese mountain? Simple. A rich Japanese businessman had a wife who was something of an Anglophile, with a particularly deep fondness for the England of olde. He had originally built British Hills for her. Later, he decided to get in on the profitable English language trade, using British Hills to lure high-paying Japanese students by giving England to them, rather than having their parents pay exorbitant travel costs to ship them to and house them in the real England.

Mr. Maki announced that he would now take us to the Admin office building, which was behind the East Wing. We had to brave the frigid outdoors again, just when I had finally warmed up.

'You'll find the staff canteen in the basement of the Admin building,' he announced as we walked back through the ground floor of the East Wing. 'That is where you will have your meals.'

We hiked upstairs to find the Admin office that served both the teachers and the Japanese administrative staff filled in a modern open plan room. The staff consisted of six men and two women dressed smartly in black and white, who were currently seated, their heads down as they worked diligently. The teachers, of course, were in the classrooms with their students.

'Ladies and gentlemen, please meet our new teachers, CJ and Ryan,' Mr. Maki announced. They all looked up and smiled warmly at us, and then went back to work without saying anything. Japanese office staff do not chit chat.

Most of them, we would discover, were friendly . . . to a point. Their roles and relationships had long been established and they'd also seen so many teachers come and go that they weren't particularly keen to go out of their way to connect with newbies.

Mr. Maki then took us to meet the school's director, Yasuda-san, who sat at the back of the office. This is actually the most prominent position in Japanese office culture. It enables the boss to watch how hard everyone is (or is not) working.

I first saw in Yasuda-san a typical salaryman. He was in his fifties, with neatly cut hair, and black-framed glasses perched on his nose. He seemed stern and much too busy to be bothered by new teachers. But he was polite (the Japanese are never rude).

Mr. Maki made a slight bow. 'This is CJ and Ryan. They are the new teachers.'

'Nice to meet you,' Yasuda-san said, standing up. 'We hope you enjoy working here.'

'Thank you. We both look forward to it,' Ryan said with equal politeness.

And that was it. Yasuda-san was a man of few words.

It's a well-known fact that when you introduce two cats to each other for the first time they hiss, scratch, and mark their territory. The same thing can happen when you bring new people into an established work environment. Behind the fake smiles and the 'nice to meet you' greetings, they can hiss at you under their breath and hide their true thoughts, feelings, and characters.

Normally, if you shove together *several* felines unknown to each other, all hell will break loose, which means a great deal of stress for all the cats. Thus, it's suggested that arranging slow, positive encounters between strange cats is the best way to make pleasant first impressions and associations. This generally involves food. Thus, Mr. Maki concluded our tour by leading us down to the staff canteen in the basement.

It was the perfect choice. It had been a long day, full of lots of strong and sometimes conflicting emotions, and I was dead tired after the tour. I was also hungry, and Ryan was ravenous.

Unfortunately, the staff canteen was white and sterile and unappetising. The kitchen was at one end, a small TV suspended from one of the walls currently offered a Japanese news show, the buffet included a salad bar, rice, the meal of the day (I learned later that most of the food we were served were leftovers from the Refectory restaurant where privileged students and guests ate). Two rows of rectangular tables for the foreign staff and two rows for the Japanese staff filled most of the room. (I quickly learned that British Hills had an unwritten rule handed down as an order from above: teachers do not sit with Japanese staff at meals.)

When we walked into the staff canteen, there were only a few people scattered about and only two teachers (the rest were still in class).

I piled my plate high with an assortment of Western and Japanese cuisine – french fries, salad, rice, miso soup, tofu and green tea. Then I sat down at a table beside Ryan. On my other side was a middle-aged teacher, clearly a Kiwi judging by his accent as he spoke to one of the Japanese admin staff who stood at the end of the table.

I wanted to be proactive at beginning to forge connections with my co-workers, but my brain froze up. I thought about asking about the quality of the food, but feared that might bring up negative associations.

'What's it like working here?' I said brightly.

'You'll see,' the Kiwi retorted. He went back to eating his food.

And that was that, which was fine by me. I was overwhelmed and tired. I didn't really want to make conversation. I just wanted to eat, get to my new house, settle in, and sleep for a hundred years.

When we finally left the staff canteen, it was approaching early evening which meant that, with the heavy overcast day, it was pitch black outside. I had to work hard to hide my yawns as Mr. Maki drove us down to our new home on the British Hills campus: a beautiful white two-storey chalet surrounded by snow-covered evergreens. Snow was piled high on the broad, angled roof. Welcoming lights beckoned us inside.

I could see other chalets within walking distance, but the forest made my new home seem solitary and magical, almost like something out of a fairy tale.

When I stepped out of the SUV, I heard the most perfect silence. Everything was still, peaceful, and wonderfully comforting. Then some of the heavy snow from the roof crashed to the ground with a loud bang that made all three of us jump.

'It sounds like we have our own bear deterrent,' Ryan said with a smile.

Bears. Wilderness. Right. Well, bears featured prominently in fairy tales, why not with this enchanted new home, too?

Brought back to terra firma, I gazed with more than a few qualms at the snow-covered driveway and wondered how we were going to get out the next morning and start our new jobs at the Manor if this thick snowfall continued. Even the tennis court next to our new home was buried under a good metre-and-a-half of snow.

The comparatively mild winters I'd known in England were fast becoming a distant memory.

Mr. Maki helped us carry our things as we walked down icy steps from the driveway and then up four steps to the front door. 'Be sure to be back in the office tomorrow morning at nine sharp for training,' he said, setting down the bags. 'See you tomorrow.' And that was that. He hurried through the cold back to his SUV and drove away.

'Well,' Ryan said, 'here we go.' He opened the front door.

'Oh my God,' I said in awe as we walked into the house.

First of all, it *was* a house, not an apartment. This would be the first time since my childhood that I would live in an actual house that was all mine. No messy roommates. Just me, and Ryan, and (soon) Gershwin.

Second, this house was the complete opposite of a converted proctology clinic. It was spacious and bigger than anything in which I'd ever lived.

The chestnut wood floors gleamed in the lamplight. The cream-coloured walls were bare. Along the whole width of the lounge were

French doors looking out into the forest. Immediately beyond the French doors was a balcony covered in several feet of thick snow. The modern furniture was a bit sparse: a plain navy blue two-seater sofa with wooden armrests that looked like it came from Ikea™, a small black TV sitting on a wicker box in a corner, and a single wood bookcase tucked into another corner.

I couldn't have been happier, because to me the furnishings and décor pretty much defined *Shibui* with its simple aesthetic and understated sense of style and every day function, everything I had read about and dreamed about before first coming to Japan and running smack into Osaka and shoebox apartments.

This house, our *house*, also had a full bath, including a small window to bring in natural light and a bathtub large enough that I could almost stretch my legs out fully. I could see myself on many a winter a day soaking away in a hot steamy bath and forgetting entirely the arctic temperatures and landscape outside.

The chalet had only two drawbacks. First, it had originally been built for summer holiday visitors, so the washer and dryer were outside to the right of the front door. (They often froze in the winter, so we had to take our laundry up to the Manor House). Second, the chalet didn't have an actual kitchen. There was no oven to be found, very few cupboards, and only a refrigerator and hotplates for heating soup or cooking pasta.

'I guess we're in for a year of communal dining,' I said a little wistfully.

'At least we won't have to go shopping in all this snow and ice, or spend time cooking,' Ryan said encouragingly. 'We'll have more time for Gershwin and TV, and I can go snowboarding.'

We climbed the wooden stairs to the first floor and got the biggest surprise of all. The entire upper level was *our bedroom*. It reminded me of a European guesthouse with its wood floor and windows at either end which promised plenty of sunlight during the day, and wonderful views if we just wanted to stay in bed and watch a morning go by. There were even skylights in the ceiling, currently covered by snow, it was true, but in the summer we would be able to lie in bed and stare up at the stars.

As night-time settled in, Ryan and I sat on the blue two-seater in the lounge and watched through the French doors the lights twinkling from ski slopes that were just a short ten-minute drive away.

'This all seems a bit full on,' I said into the silence. 'I wish we'd had a break before we started work here. We didn't learn our lesson. We went straight from work in Australia to Osaka and we paid for it. Now we're going from one job in Takayama straight to this job. It just feels too stressful.'

'Yeah, it looks like it's gonna be a lot of work,' Ryan said. 'The first few days of transition are always difficult. Let's just take it one day at a time.' He stared at the far away lights for a moment. 'I can't wait to check out the ski ground.'

'Of course you can't,' I said with a smile.

I looked around at the roomy house. It was so much nicer than anything we'd had before. We had a car to drive to Shirakawa whenever we wanted. We had a swimming pool and sauna at our disposal. All in all . . . 'I have decided I'm going to love it here,' I announced, partly to convince myself. 'But this house feels so empty.'

'Four cats take up a lot of space,' Ryan agreed.

'I can't wait to get Gershwin here. He's going to love it, too. He'll have loads of room to run around inside the house, the view from the balcony to the forest is a cat's dream and, except for bears, I won't have to worry about him staying safe. There isn't any danger from the main road.'

'This pretty much is cat heaven,' Ryan said. 'You want to call Sayuri and find out how Gershwin, Iko, and Takashi are doing, don't you?'

'Yes,' I said sheepishly.

He pulled out his mobile. 'Never put off until later what you can indulge in now.'

Chapter 14: An Umbrella to a Cat

猫に傘 / Neko Ni Kasa

My first couple of days working at British Hills were filled with ups and downs and the strong Siberian wind was so brutal it made me long to stay indoors and curl up by the heater. Up on this mountain on the northeastern side of Japan, the winter was far more severe than in Takayama. We were more exposed and even deeper in *yuki* (snow).

As I sat there contemplating snow, it was borne fully upon me just how remote British Hills was, and how even more remote this house was. There was very little here to remind me of Takayama, let alone England, which meant I would have more opportunity to focus on my new life, and all the things I could learn which might help me in my search for *ikigai*. I smiled when I thought how different my thoughts and feelings were at this new school, this new adventure, than they had been when I had first arrived in Takayama.

Just one week after arriving in British Hills, Ryan and I had settled into our work schedules, I had started getting comfortable with the staff, and New Year's Eve was upon us. I know most people look forward to it, or at least they look forward to the parties, but I've never really enjoyed New Year's Eve. It has always seemed such forced contrived happiness. I mean, what are you really celebrating anyway? Facing another year of dealing with the same issues you had last year? I just didn't get it. I was also missing Gershwin.

In my early twenties, I'd lost myself in parties and intoxication on New Year's Eve, only to wake up several days later feeling ten times worse than was strictly necessary to welcome a new year. This cycle went on for a bit longer than I'd like to admit, but now there was something appealing about celebrating without getting sloshed.

That's when I heard that old parasitic voice in my head that I had subdued for almost a year. It was gnawing at me, telling me to run from socialising, to stay home, save my money, avoid a room full of strangers. Telling me I wouldn't enjoy myself. In other words, it was playing that old tired song of my usual worries.

'Shut the hell up!' I said firmly. Eckhart Tolle would have been proud.

New Year's Eve in Japan is known as *Omisoka*, and it is one of the most important days of the year in Japanese tradition. But not at British Hills. How different this New Year's Eve was from last year. There would be no bell ringing from the tiny shrine at the end of the road, in fact, there would be no traditional Japanese festivities at all. The faculty, staff, and students would spend a typically English New Year's Eve, which meant congregating in the very British pub, or dining in the swanky and very expensive restaurant that adjoined the Manor House.

'What do you think?' Ryan asked.

I grimaced. 'I'm not sure I want to splash out on a special meal. The whole purpose of moving here was to *save* money.'

'True. But this will be the only New Year's Eve we spend at British Hills. We'll never have this opportunity again. I think we should make the most of it.'

I remembered the Japanese saying that Sayuri had taught me, *ichigo ichie* which means that moments in life cannot be repeated, and so decided to splash out on an expensive meal.

So, on New Year's Eve, I pulled on a posh frock for the posh restaurant – a little black dress I'd found in a great second hand shop in Takayama. I curled my hair, put on a little makeup and, looking in the bathroom mirror, I felt actually positive about the coming evening.

Ryan emerged from the bathroom wearing a smart multi-coloured striped shirt he'd bought in London before we left and navy blue trousers.

'*Kakkoii,*' (cool) I said. 'You brush up quite well.'

'You don't look too bad yourself,' he said with a warm smile.

We had agreed to meet at the restaurant at eight-thirty that evening with the rest of our party: Sinead, the Northern Irish receptionist; Stefan, an exuberant Bristolian whom I'd met at the sports desk; Tara, a kooky Kiwi teacher; and Hayley, a friendly young Aussie who was a dead ringer for Rebel Wilson before Hollywood turned her peroxide blonde and bleached her teeth. These were, in my opinion, the most affable people on staff.

The Refectory's restaurant design had been modelled on the medieval Great Hall (dining hall) at Christ Church Oxford. Two long wooden tables running the length of the restaurant divided by a carpeted main aisle were set with pristine white linen tablecloths and dotted with small lamps every metre or so. Twinkling fairy lights were strewn throughout the hall. A large colour photo of the Queen was hung above a grand piano. All that was missing was Harry Potter seated at the Gryffindor table.

'Oh! This was such a good idea,' I said with a happy sigh.

'The cost be damned,' Ryan agreed with a smile.

We sat opposite each other in the middle of the table and I couldn't hold back a smirk. Arrayed before me were a dozen utensils and, thanks to the table manners class I'd given a few days before, *I* knew what the tiny spoon was for and which forks went with which dish.

Almost immediately, I and the other diners were beset by Japanese waiters dressed in smart red tartan waistcoats. Even better, expensive French wine began to flow freely into our crystal glasses as we dipped through layers of crusty bread and cheese into the most delicious onion soup.

Ryan didn't seem to mind being surrounded by mostly women and the hilarious Stefan, entering easily into our conversations, which ranged from places where we'd travelled to places where we'd taught and the things we liked and disliked about each other's respective countries.

'I'm so happy. I've got a brand new Marc Jacobs handbag,' Stefan announced, holding up the tan leather bag with a big silver buckle on the front. 'Do you think it matches my shoes?'

'It's perfect,' Ryan assured him.

'I have never understood why people like handbags,' Hayley said. 'Most of them are too small to carry anything important, and they only leave you one hand free to do anything.'

'Darling,' Stefan retorted, 'handbags aren't about function, they're about fashion!'

'Oh, silly me,' Hayley said, which made him laugh. Even though she was very much a tomboy and a straight-talking dinky-di Aussie, she and Stefan got on like a house on fire.

'How are you finding it here?' I asked Stefan, who was sitting beside me.

'It's great, but I'm so homesick,' he confessed. 'I really miss my dogs.'

My ears pricked up. 'What kind of dogs do you have?'

'My family has border collies. We live in Bristol and those dogs are my sunshine on a cloudy day. Liza is a diva! I don't know where she gets it from. And Jess is a glorious chocolatey somewhat less campy guy. They are the most beautiful loving members of our family.' His eyes shimmered with unshed tears. 'It's just so hard being away from them for so long.'

'Come here, you wee eejit,' Sinead commanded as she pulled him from his chair and gave him a big hug.

Their brother-sister relationship generated over such a brief time melted my heart then and there.

The soup was followed by perfectly poached salmon, or the mushroom tarte which I had ordered.

'I'm missing our cats like crazy,' I volunteered. 'Well, only one cat now, but he puts such *life* into every day.'

'You can always tell a Protestant,' Sinead said with a grin, 'because they're the ones with cats.' Sinead, of course, was Catholic.

Throughout the meal, we were serenaded by a young man in evening clothes who played Christmas songs on the grand piano on a raised platform at the front of the restaurant under the approving eye of Queen Liz.

After we'd all had a few more glasses of wine, Ryan jumped up and stood beneath the picture of the Queen and, in his best Cockney imitation of Her Majesty, declared: 'As my Grandmother would say, I hope one has fun.' Which set everyone to laughing.

At midnight, I locked arms with Hayley and Stefan and sang *Auld Lang Syne* at the top of my voice with everyone else. A new year had begun.

As a waiter refilled my wine glass, I looked around the table and found myself surprised by an unfamiliar sensation. I was *thankful*. I was thankful, not only for the food and the wine, but also for the good company and the novel experience of dining on top of a mountain in Japan on New Year's Eve. I was thankful that Gershwin was safe and in good hands while we settled in here, and happy that we'd be reunited soon.

Unlike my previous New Year's Eve celebrations, this could not have been a more sublime evening.

I had never before felt this way on New Year's Eve, and that made me question if all the horrors of New Year's Eves past could have been avoided. Had I let myself get too caught up in resentment and fear in the past? Could I have changed my environment sooner?

Looking back at my teenage years, I finally saw clearly just how depressed I had actually been. Rather than being pushed to grow, to learn to be better, by my parents, or grandmother, or even my aunt, I had been left to my own devices. I had chosen to hide away from the world for days on end, only ever getting up to eat or go to the bathroom.

When I was fifteen and lived alone in a tiny studio, I'd miss appointment after appointment for referrals to see different counsellors or psychotherapists, because I didn't see the point. Once, I had sat in a sterile white room with a bearded fifty-something white guy listening to me in absolute silence except to occasionally mutter the occasional filler to bridge my silences. Even while I was talking, I kept thinking how useless it all was.

It never occurred to me in the depths of my depression that there were different treatment settings, more caring and helpful therapists. I didn't allow myself to think that I could actually get the help I so desperately needed.

Watching the happy people all around me who were mostly strangers, and feeling myself smile, I had to question why I felt more at peace with them than with people I had known all my life.

Mostly, I think, the reason I was more at peace in this beautiful room than with my family or friends or anyone else was that I wasn't pretending I was happy. Here on this mountain, I didn't have to compare myself to anyone, and I was new, so I didn't have any baggage as far as the others were concerned. I could re-create myself.

The next big question was, of course, if I could maintain my new level of positive feelings and thinking at future celebratory events.

Chapter 15: Three Months Is a Year to a Cat

猫は三月を一年とする / Neko Wa Sangatsu Wo Hitotose To Suru

Nothing was as easy or familiar as it had been back at our apartment in Takayama.

We were living in direct sightline of the holiday home of our landlords, a middle-aged couple from Tokyo who spoke no English and were not very friendly. While vacant through most of the week, it would often be occupied on weekends, which meant our privacy would be almost entirely lost, unless we closed every curtain and stayed inside. More importantly, Gershwin would be rejoining us in March. I spent a lot of time worrying that he might be discovered by the owners one weekend and we would be given an ultimatum: remove our beloved cat or quit our good-paying jobs.

One major worry had been removed, however. A week after we moved to British Hills, the notice we had posted about Iko at our Takayama vet's office finally bore fruit. A woman in her forties wanted a feline companion for her white cat and, even though the vets had other re-homing cat notices, Dr. Iguchi very kindly steered her to Iko to help us out. It looked like a great combination. The new owner even sent us pictures of Iko living happily in her new home with her new "sister." My gratitude and relief were vast. Guilt and worry were gone. I could now focus entirely on my new job, my new world, earning enough money to bring Gershwin to British Hills, and my search for *ikigai*.

Teaching Japanese teenagers at British Hills was very much different from teaching working class English kids back home or the unmotivated high schools students in Takayama. Certainly, there were the occasional Tokyo teenagers who considered themselves too cool for school, like the *Ganguro* girls, who looked like Christina Aguilera with their tanned skin, bleached hair, and colourful makeup.

These students were a far cry from Takayama's comfortable housewives and cute kindergartners.

While the classes were enjoyable and unmonitored, Ryan and I both chafed under the micro-management at British Hills, which chose what food we ate and when, strait-jacketed us into suits, and forbid us to offer an opinion let alone challenge something we thought was unfair or unjust. British Hills, for all of its expansive grounds and buildings, sometimes felt like a very small suffocating box.

'It'll take us a while to get the hang of it,' Ryan would say which, as far as I was concerned, was a vast understatement.

About two weeks after moving into our snow-bound home in Fukushima, I sat gazing out the lounge's French doors into the snow-shrouded forest thinking about Takayama and its easy lifestyle where I had the ability to drop in on my friends on a whim, cycling through the city and hearing the water running through the many open drains.

Just enumerating these things made me realise that the truth was I was homesick. I was missing Takayama, my friends, and, of course, Gershwin. *This house will feel more like a home when he finally gets here,'* I told myself. Often several times a day.

Ryan felt pretty much the same way about British Hills as I did, although he quickly made good use of the nearby ski slopes and he'd already found some Blokes on the staff with whom to share a pint and talk endlessly about football at Falstaff, our one and only pub. Simon was Canadian. He had dark brown hair, was very tall, and very eccentric. A major Anglophile, he knew more about the UK and English music than I did. He had actually been an undertaker at one point, a job at complete odds with his *joie de vivre*. He was one of the funniest guys I had ever met, constantly speaking in innuendos and breaking out into a Mike Myers/Austin Powers impersonation ('Yeah, baby!') at the least opportunity. Like Mike Myers, he was from Canada, so naturally we referred to him as Canadian Simon.

Another bloke who joined our core group of mates, and quickly became one of my best British Hills friends, was Stefan. A bunch of the teachers, including Ryan and I, had journeyed to a Shirakawa restaurant in search of different food and a more attractive environment than the staff canteen provided. With sufficient alcohol-based courage, everyone was taking turns going up on the stage of a makeshift karaoke bar in the back and singing typical karaoke songs. Then Stefan – who was always flamboyant and, unknown to us, a superb Gloria Gaynor impersonator – walked up to the mic and began belting out 'I Will Survive,' strutting around the tiny stage with outrageous flourishes. He instantly supercharged the restaurant. Everyone was cheering and whistling. From that day on I called him Gloria (To this day, when we email or text each other, he always signs off #GloriaForever.)

Even with 'Gloria,' Hayley, and Sinead forging friendly ties with me, Ryan was still much more keen to socialise than I. So generally three nights a week, after work and dinner, we'd drive home, he'd shower, I'd stay home to read or watch TV, and he'd head off to the pub. Occasionally, I'd join him, but the Commonwealth guys usually drank much more than made me comfortable, at least on week nights. I didn't want to have to teach the next day with a hangover.

Twice a week after dinner, Ryan and I would swim and sauna and sometimes lounge in the Jacuzzi at the Manor. This was a British Hills perk that, along with the friends we were making, helped make us feel this was a good decision. But the tug to Takayama was still strong in me.

About three weeks after we moved to Fukushima, Ryan and I walked into the Admin building and there, plonked on my desk, was a bulky brown envelope on my desk.

'Interesting,' Ryan said, examining the package. 'It isn't your birthday. Have you been internet shopping again?'

'No, not this time, and this has *my* name on it,' I retorted, plucking the surprisingly heavy envelope from his hands. Curiosity running rampant, I ripped open the brown packaging, being careful not to damage whatever was inside.

I pulled out a paperback novel-sized black and white photo album with a picture on the cover of a tabby cat that looked like Takashi. I turned to the first page and there was a picture of the real Takashi staring back at me. Beneath the picture, carefully inscribed in Japanese and English upon red and pink square paper, were the words: *Thanks for my life. I am Takashi.*

My eyes started to well up. This was the sweetest present anyone had ever given me, and it was unmistakable who had created this special album of memories. Sayuri, that most generous and sweetest of friends, had sent me a treasure. I turned to the next page to find a photo of the little shrine at the end of our Takayama road in autumn covered with rustic leaves and the inscribed words, *Those make yellow carpet.*

With Ryan looking over my shoulder, I slowly turned page after page. Each one had a picture of one of our favourite spots in Takayama: Bagus, a restaurant, a shop, and of course the vets. Sayuri had captured the moments we had shared, and had filled these pages with the special people and places I loved.

I was actually shaking a little. No one, not even Ryan, had ever given me such a loving and thoughtful gift. Sayuri's kindness filled my eyes with thick, blurry tears. Her compassion overwhelmed me. I started to laugh and cry simultaneously as I flipped through the pages. Then, I suddenly emitted a gigantic roar of laughter when I came to a picture of Gershwin dressed in a blue nurse's uniform with a hat that had the Red Cross drawn on it. He was caring for me while I was sick in bed with the flu just two months before we moved.

The rest of the office must have wondered what had come over me as I laughed and cried at the same time.

'That's so sweet of her,' Ryan said, a little teary himself.

When we got back home at the end of the day, I put the album on the bookshelf next to a photo of Gershwin so that I could look through it every day. It was a constant reminder of the people, places, and cats I loved, and of the deep friendship I had forged with Sayuri in the last year. I couldn't wait to thank her in person for her wonderful gift.

In March, three months after we had settled at British Hills, it was still quite cold. Much of the heavy snowfalls had passed, but the snowbanks remained. At night, the temperatures were frigid. But the stars had finally aligned. Gershwin was coming home to us.

Ryan and I hadn't been able to ask for time off so soon after starting at British Hills to go back to Takayama to bring him to his new home. Nor did we have any room on our credit cards to pay for the trip. (It was bloody expensive travelling from Takayama to Fukushima and back.) So, for three months we'd been saving and finally Ryan and I had enough money to bring Gershwin to us courtesy of Sayuri, who had finally been granted a holiday from work. So, one March morning, she bundled Gershwin into his carrier and set out for Fukushima.

To take a cat across the country on a train in the final throes of winter was a massive task for anyone, but Sayuri assured me repeatedly on the phone that she was happy to reunite Gershwin with his family.

Of course, we paid for her roundtrip ticket, and we'd take extra special care of her while she was visiting us, but still I doubt there are a lot of people in this world who would go so far out of their way for her friends as Sayuri was doing for us.

During the week before they arrived, I was almost ridiculously excited to finally have Gershwin coming home. Ryan was excited, too.

I was buzzing with anticipation and, to work off some of the energy, I spent many an hour planning everything I would do with Sayuri when she arrived. (Ryan, of course, planned to take Sayuri to our new local ski ground for a day of snowboarding.) I soon had a long list, with everything from taking her to sample some British pub grub to visiting some of Fukushima's local attractions, like Mount *Nasu*, which had sulphur geysers and pools and great hiking trails.

I walked around practically vibrating with excitement at having Gershwin back in my arms. At least twice a day, Ryan would say 'He's coming!' with a huge grin on his face, unable to contain his excitement about being reunited with his best friend.

We had asked Sayuri to arrive in Shirakawa at night, so we could smuggle Gershwin into the house under cover of darkness. Hopefully, our neighbours wouldn't see our illicit contraband.

On the night Sayuri and Gershwin were due to arrive, Ryan and I were both so excited, that we left for the train station early, driving down the treacherous, icy road to Shirakawa station and going over again and again our plans to smuggle Gershwin into the house and keep him hidden once he was home.

Of course, we got to the station early. We had told Sayuri to take the rear exit from the train station where we'd be waiting for her. So, we parked, facing the station, with the motor on to keep the heater blasting. The minutes between parking the car and the train arriving seemed to take an extraordinary length of time to pass.

'I can't wait to see him,' I announced, my fingers drumming frenetically on the arm rest. 'What if Sayuri missed her connection in Tokyo? What if – '

'Don't worry, CJ,' Ryan said, 'this is Japan, where there are never any problems with transport or delays, where everything always works, and

141

everyone and everything always arrive on time . . . like that train about to pull into the station.'

With a gasp, I looked up to see a bullet train glide gracefully and precisely to a stop at the Shirakawa station platform. As the train doors slid open, Ryan and I jumped out of the car. A small bundled-up figure walked toward us under the yellow lights of the fluorescent-lit station. She looked at ease despite being a little over-loaded with a cat carrier and a large black duffle bag. I was thrilled to see her.

'*Gershwin*!' I yelled.

He stood up in the basket and emitted the loudest meow I had ever heard him make. His eyes, green as a spring forest, met mine and, despite the usual cat aloofness when being reunited with a human who had abandoned him for so long, I saw recognition and happiness.

I gave Sayuri a huge hug, thanking her again and again for bringing Gershwin to us. Ryan reached out for Sayuri and hugged her, too, saying '*Ohisashiburi desu*' (Long time no see).

Even though I was desperate to take Gershwin out of the carrier to hold him for a moment, I knew this wasn't a good idea. He might be so freaked out by the trip that he ran away. And I couldn't let him out in the company car, where he might also freak out and attack everything in sight. I could just imagine explaining claw marks to Gavin and Mr. Maki.

All I could do for now was peek inside the carrier. Gershwin was bigger than he had been, more of a cat now than a kitten. I got a little teary at having missed the last few months of his kittenhood. But I didn't have time to get maudlin, because Ryan was bundling all of us and Sayuri's luggage into the car.

All the way back up the snow-covered mountain, Ryan and I pestered Sayuri with questions about Gershwin, demanded updates on Bagus, and asked about all of our other friends in Takayama.

When we got home and parked the car, Ryan and I got out first and looked to make sure that our neighbours had their curtains closed and the owner's house was still dark. Then, Sayuri got out of the car with the cat carrier.

'*Sugoi*!' Sayuri exclaimed when she saw the house. 'It's so nice.'

'Wait until you see inside,' Ryan said.

We opened the front door and ushered Sayuri and Gershwin into our home, the lights and heater left on to welcome us. *'Kore wa kirei desu ne,'* (This is beautiful, isn't it?) Sayuri said.

As soon as we got into the lounge, we opened the cat carrier. Gershwin ran out cautiously, legs and tail close to the floor, his ears pricked. His green eyes darted about the room. Then he began to explore, running first to the French doors. Then, he sniffed the corners. Suddenly, he launched himself up the stairs, his first venture to an upper floor. Our silver Ninja Cat sprinted up to the bedroom to investigate.

I wanted to follow him, but I was busy making tea for everyone in the mini-kitchen, so I just let him explore on his own. A few minutes later, he came galloping down the stairs looking supremely happy with himself and his new home.

He continued exploring the main floor, relishing the freedom after such a long confinement in his small travel basket and enjoying the much larger living space in which he could race around and leap from bookcase or counter or the back of the sofa.

After I had got my Gershwin fix, cuddling and petting him and absorbing his loud purr, Ryan announced that he was hungry, and Sayuri was undoubtedly starving. Food. Right. Practical matters in the midst of joy.

So, leaving Gershwin to settle in, we bundled up again, got into the car, and drove up to Falstaff's. It had, of course, become our home away from home. The pub reminded me of an old country boozer, from the exposed wooden beams and white washed walls to the large wooden carving of a salmon hanging over an open fireplace. I always found it hard to believe I was actually in Japan when I was propped up on a tiny wooden stool at the bar balancing a pint in one hand and a chip in the other. To my surprise, Falstaff's wasn't as busy as I had expected, which meant we managed to find a table close to the bar.

'You have to have your first pint of English ale,' Ryan declared when we sat down at our heavily lacquered table.

'And fish and chips. There's nothing more gastronomically English than fish and chips,' I insisted.

I'll never be sure if Sayuri really enjoyed English beer and food. She was Japanese and too polite to do anything but smile and drink and eat up. I, however, loved it. I loved being in an English pub with my boyfriend and my best friend, and with Gershwin waiting for me at home.

Sayuri did enjoy meeting all the other *gaijin* staff and listening to their imperfect Japanese. We introduced her to Sinead, the Northern Ireland receptionist, and Simon. They quickly became engrossed in talking about music and travelling.

British Hills had just transported me back to my university days, when the only things that had seemed important were music and friends.

When we got back home, we made up an extra comfortable bed on the floor in the lounge for Sayuri.

Gershwin slipped under the covers with Ryan and me, purring happily as he drifted off to sleep between us. I was so happy, I almost wept.

The next day, as I stood outside in the snow beneath the whispering Japanese pine trees at the back of the house, I felt a sense of hope and peace that things were about to get a whole lot better. One silver-furred cat with large green eyes had finally settled me into British Hills.

Chapter 16: To Indulge a Cat

猫かわいがり / Neko Kawaigari

Needless to say, Gershwin got special food treats and an abundance of cuddling his first days at British Hills. Whenever I was home, I couldn't stand having him out of my sight. Ryan was constantly petting him and cuddling with him on the sofa. He accepted all of this as his due and settled contentedly into his new home.

Sayuri had brought Gershwin to us on a Friday, so we had an entire weekend to chat and reminisce and show her our favourite places, and discover places we hadn't yet had time to visit.

On Saturday, we all drove down to *Ubudo Nasu*, a Balinese village. It was purpose-built for all of the Japanese who love foreign climes but have neither the time nor generous annual leave to visit those climes. They get a taste of other cultures by visiting places like *Ubudo Nasu*, and British Hills.

The village was about an hour's drive away in the northern Tochigi Prefecture. It was also near Nikko National Park, which is famous for its temple with the three wise monkeys (See No Evil, Hear No Evil, Speak No Evil), the same ones my grandmother used to have on her mantelpiece so many years ago. I had always thought they were some sort of reference to the Bible. This trip to the shrine taught me how silly that assumption had been.

The philosophy 'see not, hear not, speak not' came to Japan from China in the Nara Period, the eighth century, as part of a Tendai-Buddhist legend and was popularised by carvings on eight panels at the Tosho-gu Shrine. The carvings are said to represent the Confucius Code of Conduct. The monkeys were introduced as both a sly play on Japanese words and as a means of depicting the human life cycle.

After we finished up our shopping at the Balinese village, we visited Nasu Animal Kingdom, a forty-three-hectare animal park that was just a fifteen-minute drive away in a valley. The park's slogan was 'Shake Hands with Nature.' It had indoor and outdoor displays of over six hundred animals and was unlike any animal park I had ever seen in the UK or Australia.

It had farm animals – horses, sheep, geese – in fields and a bird park in an enclosed building, which upset me on many levels. First, the poor birds, who were born to soar in the skies, were trapped between walls and beneath a roof. Worse, many of the birds of prey like hawks, eagles, and owls were chained by their legs to wooden posts. They could not fly. They could barely move. I got out of there fast.

Ryan, who'd been a member of the Young Ornithologists' Club as a child, and Sayuri, who was an avid animal lover, were equally upset when they saw the tethered birds. '*Kawaisō*' (poor things) Sayuri said over and over.

We escaped to the indoor Penguin Village where we had missed the most recent performance. In the Rabbit Kingdom, we pet a couple of Flemish Giants, billed as the world's largest breed of rabbits. I had been expecting to see rabbits the size of a basset hound, but these long fluffy brown giants were only about as large as Gershwin.

Next, we walked to the outdoor aquatic park, which of course had seals that gave several shows daily – balancing balls on their noses, sitting on podiums and blowing into horns, jumping and diving for fish, that sort of thing.

Nasu Animal Kingdom was making it abundantly clear that many Japanese considered animals as simply a form of entertainment. Observing them in their natural habitats was not sufficient. They had to perform.

One wing of the park was devoted to different breeds of domesticated cats. No tigers. No lions. Just twenty large fluffy felines roaming next to skinny short-haired tabbies and perching on fake trees and posts. There were also vertical platforms they could climb or jump up to, little wooden houses to sleep in, and slightly raised tracks they could walk on around the wing. The back wall was painted with green leaves to make it look like they were in a forest. (The people who worked in the cat wing wore pink jumpsuits and had cat ears on their heads.)

There was also, according to our brochure, a cat show – not an admiration of breeds, but performances in which the cats climbed five-metre-tall trees, jumped through hoops, navigated through an obstacle course, and walked across tightropes. We had come at the wrong time of day and missed it.

'How can so many different types of cats be living together in harmony like this?' I demanded. 'How can they live together and not fight?'

Sayuri shrugged and smiled. 'They are Japanese cats, so they must behave politely toward each other.'

The next morning, while Ryan and Sayuri were off snowboarding, I sat on the sofa with Gershwin purring on my lap and thought about the animal park, not only about all of the things I had disliked about it on the animals' behalf, but also about how much I had enjoyed being amongst the cows, horses, seals, penguins, and cats. It struck me that, for as long as I could remember, I had wanted to work with animals.

For most of my childhood, I had been fortunate enough to spend most of my free time at my Aunt Cora's riding stables. All of my fondest memories were there in the muddy fields with the horses, the stray mongrels, the barn cats, and even the mountains of manure.

Whenever I ran away from home, I would go there, hiding in the darkness, breathing in the familiar, comforting scents. I might have been cold and alone, but – until the police inevitably came, found me, and took me back home again – it was my little piece of happiness in a family that didn't seem to know the meaning of the word.

I had always been told from a young age that there was no money in horses, even though my aunt ran a successful stable and riding school. 'When you grow up,' my grandmother would say, 'you ought to work in a bank. Something respectable and dependable.'

This advice always had the reverse effect on me. I knew even in primary school that I most definitely did *not* want to work in a bank or anything smacking of a corporate environment. I would work with animals; I felt it in my young bones.

When I was twelve and my Aunt Cora married suddenly, closed the riding stable, and moved away, all the things I held dear were gone, all the animals, all the friends I'd made, all the safe distractions disappeared within a month. My safety net from the rest of my family was gone. I was stunned.

I still remember standing shell-shocked and weeping as I watched the horseboxes take away one beloved pony after another. Almost immediately it seemed, my mother left me to move with her new husband to South Africa. She returned to England a year later, and a year after that she died. For all the times she had hurt me, she was my *mother* and she was gone.

Losing my aunt to marriage, my refuge in the stables, and my mother to South Africa and then to cancer broke me in two. My life felt distorted and I turned to all the wrong people and all the wrong activities – as I sought some sort of comfort. I never found it. I had been pulling myself out of that pain, that distortion, and those choices ever since.

Since coming to Japan, my old desire to work with animals had been resurfacing. Visiting the animal park confirmed what I had learned in Takayama. From the moment Ryan and I had rescued Gershwin, I had rediscovered my love of animals and my connection to them. I realised now, with Gershwin stretching and resettling himself on my lap, that I was desperate to find a way, not only to help the animals I found, but also perhaps to find a career with animals that would take me far away from teaching teenagers.

I just had to figure out what that career would be and I would have my *ikigai*.

Chapter 17: Give Catnip to The Cat and Save Your Gold Coins for The Prostitutes

猫にまたたび、御女郎に小判 / Neko Ni Matatabi, Ojorou Ni Koban

Wrapped in the cocoon of blindingly white snow drifts, the welcoming comfort and ease of my new home, Ryan's wonderful ability to let me be independent, and Gershwin's unwavering affection, I spent the rest of my winter at British Hills teaching and going deeper and deeper into contemplation of who I was, who I had been, what I wanted to change, and where I wanted to go.

As the strong winds from the north calmed, blizzards turned to flurries and then to rain, and a light warm breeze blew delicately through the pines. Spring takes its time coming to the northeastern prefectures on the island of Honshu. It was late March before it was possible to walk outside without digging through dense snowbanks. It was April when most of the snow had finally fled to be replaced with eager spring flowers and leafing trees.

Since Gershwin's arrival, I'd spent most weekends worrying we'd get discovered for having a cat. My hair would stand on end, every time I heard a car door close, and see Gershwin sitting by the window cluelessly grooming himself in full view of the owner's house. Fortunately, this was all about to end when I heard that they'd be spending some time overseas. This meant my feline contraband would be safe for the next few months at least.

After the long drawn out winter, I was desperate to get outdoors and make the most of our neighbouring tennis court. When the spring sun started to melt the snow, clay patches appeared and I was able to use the court as a safe place to train Gershwin to walk on a leash.

My Ninja Cat on a leash. It sounds impossible, I know, but the lessons went surprisingly well. At first, Gershwin thought it was a game. He chased the leash and attacked his harness with its red, white, and blue stars with his teeth. Then there were the times he lay on the ground and refused to budge. But gradually, he got more and more used to the harness and walking on a leash and began to accept them. After just a week, he was taking it all in his stride. He would run toward me, his tail raised in excitement, when he saw me pull out his harness and leash from the drawer.

Both amused and impressed, Ryan called G 'the Circus Cat,' because of his astounding acceptance of the leash on his walks.

When all traces of snow had gone, Ryan and I could actually play tennis on the court two or three times a week and I could take Gershwin beyond the green fenced court to stroll along the little unpaved lane next to our house where new grass was starting to grow.

On the morning of Gershwin's first spring stroll, I made sure that he was safely secured in his harness. Together, we walked outside into a relatively warm sunny morning.

No sooner had we made our way up to the main driveway than Gershwin made a beeline for the thick fern overgrowth to the right of our driveway, stretching the extendable lead to its maximum length. He was sniffing happily, investigating the scents of new growing things and all the other critters who had trespassed here. Suddenly he froze, his green eyes staring straight ahead.

Something in the bushes had transfixed him. *'Probably a mouse,'* I thought as I tried to pull him away. He wouldn't budge. Again I tugged on the leash. Gershwin was immobile. So, I crouched down to see what was so mesmerising.

I froze too. In front of us, with a long protruding tongue, was the longest, greenest snake I had ever seen. Its hose-like body was wrapped around and around in an emerald turban. And it was licking its reptilian lips, as if thinking that a cat would make a tasty lunch.

Not on my watch. I scooped Gershwin up into my arms and sprinted back to the house, shutting the door firmly behind us. Thus ended our first spring walk together beyond the safe confines of the tennis court. Fortunately, it had been a relatively painless lesson to learn. I vowed on future walks to be extra vigilant and to keep Gershwin away from anything that was overgrown.

Soon, Gershwin and I settled into a comfortable (and safe) rhythm for our outdoor walks. I walked him almost every afternoon after work and on weekends, sometimes with Ryan, and sometimes it was just Gershwin and me.

During the week, when it was quiet and free of weekenders, we'd go down to the Regina Forest Resort in the lush Hatoriko Highlands. The resort had been built around Lake Hatori and it was pet-friendly. Campers often brought their dogs or cats to enjoy nature with them. Spring also brought group after group of weekenders from Tokyo who had come to forage for prized *sansai* (edible mountain plants). Their diligence, bordering on obsession, as they hunted for *sansai* was fascinating. *Sansai* is said to be 'the taste of spring.' They are actually quite bitter, but most Japanese enjoy them.

From Monday to Thursday, though, Gershwin and I had the place pretty much to ourselves. We would walk around the dark blue lake. He would explore while I enjoyed the beautiful and peaceful views, the rich scents of earth and pine, and the sounds of birds singing or calling to each other, broken occasionally by the sound of a car on the main road. Sometimes we'd visit the Wetland Garden. I'd study the different vegetation, like the *Shojobakama*, the Japanese hyacinth, and Gershwin would explore the marshy undergrowth.

We were, in our own way, participating in *Shinrin-Yoku*, Japan's National Public Health program. Basically, it's 'forest bathing.' The government wants its Type A Japanese citizens to forget work and responsibilities for a little while and instead drink in the power of the natural world by going into the woods to sit and relax, breathe deeply the forest air, and accomplish absolutely nothing. I was becoming a model for *Shinrin-Yoku.*

On our nature walks, Gershwin would forage for lizards, his latest favourite plaything. Sometimes, swarms of *tonbos* (dragonflies) turned him into a prowling mass of fur, tail, and leash as he struggled desperately to capture one of the double-winged insects. Try as he might, though, he never succeeded. That didn't stop him from launching himself into the air in a daily attempt to catch one. In Japan, the dragonfly symbolises perseverance, never giving up. Gershwin was a true Japanese cat.

We became wrapped up in our own natural world, the only creatures walking through the forest. It felt as though we had the whole pristine mountain to ourselves. No human being or four-legged leashed pet disturbed our solitude. Birds and the sound of cicadas were all that could be heard for miles around.

Before coming to Japan – in fact, ever since my Aunt Cora had closed her stables – I had made a conscious effort to walk as little as possible. I certainly never sought out a park or a woods in which to stroll and commune with Nature. Looking back, I think I was determined to avoid my body, the natural world, and my place in it.

In Takayama, though, with Ryan's enthusiasm for all outdoor sports rubbing off on me, I had taken to going on actual hikes and now, at British Hills, with no urging whatsoever, I walked through forests and meadows and up and down mountain trails as often as possible every week. I realised that my happiest time as a child had been rambling the Surrey countryside, often on horseback. I had no horses at British Hills, of course, but I had a cat with whom I could hike. I discovered on our rambles that I was becoming happier and happier.

Sometimes I walked alone, often Gershwin accompanied me, and sometimes Ryan joined me on these walks. Despite our generally outgoing personalities, which leads many to think we are extroverts, both Ryan and I are actually quite introverted characters. We needed time to retreat into silence after being busy with students all day long.

More and more, though, I found myself taking and relishing solitary walks. I loved being alone, not distracted by anyone or anything. I could be fully at ease in my body and my thoughts. I could contemplate without interruption my life, passion, animals, and how I might blend them all together into a career. I thought how much just having Gershwin in our British Hills house had settled me, fulfilled me. I thought about all of the cats in that grungy Takayama apartment who had, through their boundless affection, their perfect unselfconscious ease in their own skins, and their playfulness helped me to really start healing from all the pain and loss of my childhood and adolescence. Cats (and other animals) as therapy. Perhaps this was something I could share with others.

I began hauling my laptop up to the Admin building to do some internet research at my desk. I couldn't find any animal-based healing programs near me in Japan. In England, I was happy to see, had a treasure trove of programs that appealed to me in various locations across the country. Tentative plans began to form in my mind. When Ryan and I returned to England in the autumn, I would not return to teaching. Japan was giving me the courage to take a new path.

Thoughts of returning to England, even as I immersed myself in my life at British Hills, naturally made me think of how to get Gershwin into the UK. Smuggling him on a night train was not an option in returning to England. I would have to get him in legally, and that required many months of planning and working my way through miles of bureaucratic red tape.

There are pet courier companies that can do the heavy lifting for you by taking on all of the monumental restrictions and hassle associated with international pet travel, but this can cost an arm and a leg, and Ryan and I could not spare either. We simply couldn't afford to hire someone to help us. I needed to take action myself to get Gershwin's pet passport ready for entry into the UK.

Of course, I couldn't do it on my own. I needed help. Friendly unpaid help. I had several Japanese documents I needed translated, so I looked around and decided to ask one of the younger staff members, Ayumi, for her assistance. She was in her late twenties, very slim, very pretty, and always approachable. I'd had a few conversations with her before in the staff canteen, so I didn't feel too awkward seeking her out. Despite the fact that she had seen so many foreigners come and go at British Hills, and witnessed the sometimes reckless behaviour of young Western teachers, which had left her with a bad taste in her mouth, she agreed to help this most grateful *gaijin*.

I had assumed that a basic translation from Japanese to English for someone who was bilingual would be relatively easy. I couldn't have been more wrong. She stared at the pet permit form and other travel papers, her eyes crinkling, her mouth crimping.

'Some of these Japanese words and symbols I don't even understand,' she announced, and then smiled awkwardly. 'They have used complex *Kanji* characters on this form. I'm going to have to check the meanings on my computer. Hold on a minute.' She turned in her chair to her computer.

I waited apprehensively as she tapped away on the keyboard, mystified that a language (and process) could be so complex that even an educated Japanese woman had to turn to a computer to explain her own native words. Frustration and impatience welled within me as the minutes ticked by. Just as I was about to break out into hives, Ayumi clicked a button, the printer whirred, and she handed the finished product to me.

'Here you go,' she announced. 'Just show this to the animal *Sensei*. He'll know what to do.'

I released the breath I had been holding for what felt like hours. The relief was wonderful. '*Domo arigato*.' I said fervently. Hopefully (I mentally crossed my fingers), the vet *would* know what to do next.

'*Dōitashimashite*,' (You're welcome) she said, hiding, I suspect, her amusement.

Helping a foreign worker send her cat overseas went way beyond Ayumi's job description, and then she went further. As I slipped the document carefully into my pet travel folder, which had doubled in size since I had started the Gershwin Emigration process, Ayumi called the local vet to make an appointment for him.

Real (selfless) help equalled real movement forward. I walked out of the office thinking I just might succeed in getting my Japanese cat into England.

The next morning, with my first class not scheduled until two o'clock, I set off early. By now, I had taken Gershwin in the car with me many times. Heading to town, he assumed his favourite travel position: riding shotgun until we hit the main road. His pink nose and white whiskers poked out the small gap in the window, nervously sniffing the crisp mountain air. I turned on the car stereo and played some soothing classical music, which usually helped mellow him out. The winding roads made most people and animals suffer from motion sickness, so I drove carefully to avoid any feline pongy mishaps on our long descent into Shirakawa.

We passed an elderly couple out on their morning walk. They waved and smiled widely as they saw a taut bundle of silver fur and big green eyes poking out the window. Smiling, I waved back. I loved country life. It was friendlier and slower-paced than city life. People had more time for each other. You could even find a place to park without giving into – or encountering – bouts of road rage. What could have been a stressful drive to the vets was made easier and happier, because where we lived.

Amazingly, I found the animal doctor without much trouble in a residential area of Shirakawa I'd never been to before, away from the big shopping centres I usually visited. I parked, loaded Gershwin into the cat carrier (much to his disgust), and walked into the vet's lobby, which was empty, perhaps because it was early on a weekday.

I walked up to the reception counter and gave my name and Gershwin's name to the pretty twenty-something receptionist, and then sat down on one of the hard grey plastic chairs with Gershwin beside me to wait our turn. After just five minutes, a veterinary assistant called:

'Gershwin-sama.'

I smiled. I loved how vets in Japan always called the name of the pet, instead of the owner.

I carried Gershwin into a compact exam room with wooden furnishings. The vet, Dr. Taro, walked in almost immediately in a pristine long white lab coat. He was an older gentlemen in his late fifties with greying hair and no smile. No chit-chat. He did not even pet Gershwin. He was very business-like. I missed the warmth and casual friendliness of Dr. Iguchi, our vet in Takayama.

But I had come for help and Dr. Taro, however cool, could provide it. So, I told the *Sensei* about our travel plans while he ran his hand over Gershwin's silver coat in a basic examination. I handed him instructions from Ayumi about the pet permit. He looked puzzled, then uttered those now familiar words '*Sou desu ka?*' (Is that so?)

The veterinary assistant came in, and talked to the *Sensei* for a few minutes in Japanese.

'You must come back next week,' the assistant suddenly announced to me.

'What? Next week? Why?' I asked plaintively.

The pair were tight-lipped. (I was in Japan and had made the *faux pas* of questioning authority.) I was finally able to glean that they needed time to do some research about how and where to send Gershwin's blood tests off to a government-approved laboratory. So, my heart sinking, I agreed to return in one week.

I smiled weakly and put Gershwin back into his carrier. I managed to say '*Domo arigato*,' then carried Gershwin back to the car.

I grumbled and worried and complained to Gershwin all the way home. I walked back into the house and let Gershwin out of his carrier (he zoomed for the comfort of the upstairs bedroom heater).

When I tracked Ryan down that afternoon before my first class, and before I could launch myself into a recitation of all of my grievances, Ryan smiled and said 'How about going to Lake Inawashiro tomorrow?'

That stopped me in my tracks and shifted me instantly out of my trials and tribulations. Instead of focusing on my pet passport woes, I was suddenly contemplating the delights I might find tomorrow at the beautiful lake where Japanese swans chose to winter.

'That sounds great,' I said. Getting away from travel planning and Japanese and British red tape for a day seemed suddenly very necessary. I had begun to feel myself getting stressed out over a move that was still eight months away. Spending a day relaxing by Lake Inawashiro would break that tired knee-jerk pattern and return me to sense and good humour.

I shook my head wryly at Ryan. He had known exactly what was going on and had also known just what I needed.

Chapter 18: Act Like a Cat, or Act Like a Tiger

猫にもなれば虎にもなる / Neko Nimo Nareba Tora Nimo Naru

We woke early on Saturday, packed some juices, and stopped off at Daily Yamazaki, the nearest convenience store, to get some *onigiri* for lunch. We both loved the triangular rice balls with unusual fillings like red adzuki beans or *umeboshi* (pickled plums).

The hour-long drive to Lake Inawashiro north from British Hills was on a mountain road that wound through lush forests of ancient cypress, green beech trees, and creeping pines. Search as I might, I found very little signs of wildlife, just the odd rabbit running beside the road and the usual hawks soaring overhead looking for lunch or just simply enjoying riding on the air currents.

In the distance, I could see towering mountains still white with snow. But here, on this mountain road, it was a lovely warm spring day and Ryan and I were embraced by all the glories of an untamed natural world. We remained silent as rolling forested hills led down to a small emerald green valley filled with rice paddies. You can enjoy something together, like the spectacular beauty of the natural world, without having to speak.

We didn't pass a single car until we reached the lake, which was a few kilometres beyond the rice paddies.

Oval-shaped Lake Inawashiro is the fourth largest lake in Japan. Encircled by hills and forested mountains, it has been nicknamed 'Heaven's Mirror' and 'Sky Mirror Lake,' because the deep blue sky with its big white clouds is reflected on the cold glassy water. The lake also has several strips of rather narrow beaches, ranging from white sand to rocks.

As we drove closer to the lake, I saw many people walking, strolling, and playing along the lake on a white sandy beach. Ryan wasn't the only one with a good idea. We parked on the side of the road and walked down to the lake.

'I do like this part of Japan,' I announced. 'I can go for hours without seeing any western influences, apart from the odd discarded box of cigarettes or soft drink can.'

'Pristine,' Ryan said.

'Yes,' I said with an answering smile. My smile grew. 'This has got to be one of the pet-friendliest places I've ever seen in Japan!'

Big dogs, little dogs, and everything in between were trotting along the beach and running in and out of the crystal clear water, thrilled to be freed from four walls and eager to discover every single scent and every possible game that beach, water, and people could provide.

I pulled out our picnic blanket and we settled down on a patch of grass on a quiet end of the beach, leaned back, and drank in big gulps of fresh mountain air.

'Gershwin would love it here,' I said with a happy sigh.

'The dogs would eat him,' Ryan pronounced.

'Maybe not. Look,' I said, pointing at one of the sweetest things I'd ever seen in Japan.

Sitting at attention beside a red tent and an enormous chocolate-coloured dog was one very small tabby cat. Ears pricked, every sense alert to its surroundings, the cat just sat, acting as if the great outdoors and the hordes of dogs on the beach posed no direct threat.

'He's got a bodyguard,' Ryan said, nodding. 'That dog is bigger than any other canine here. No one would dare mess with him, or his cat. And we're having lunch first.'

I raised my eyebrows in an unspoken question.

He grinned knowingly. 'I want to eat something before you throw yourself at the poor unsuspecting owners of the tabby and interrogate them from now until sunset.'

'I would be more considerate than that,' I said loftily.

'Of course you would,' Ryan said,

'Besides,' I said with a grin, 'I'm starving, too.'

Chuckling, he reached into our food bag and pulled out our *onigiri*.

There are two things that can distract me: animals and food. I gave in to the latter and enjoyed a delicious lunch.

Once hunger had been sated and rubbish carefully put away, Ryan stood up and pulled me to my feet. 'Don't overdo it,' he said with a wink as we walked over to the little tabby, gigantic dog, and their owners. 'Remember, they are probably on holiday and they're very polite, because they are Japanese, so they won't brush you off. Try not to ask too many questions, alright?'

'Got it,' I agreed.

Of course, that was much easier said than done.

As we walked over to the human, feline, and canine campers, I was reminded of an article I'd read claiming that the Japanese now preferred pets to parenthood and the staggering statistic that there were now more pets than babies in Japan. As a result, pets are treated like family members and the market has responded accordingly with everything from pet prams to pet gyms for overweight pets.

This cat and dog, however, seemed in excellent health. Their owners – slim, friendly, and fashionable in their jeans and sweaters – were in their late twenties and sitting by the lake in camping chairs, drinking tea from flasks.

Ryan and I bowed and he introduced us in pretty good Japanese.

'*Sumimasen. O nami wa?*' (Excuse me. What are their names?) I asked, pointing at the cat and then the dog.

'*Kore wa Eri-Chan desu*' (This is Eri-Chan), the woman said as I pet the tabby. '*Kore wa Cocoa-Chan desu*' (This is Cocoa-Chan), she said with a smile at the big dog, who looked at her eagerly when he heard his name.

Ryan smiled as I petted both the cat and the dog and struggled with my inadequate Japanese to ask the owners about travelling with both a cat and dog and how well they got on together, especially in strange places.

I could sense Ryan was trying to shuffle off, and I started to politely end the conversation. But then I got a better look at Eri's right eye. It seemed the little cat was blind in that eye and my curiosity was piqued.

'What happened?' I asked in Japanese.

'Eri-Chan is very old, the woman said.

'*Nan si desu ka?*' (How old?)

'She is eighteen years old.'

'*Sugei*,' I said, impressed. (Using the cooler more informal version of *sugoi* meant 'great.')

Ryan was now pretending not to listen anymore. He had turned and was studying the lake.

I ignored the hint. 'Do you live here?' I asked.

'No, we're from Yokohama. We're on holiday here,' the woman said. 'Eri and Coco love camping. We've holidayed together since they were young.'

I was amazed that a multi-pet household went camping *regularly*. Safely. When I was small, my parents and I had taken Lucy, my grandmother's slightly disagreeable tabby, to the New Forest with my Grandmother. One night, Lucy went off on her own and was never seen again. It had ruined our holiday, I was heartbroken, and my grandmother never spoke of Lucy after that.

Unlike Eri, Lucy had not been trained properly and had certainly never seen a stylish cat harness, much less worn one, in her life.

I wanted to ask the couple details about how they had trained their cat and dog to not only live together in harmony, but to go camping without getting eaten, attacked, or lost, but Ryan had disappeared, a not so subtle hint that I had taken up too much of the Japanese couple's time. So, I thanked them and said my *sayonaras* to the cute couple and their equally cute pets. Then I hurried off to catch up with Ryan who was buying an iced tea from an outdoor vending machine.

'Can you believe that?' I exclaimed. 'They actually holiday with their pets!'

Ryan regarded me silently over his soda. The message was clear: 'Don't get any funny ideas.'

Too late. I already had lots of them. I smiled cheerfully back at him.

When we got home that evening, I cuddled with Gershwin on the sofa, which made me think of the complications of returning to the UK with a Japanese cat in tow, and *that* brought me smack dab against the subject I had been trying so hard to keep at the back of my mind: my estrangement from my family which had now made me ignorant of where any of them were living, let alone what they were doing.

The problem was, as a young child I knew that my Aunt Lydia on my father's side of the family had taken her three dogs and one cat back and forth between America and the UK for many years. She was bound to be a fount of information for our upcoming return to England, but I hadn't spoken to her since I was ten years old when there had been a huge family argument over Christmas. Then my father remarried and I got a new stepmother. When he moved overseas, he lost contact with his family, which meant I lost contact with them, too.

I always thought Aunt Lydia and her family were busy living their own lives and unconcerned about me. Later, I became pre-occupied with studying at university in London, and then working. The family disconnect turned into nearly two decades of silence. All I knew was that my Uncle Frederick was a successful businessman, my Aunt Lydia was an interior designer for the well-to-do, and that both my cousins had gone to private school and then a university in New York.

It occurred to me, as I contemplated my separation from my American-based relatives, that I had actually surrounded myself with a thick protective wall that had kept almost *everyone* away from me. Until now, isolation had been good. Isolation had been safe. Looking closer, I thought that perhaps my self-imposed boundary against Aunt Lydia and her family had been driven, at least in part, by my feelings of personal inadequacy.

Yet, here I was, on top of a mountain in Japan with a happy loving family – Ryan and Gershwin – and a beautiful home. So much of my life *was* good . . . and *I* had made that happen. Yes, fear had been present, but I still had made the decisions that had brought Ryan into my life and kept him there. I could have said No to Japan at any moment, as I had in Osaka, and Ryan would have flown back to England with me the next day. But I had chosen to stay in Japan, to learn, to grow. Rather than fending off love and attachment, I had welcomed new friends and Gershwin with an open heart and was now doing everything necessary to keep them.

Yes, it was scary contemplating breaking through nearly two decades of silence and negativity and assumptions. But I needed help and my Aunt Lydia might be able to provide it. Sitting on the sofa with Gershwin sleeping contentedly on my lap, I made the decision to take the first step in a *rapprochement* with my father's family. Once again, Gershwin was helping me break free from my past and grow into more of the person I wanted to be.

Feeling brave, that night I took my laptop up to the Admin building and searched on Facebook for my cousin Jessica, the eldest daughter of my Aunt Lydia. I hadn't seen her since she was a baby. I hadn't communicated with her at all. But right now, it felt easier to reach out to someone closer to me in age than to find and connect directly with my Aunt Lydia.

To my surprise, I found Jessica fairly quickly. According to her Facebook page, she had got a degree in Politics and International Relations (the same as me! We had something in common) and was now living in London and working for a PR company. Based on the picture she had posted, she even had my blue eyes. Heart pounding, I started typing a message:

Hi, Jessica,

You don't actually know me, because I haven't seen you since you were a baby, but we are cousins and I wanted to reach out to you. I have often thought about you, but was never sure how to go about contacting you. I finally found you on Facebook.

I finished university about five years ago, I lived in Australia for a year with my boyfriend, Ryan, and we're now living in Japan teaching English at a British-themed school.

How are you? I'm a little stunned that you studied Politics and International Relations at university as well. Family genes and dynamics are interesting!

What has your life been like and what have you been doing since university? It would be great to hear what has been happening with you. We have two lifetimes to catch up on!

I'm also hoping you can give me some advice about travelling internationally with pets. I know your mum has done this a lot over the years. I was wondering if you could give me some tips. As I mentioned, I'm currently in Japan and I need to bring my cat Gershwin to London when Ryan and I return to the UK.

Hope you are well.

CJ xx

School and walking Gershwin kept me so busy (or at least that's what I told myself), that it was a few days before I logged onto the computer again. I opened my email box and jumped a little.

My *Aunt Lydia* had written to me. Not just a few brief words like 'bugger off,' but an actual letter. A long letter. To me. Nervous, curious, and even a little hopeful, I began to read:

Dear CJ,

Your cousin sent your message to me. I hear you are living in Japan now. That must be quite different and exciting. We are back in the UK at the moment, living in Oxford. You will have to come to stay when you are back. Bring Ryan, too. We would love to meet him.

I was going to say you don't know how sorry we feel about the lack of contact, but I think you do.

When you send your pet, make sure he will be on a direct flight unless totally impossible. To come into the UK, you probably know you need a pet passport or he will have to go into quarantine. Although it sounds complicated it's not. But the sooner you start the better. Where are you going to? If you both need somewhere to stay while you re-group, we have plenty of room. Just let me know.

All is going well. It looks like your Dad and Krystal will be off on Monday - hope he knows what he's doing!

If you need any more info just let me know.

Love LL x

I stared at the letter utterly astounded. Nearly twenty years had passed and she had written to me like she'd spoken to me only yesterday! I wondered what she'd been told over the years of my activities and whereabouts and I prayed that it was something resembling the truth. She was treating me so nicely, and I didn't want her to think badly of me.

I re-read the letter. It was still as friendly as the first time I had read it.

I re-read the last bit again and wondered how often she spoke to my Dad. Wasn't there supposed to be a family estrangement?

The biggest question of all was: where was my Dad going on Monday, and who was Krystal?

The juxtaposition of reconnecting with an aunt happy to communicate with me and learning that she knew more about my dad and his activities than I did was painful. And sobering.

The time had come for some equally painful and sobering soul-searching.

It wasn't merely that I had to decide how best to answer my aunt's letter. I had to decide if I was willing to open the lines of communication with my father, what I wanted from a relationship with him, and if I had any hope of getting it.

Chapter 19: When a Cat Washes Its Face, It Will Rain

ねこがかおをあらうとあめがふる / Neko Ga Kao Wo Arau To Ame Ga Furu

It was late August, almost typhoon season in Japan, and British Hills had turned into an even greater storm of activity. The staff were busy preparing for the impending arrival of students and teachers from Keio, one of Tokyo's most prestigious universities, who were coming for three days of study, cultural immersion, and a speech contest – the standard British Hills package. But they were from Keio, so everything had to be perfect for them.

Every effort was being made to ensure their brief stay was a memorable one. Not unlike a scene from *Downton Abbey*, I watched as cutlery was given an extra shine, freshly cut flowers were placed in expensive vases, and the waiters and waitresses carefully groomed themselves to look extra smart. The teachers, as usual, were given no special instructions. We were expected to know how to prepare for this visit and how to perform during it.

All of this hustle and bustle and bending over backwards for students from Japan's best families made me wonder how these super-privileged elite university students would compare to their British counterparts. Would they have the same aristocratic airs, the same level of snobbery, as did students from Eton and Harrow, Oxford and Cambridge? (And how would I feel being around that snobbery again?)

I considered all of this extra activity a blessing, however, because it gave me the perfect excuse to avoid immediate further contact with my Aunt Lydia. Despite her kind, friendly email letter, I was still unsure how to respond after having gone nearly twenty years with silence between us. So, I used every excuse to sidestep my laptop computer.

Helping me enormously in my continued avoidance of family connection was one of my favourite Japanese BH staff, whom I'll call 'K.' He was more British than the British. I'd been told he was some type of Baron (*danshaku*). While the aristocracy (*kazoku*) and their five tiers of titles had been abolished in the 1946 Constitution of Japan at the end of the Second World War, many descendants of the *kazoku* families continue to hold influential positions in the country.

K certainly dressed with the kind of grace reserved for the aristocracy: perfectly tailored tweed suits with a perfectly placed handkerchief in the breast pocket. He roamed the grounds with a permanent stiff upper lip engrained on his face. He would not have looked out of place in the House of Lords among the blithering and privileged elite.

No one was exactly sure what K's job entailed. He simply turned up once every two weeks to sit at the back of the Admin office, make phone calls, and watch everyone. I enjoyed watching him in turn.

Although I had been at British Hills for nearly nine months, I first met K in July in the Admin building by the photocopier. I said 'Good morning.'

His ears pricked up at my accent. 'What part of England are you from?' he asked without any preamble.

'I grew up in Sussex, but I lived ten years in London before I left.'

'Ah, Great Britain,' he replied keenly. 'Country manors and rose gardens. I have been many times, you know?' He smiled and then said to me, and would repeat on more than one occasion: 'Japan and Britain, two great islands who share a great love of tea.'

At first, I'd avoided talking to K. I had assumed that we would have nothing in common. I couldn't have been more wrong. K was always a true gentleman, courteous and genuinely interested in others' opinions and experiences.

I seemed to have endeared myself to him when I suggested that the local village of Ten'ei ought to be twinned with a British village. He agreed with as much enthusiasm as his stiff upper lip permitted. Ever since that conversation, whenever he saw me he'd always smile and go out of his way to engage me in a chat about a Japanese-British sister city.

I have always been drawn to people I never fully understand. I liked K's friendly eccentricity. Besides, distracting myself with K was another way to help me avoid replying to my aunt.

On the day of days, K was standing by the main entrance to the Manor House that Thursday summer afternoon as he greeted the four teachers and the nearly one hundred and fifty Keio university students as they got off the coach. Everyone filed into Ambassador's Hall quietly and respectfully, which was pleasingly different from the chattering high school students who usually came to British Hills.

I fumbled a little with the papers in front of me on the lectern as I looked out at my audience. Then I breathed in deeply. Public speaking was no longer terrifying, or even worrying. I now had a lot of experience, which had given me the confidence I needed to make my standard speech to these more mature students. I ran through the registration procedure and the house rules calmly.

The moment I finished my little speech, K appeared. He gestured to the university's Head Teacher, with whom he seemed well acquainted. The two of them left the Ambassador's Hall together, probably to walk the grounds and commiserate about the modern era.

I took my usual position at one side of the Hall as Gavin, the head teacher, gave a final welcome to the students. Then, I heard someone query in perfect Queen's English: 'Will we be having tea?'

I turned to see a smiling, refined Japanese gentleman in his senior years, another chaperone responsible for the equally refined group of boys and girls sitting in the auditorium.

'I certainly hope so,' I said with typical British pessimism and an answering smile. 'I'm CJ.'

'Nice to meet you. I am Tomohiko.' He reached out and gave me a firm handshake that took me by surprise. The Japanese don't usually offer such an assured handshake. His BBC-accented English was flawless and so were his manners. 'These bright boys and girls are the future of Japan,' he said proudly. 'Our former students include some of the brightest minds in the country, and former prime ministers, too.'

'Really? Who?' I enquired.

'Koizumi, among others. Keio has one of the best reputations in the country.'

I felt a little out of my league talking with this perfect gentleman who represented a class and a level of education that were so far above me they could cause nose bleeds. But I was also curious. 'Were you educated in Britain or did you work for the BBC?'

He chuckled softly. 'Neither. You know, when I was younger, British English was the preferred choice for a second language in Japanese schools, but that's all changed. Nowadays, everyone wants to have an American accent.'

'Will you be judging the speech contest?'

'Yes. I look forward to it.' Although, at that moment, I wasn't sure I had the right or the ability to judge the speech of any upper class university student, let alone the speeches of the future Prime Ministers of Japan.

'It's a very good opportunity for our students to come here and be judged by the teachers of British Hills,' said Tomohiko. 'A great experience for everyone involved.'

We parted as Gavin finished his speech and the students rose to go find their assigned rooms.

Once everyone had settled in and had lunch, we launched the Keio students into their first classes. I did two cooking classes that afternoon, making scones, which went seamlessly.

The next day, Friday, each teacher was assigned a group of university students to tutor and prep for the climax on Saturday: the speech contest finale. I was lucky. I got an attentive group of twelve students who listened intently to me as I explained the judging criteria: good content, a clear voice, eye contact, timing, and gestures.

'Could you give us some examples of gestures, please?' said Kenta, one of the taller and more confident boys in the class. 'And when is it correct to use them?'

'The easiest hand gesture is numerical,' I replied. 'Whenever you say a number, make the corresponding gesture: hold up one finger for one, two fingers for two, three fingers for three, like this,' I said, demonstrating. 'You can also raise a clenched fist when making a point you're passionate about. Also, try spreading your arms wide to indicate the world or the world around you. Remember, using hand gestures will help make people focus more on what you are saying, and what you are saying is very important.'

To be honest, I felt humbled that these kids, the children of ambassadors and CEOs, the *crème de la crème* of Japanese society, were taking advice from me, someone who had spent more time on a housing estate than among the (future) elite. I guess that's the power of the

168

English language: it can transcend borders, classes, and perceptions (as long as you're not anywhere near Eton).

I spent the next few hours working one-on-one with each student, reading through their speeches and helping them to edit and streamline them to meet the time requirements and to strengthen their arguments. The range of subject matter was impressive, from the global economy to the environment and refugees. If this was the future generation of Japanese leaders in my classroom, the country would be in safe hands.

While I was working one-on-one with a student, the rest of the class practised their English pronunciation and timed their speeches to make sure they didn't go too long.

The morning, for me, was a revelation. I had never encountered such intelligent, polite, and sophisticated young men and women from the upper crust of society. They were completely free of arrogance. They were grateful to me for the coaching I provided, supportive of each other as they rehearsed, and concerned with the world far beyond themselves and their university. My morning with them felt like a gift.

After class, they headed off to the Refectory for lunch while I walked over to the staff canteen.

'How are yours doing?' Simon asked as we stood in line to serve ourselves.

'Pretty good, I think. They seem to be asking the right questions and taking my advice. What about yours?' I asked.

'Well, they're not exactly Winston Churchill, but I guess we can't expect them to be, can we?' he said with a wry smile.

After lunch, the afternoon classes were devoted to fun subjects – cooking and British sports – so the students could let off some steam. Then, we went to the Ascot Tea Room to practise conversational English.

It was one of the best days I had ever spent at British Hills.

The next morning, students in each class made their presentations and the teachers selected the eight finalists for the speech contest. From my original dozen, I chose the shy daughter of a Chinese businessman who planned to study to be a vet. I could tell she feared talking in front of the other students, but she did it and she did it well. I thought her speech, her determination, and her attitude were worthy of nomination.

After lunch, the tension of the students was palpable as we filed into Ambassador's Hall for the speech contest. I sat in the front row with the seven other teacher judges as Gavin welcomed the university students and opened the contest.

As I listened intently to each of the eight finalists give their speeches, there was no doubt in my mind who the winner should be: a boy who looked as if he came from a mixed race family. The Japanese would call him *halfu*. His hair was short and noticeably wavy. His skin was darker than that of the other students. He gave a brilliant speech on border control and social integration. Not only were his arguments and his English excellent, his presentation held the audience's rapt attention. When he concluded with a passionate plea to 'free all borders,' everyone rose as one and gave him a standing ovation. Even the Keio teaching staff clapped longer for this boy than for anyone else.

When this boy was announced as the winner and he walked up shyly to accept his award, the applause grew louder and louder. Racism did not exist in this auditorium. It seemed that Japanese society was changing in the younger generations in this modern yet deeply traditional country.

After the Keio students had filed back onto their coaches and headed back south, Ryan and I went with most of the British Hills staff down to the pub. The sojourn was now very much part of our daily routine. Falstaff's was a good place to catch up with the other teachers and, between pints, put the world to rights.

On this day, some of the new holiday hospitality staff – temporary waiters and waitresses working in the Refectory, tea rooms, and pub – had finished their first shift in the Refectory and had decided to sidestep the Admin office to come to the pub instead to unwind and meet the teachers and other staff. When we arrived, three new staff were already busy downing pints.

No sooner had Ryan and I stepped up to the crowded bar to place our orders than beside us a twenty-something fair-haired Australian with the typical carefree attitude of an Aussie on a gap year started talking.

'Hey, I'm Phil. Good to meet you.'

'I'm CJ. How you finding it so far?' I said.

'It's seems pretty easy at the moment, but it was only my first shift.'

'What city are you from?' I asked.

'Radelaide,' he joked, using the colloquial term for the South Australian city.

'We were in Sydney for about a year, and we loved it,' I said.

'How long since you were there?' he asked.

'It's hard to believe, but it's been almost two years. We'd love to return, but it's difficult because of the visa restrictions.'

Our conversation was interrupted as more teachers and holiday staff piled into the pub and ordered their own drinks. The noise level in the pub rose exponentially.

'What do you want to do when you leave Japan?' I asked Phil after taking a sip of my ginger beer and vodka.

'I might go travelling in Europe after this. Mum's English, so I have a British and Australian passport.'

'Lucky you! You can go back to Australia whenever you want. I hope I get to return to Australia one day.'

'Well, you're talking to the right person,' Phil declared. 'My Dad runs an immigration agency, so if you ever want to go back . . .'

I could feel a stirring in my stomach – that unmistakable feeling I used to get as a kid before competing in horse shows. Excitement. At the same time, my mind went into overdrive with a zillion questions like *If we get a visa, what will happen with Gershwin? Where will we live? How will we live?*

'I'm not sure it's that easy.'

'He can get you work,' Phil insisted. 'It mightn't be a job you like, though, or where you want to live, but still, you'd be in Australia. Look. I'll give you his email address. You can contact him yourself and figure it out. You could be in Australia in time for Christmas at the beach. He's pretty good at what he does. Trust me.'

The words *never trust anyone who says 'trust me'* ran through my mind. 'Okay,' I said, still unconvinced that fulfilling a dream was that simple.

I stood in the noisy pub beset by excitement. Standing there, I realised that this was not how I usually responded when change was offered to me. Although I had a plan in my head as to what Ryan and

Gershwin and I would do when we left Japan, now, everything could potentially be knocked cockeyed. I was being offered everything I said I wanted, but it meant change, big change, and that did worry me.

Ryan drove us home that rainy night and I told him about Phil's unexpected offer.

'So,' I said with feigned calm, 'what do you think about Phil's Dad's agency?'

'It sounds promising,' Ryan said above the noise of the windshield wipers and the rain drumming on the car. 'But what do *you* really want to do? I don't want us to go to Australia and regret it.'

'I've always wanted to go back to Australia. This *is* a great opportunity. We'd be stupid to miss it.' My stomach felt tight. 'But we're all set to return to England. We've made plans. What do you think?' I said, shifting the responsibility back to him.

'Look, I'll email him and see what happens. It can't hurt can it?'

Chapter 20: A Cat That's Always Mewing Doesn't Catch Mice

鳴く猫はねずみを捕らぬ / Naku neko wa nezumi Wo toranu

The next day the rain continued. Not just a heavy shower, but relentless torrential rain that seemed bent on flooding the world. It was still pounding away that evening as Ryan and I drove up to the staff house where the foreign hospitality staff lived. We were attending a welcome party for British Hills' new (albeit temporary) recruits. The car's window screen wipers thrashed violently from side to side to little effect. It was nearly impossible to see the road on this drenched and gloomy night.

We left the Nissan Laurel in the car park and dashed to the staff house through large pools of water that had sprung up with the storm. Our umbrellas had no effect. My coat was soaked by the time we reached the staff house. I took it off with relief once we got inside. My jeans were damp and clung clammily to my legs. My feet were saturated.

The main entrance was cleaner than usual, which was a relief. Someone had even hung pink fairy lights around the staircase to welcome guests. Loud distorted dance music was blaring from someone's laptop in the living room. The kitchen was packed with people making cocktails.

I usually did my best to avoid these sorts of social events, preferring the peaceful solitude of Villa Fuji to the hi-jinks of the twenty-somethings who called this place home. Yet for some reason, on this occasion, I had felt myself swayed by the offer. I really had nothing to lose (apart from sleep) and, the truth is, I was hoping I might be able to corner Phil and pick up our Australian immigration conversation.

No sooner had I settled down on the lumpy stained sofa to enjoy my vodka cocktail, however, than I was distracted from any thoughts of Australia at Christmas. Walking gingerly through the room, carefully avoiding being trod upon, was the friendliest bundle of calico feline love I'd ever seen. As if compelled by some psychic power, she walked over, sat down right in front of me, and stared up with big greenish-yellow eyes. Clearly, she expected me to do something for her.

Known in Japan as *mi-ke* (triple fur) because of the mixed orange, black, and tan colouring, this determined female resembled Tama the Station Cat, the feline who saved a train station and was made its honourary station master. She even reminded me of the cats depicted in prolific nineteenth century artist Utagawa Kuniyoshi's famous woodblock prints. In fact, calicos appear frequently in Japanese art and culture. It's said that the famous Japanese *Maneki-neko* (beckoning cat) is a calico cat, although in some books she's thought to be a Japanese Bobtail.

Long before the likes of Tama the Station Cat and Hello Kitty pawed the global stage, the Japanese openly admired felines. It's said that cats arrived in Japan about the same time as Buddhism, and they have played a big part in Japanese art ever since. The earliest work of Japanese literature featuring a feline is *The Tale of Genji* by Murasaki Shikibu. Written in the eleventh century, it is considered by many to be the world's first real novel.

The more I studied cats in Japanese culture, the more I found. From the Unrinji Cat Temple in Yamaguchi to the cat islands of Aoshima and Tashirojima, where I planned to visit soon.

I was particularly keen on the Japanese folk tale of the shape-shifting *Neko-Mata*, with its tail that splits in two or *Bake-Neko*, which is known for being fond of hitting the dance floor. The city of Nagoya has several famous images of cats dancing with towels on their heads.

Bake-Neko is also feared for its ability to control the dead and its retribution on anyone who hurts its owner.

I doubted that the feline sitting before me had the ability to shapeshift or rain down retribution on someone. She was far too cuddly. She was impossible to resist. I had to pet her, even as I wondered what she was doing here. I knew as well as anyone that pets were forbidden in staff accommodation. So, how had this pretty and clearly well-cared-for *neko* (cat) found her way into this party house?

The answer appeared the next moment in the form of Claire, a soft-spoken Queenslander who worked in the Refectory. Tall and thin with long fair hair worn scrapped back in a pony-tail, she sat down beside me.

'I see you've met the cat already,' she said with a smile.

'What's her name?' I asked as I scratched the calico under her chin.

'Well, she started out as Snookums, but somehow her name has become Nyan-chan, sort of a variation of the English word 'meow.'

'Where did you find her?' I asked.

'She and her sister were heartlessly dumped outside the school gates in a cardboard box a few weeks ago,' Claire said indignantly. 'One of the Japanese hospitality staff who lives off campus took the other sister and I took Nyan-chan. I couldn't leave her to fend for herself, not with all the predators in the forest and the cars going up and down the road. So, I smuggled her into the house. She has food and shelter, but now she's at the mercy of the working holiday staff and I have to worry about management finding out about her and giving me the boot.'

The bond the pair had struck up in such a short time was clear as Claire picked the cat up and cuddled her tightly. Equally clear was Claire's palpable worry.

'Look, I can take her back to my house if you like,' I offered without consulting Ryan who, in a slightly inebriated state later in the evening, might be more amenable to taking in another cat. 'We never have visitors, especially not management, and the house owners are overseas at the moment so they're not around. That way, you'll both be safe while we figure out the best thing to do for Nyan-chan.'

'That would be awesome!' Claire cried as she gave me a rib-crunching hug.

'Besides,' I said *sotto voce*, 'I think my cat Gershwin would like a girlfriend.'

Her eyes went wide when she realised I had smuggled my own cat onto the hallowed grounds of British Hills. A grin tugged at her lips. We were officially co-conspirators.

'I'll collect her tomorrow night and keep her safe while we figure out a more permanent solution,' I said.

The next morning, I called Sayuri and, among other news, told her the story of the calico cat who had been dumped at British Hills.

'That's so sad,' she said and then paused for a moment. 'Maybe I can help. Give me a few days. I'll call you back.'

Sayuri being cryptic always filled me with hope.

Ryan, even without the mellowing help of alcohol, was fully committed to smuggling Nyan-chan to our house. I think he felt sorry for the cat being stuck in the rowdy staff house. After our successes at re-homing Iko, Niko, and Takashi, he didn't seem worried about temporarily taking on a new cat. All of the foreign staff knew we had Gershwin and they hadn't ratted us out. Nor was he worried about being caught by the owners, since they were overseas.

'But how will Gershwin react to a strange cat entering his domain?' I said the next morning as we drove up the hill.

'This calico is in need just like G was,' Ryan replied. 'I'm sure he'll understand.'

The rain continued pounding down on the campus throughout the next day. After classes ended, I met Claire at the staff house. Fortunately, most of the other residents were in the pub, so there were no witnesses to our criminal deed. Nyan-chan waited patiently in an old orange plastic shopping basket with a worn blue towel spread over the top to hide her.

'She'll be safe,' I promised Claire as I picked up the basket. 'I'll do my best to find her a forever home.'

'Thank you so much,' Claire said, her eyes welling with tears as she bid goodbye to the cat she had come so quickly to love.

I hurried through the unrelenting rain to the car where Ryan was waiting. Nyan-chan and I were damp, but not as drenched as Ryan who helped to complete the final link in her escape from management's prying eyes. Surprisingly, unlike every other cat I've known, Nyan-chan was silent during the whole drive. 'She must realise we're trying to help her,' I said.

'Cats are intuitive creatures,' Ryan said.

With the rain drumming on the roof and hood of the car, he parked in our driveway. I collected the orange basket from the back seat and then dashed through the rain to the front door.

Once inside the house, I put the basket on the floor. Gershwin appeared out of nowhere and began prowling around the basket, sniffing it. Fortunately, Nyan-chan did not hiss or react with fear or aggression. So, I let her out of the basket. The pair touched noses. Gershwin looked up at me with excited green eyes and gave me a cat smile. Ryan had been right: Gershwin seemed to know that Nyan-chan was a feline in need.

The two warmed to each other almost immediately. I think Gershwin liked having another feline friend around and seemed to sense that she was a temporary cat rather than a threat to his kingdom.

That evening, Ryan headed off to the pub while I stayed home to further settle the cats. I even dished up some tasty tuna to encourage the bonding between Gershwin and Nyan-chan.

I sat back on the sofa and watched the two cats eat their dinner. I was surprised that I wasn't panicking. I wasn't even filled with the usual self-recriminations like *What have you done?* I had done what I felt was right. I also knew that I couldn't keep Nyan-chan – shipping one cat out of Japan was more than enough stress – so I had already begun protecting myself from becoming too attached to her.

After their dinner and after-meal bathing, the two cats sat on the couch side by side looking out the French doors and that is pretty much what they did every day. Nyan-chan was a very docile cat and that rubbed off a little on Gershwin. I think, too, that he had been missing Iko, Niko, and Takashi and was glad to have another cat to whom he could cling. At night, however, Nyan-chan slept on the couch and only Gershwin slept with us. I think he had made it clear to her that Ryan and I were his property and she was not to interfere.

A few days later, Sayuri called as promised.

'I have a home for your new cat,' she said without preamble. 'My Grandfather passed away a few months ago and I think the calico cat will be a good friend for my Grandmother. What do you think?'

'I can't believe it. That's a perfect solution!' I said excitedly. 'I have some time off in about a month, so I can bring Nyan-chan to Takayama.'

'Even better,' Sayuri said happily. 'I can't wait to see you again.'

Several more days passed and along with them grew my guilt. I had not yet responded to my Aunt Lydia's kind email. The last thing I wanted was to offend her and start a new estrangement. So, I finally made myself go up to the Admin building to email her. I sat in front of my desk, braced myself, and opened up a new email message. The safe course was to use Gershwin as the main focus of the letter so I could avoid more serious discussions about family. I wasn't ready for them yet.

I began typing. I thanked her for her kind words and advice and finished by writing: 'Do you realise we may never have spoken if it wasn't for Gershwin?'

She responded a few days later with a note that was reassuring, succinct, and perfect: 'One little cat and we found our way back to you. What a blessing.'

The internet was truly my friend that month.

Yet, whenever I probed my aunt further about the mysterious Krystal and her relationship with my father, she'd grow circumspect and say that she didn't know much about their relationship. I never learned any more about her perhaps it was best that way.

Ten days later, Steve, Phil's dad's business partner, replied to Ryan's email inquiry, which had included both of our CVs. Ryan read the email and his jaw literally hit the floor.

'You won't believe it, CJ!' he said excitedly. 'Steve contacted my former boss at the press agency and he wants to give me my old job back on a longer work visa, and it's in Sydney!'

The job was perfect for Ryan, and Sydney was our first choice if we ever had a chance to live in Australia again. 'That's amazing!' I said, dumbfounded, as I hugged him and read the email over his shoulder.

My initial rush of koala-crazed euphoria was crushed almost immediately, however, by a tower of anguish and worries. This was September. Our plans, my expectations, were all set for returning to England in December.

Had all the time and effort I had invested in planning our trip home been for naught? How were we supposed to get Gershwin into Australia? Was its pet import policies and process different from those of England? Were they even more complicated and stringent?

How far would my yen go in Aussie dollars? Was it worth going back to Australia and gambling with our future now when we'd finally made a dent in our debts back home? I was pretty much assured of getting a job in England, but did I have any assurance of getting a job in Sydney? Our friends and families were in England. When we'd last been in Australia, we had travelled so much that we hadn't really formed any firm friendships. Did it make sense moving to a country where we really didn't know anyone and where we didn't have the safety net of a school with its built-in set of friends and acquaintances? Would it be more sensible to go home and make a go of it there?

I didn't want to dampen Ryan's excitement by dumping all of my worries on him, so that night at dinner in the staff canteen I enumerated them one by one to Davina, a colleague and friend.

Davina was short, but what she lacked in height she made up for in personality. She was a straight-talking pocket rocket brimming over with self-confidence. Other people were scared of saying the obvious. Davina saw through other people's BS and called out the two-faced and the stupid.

I always felt safe telling Davina about my doubts and fears, because I knew she would tell me the truth untainted by any baggage.

'Everything happens for a reason, CJ,' she assured me over dinner. 'Don't let your doubts consume you and win. Everything is aligned for you to go to Australia. So go with the flow.'

'True,' I said, ignoring my chips and salad. Concerns over the move had left me with no appetite. 'But isn't it a bit risky? I mean, we'll have nowhere to live when we get there. I'll have no job, no savings, and a cat to take care of when we arrive.'

'That's all part of the fun,' she said and winked. 'It's an *adventure*, CJ!'

'I suppose so,' I said, still unconvinced by this optimistic go-getting Queenslander who wouldn't let a single opportunity pass her by. She'd grab it with both hands and worry about the consequences later. And maybe that was why I had chosen her to confide in. I needed a different mind-set, something that would pull me free from all of my usual miasma that had held me back for most of my life from living the life I wanted.

'Jeezus, CJ, things like this don't happen every day, mate. Jump on board and enjoy the ride,' Davina commanded.

Davina was right. If I spent as much time thinking about all of the good things that could happen by moving to Sydney as I usually devoted to dwelling on the possible bad, I just might find myself happily embracing this amazing opportunity.

My mother and grandmother had tried to shove hope out of my thoughts. My pessimism was their pessimism. Both had returned early from their overseas adventures (South Africa and Canada) after things hadn't worked out exactly the way they'd wished. Or, maybe the truth was that they hadn't the courage, the internal fortitude, to forge ahead even in the face of adversity.

Had I the strength and courage they had lacked? I thought I might. I hoped I might. And I had Ryan, someone who had adventure in his soul. And, of course, I had Gershwin, whose playful affectionate presence always chased away sadness and loneliness.

I sat beside Davina in the staff canteen and I knew I had a decision to make, one that might affect the rest of my life. I could let doubt and fears overwhelm me, succumb to my mother's and grandmother's pessimism, and return to the known safety of England. Ryan would be disappointed, but he would support my choice.

Or, I could use all the energy for something far more practical and positive: taking control of my choices and planning a new adventure, the one I had said I wanted from the moment Ryan and I had left Australia two years ago.

I could worry and complain, or I could get what I really wanted. There was, I realised, a great deal of truth in that old Japanese saying: *A cat that's always mewing, doesn't catch any mice.*

It was time to stop mewing and catch me some happiness.

Chapter 21: A Cat's Tail

猫の尻尾 / Neko No Shippo

As the colder days of autumn set in, the arrival of a new season also brought the arrival of a childhood friend.

The Japanese have a special word, *kouyou,* for watching the changing autumn leaves. As in spring when the cherry trees blossom, across the country people gathered to view the changing colours autumn brings.

Gershwin was now a fully-grown male. His wiry fur had turned into a smooth shiny coat and his long hind legs were now more in proportion to his athletic body.

Gershwin had adapted well to his new home and new friend. I wondered if the next stage of this inquisitive feline's life would be quite so smooth. With our long-desired return to Australia handed to us on a silver platter, complete with a job waiting for Ryan when we arrived, Ryan and I had changed all of our plans. We were moving on to Australia, not returning to the UK.

We had planned to fly to Sydney just before Christmas, but our plans got pushed back thanks to some missing documents we needed for our visas. This was actually a happy delay, because British Hills was quite keen for us to continue teaching, which meant we could save even more money before we finally relocated.

I was even well on my way to getting Gershwin's permit for Australia finalised, so all was pretty much right with the world.

Ryan, meanwhile, was tracking down his university transcript and chasing previous employers for references.

It was around this time that I got the long-awaited news that my oldest friend, Karina, was finally coming to visit. We had grown up together in the same small town and we shared the same hunger to get more from life than staying in that town.

We wanted more and we got it. I was now moving to Australia and pursuing the marriage of passion and practicality in *ikigai*. Karina had gone to night school while working full-time and, after some difficulties, had landed a good job at a prestigious interior design company.

Our shared history kept us close, as did our differences. I liked her laid back attitude to life, while she always referred to me as a 'stress head.' I wondered if she'd call me that now.

Karina and I decided that we would meet first in Tokyo and then visit Tashirojima, known as Cat Island, northeast of Tokyo, which had become famous for its large cat population. Karina was a sister cat-lover and I had long wanted to visit the island.

While Ryan was teaching at BH, I took the eleven o'clock train down to Tokyo on a sunny October morning. Karina's flight had arrived extremely early that morning and she had wanted time to rest at an airport hotel while I travelled down from Tokyo. We would be meeting at Ueno Station.

The moment I stepped out of the Tokyo train station, I was surprised at seeing so many people from distant lands like Brazil, India, and Germany. I had grown accustomed to a more homogenous society in Takayama, and certainly at British Hills. I had fun people watching and listening to the many different accents and languages. Tokyo was more cosmopolitan than I remembered, and I realised I had missed human variety.

I had arranged to meet Karina at the main gates for the Keisei Skyliner. I watched the train pull into the Ueno Station and easily spied her amidst the masses of people. As always, she was smartly dressed. Today, she wore a black dress, knee-high boots, and carried a designer bag. Her long black hair flowed down her back. She looked surprisingly unruffled by the nearly six-thousand-mile journey, taking it all in her stride, as if she had just got off the tube at Trafalgar Square. I smiled ruefully at the vast difference between her laid back ease today and my meltdown when I had arrived in Osaka two years ago.

Our eyes met and we hurried through the crowd to each other. I reached out and gave her a big hug. 'So, you made it in one piece then?'

'Yes,' she said with a warm smile. 'The flight left on time and I made my way through most of the red wine on board, so it's all good.'

I laughed, looped her arm through mine, and led her through the train station, Karina easily rolling her single piece of luggage behind her.

'I'm sure I can hear owls,' she said.

I chuckled. How that comment took me back to all the odd sounds I had first heard in Osaka, and later Tokyo. 'Oh, it's recorded bird songs to help people with poor or no vision find the exit,' I said.

'I thought it was me being jet-lagged,' Karina said, laughing.

We walked out onto the street, which was not terribly busy or jam-packed. Most of the city's office workers were busy at work in all of the surrounding glass and metal skyscrapers, and the height of tourist season had passed.

The sun shone brightly, making it a little difficult to use Karina's iPhone to get directions to our hotel.

We turned and began walking. As we crossed one street at the traffic light, a kindergarten bus with a black and white panda face on the front stopped and the driver flicked the front lights (the panda's eyes) to wink at us, which made Karina and I laugh.

She looked around at all of the buildings, traffic, frenetic advertising, and people. 'There's so much distraction here, it's impossible to think about negative things like all the usual hassles at work,' Karina said.

'I know, right?'

Although she'd only just arrived, I was happy to see that she totally got it. With so many things to take your mind off what could potentially get you down, it was virtually impossible to dwell on dark thoughts, at least not for long. Japan had not only distracted me for nearly two years, it had started to heal me.

I had come to Japan to earn money to pay off my debts and to experience a country and culture quite different from my own. I had got that and so much more. Without the stagnant safety of my usual environment, I had been pushed to learn more about myself, to examine all the weaknesses and poor decisions I'd been able to avoid examining in England.

We grabbed some red wine from a convenience store and went to check-in at our hotel, a cheap place located near the Sumida River that I'd found online.

The next morning, we left our hotel early and wove in and out of what seemed like an endless sea of surgical masks on our way to Ueno station to catch the bullet train north.

Inside Ueno Station, we passed an older woman in her fifties wearing a black and white tee shirt with a picture of two cute kittens and the words, '*The Big City Makes Us Sad*.'

I wondered if this was true for me anymore. I had certainly felt that way in the past, but now? I was happy to be back in Tokyo and happy to be sharing it with my friend.

As we boarded the bullet train, we struggled to find our seats and the correct carriage while a trainload of bemused Japanese faces stared back at us. We must have looked like stereotypical scatter-brained Western girls totally unprepared and unorganised for their trip, which wasn't far from the truth.

We sat back to enjoy the rest of the more than hour-and-a-half-long journey as the bullet train sped north through the outer Tokyo suburbs.

As the train powered northward through eastern Honshu, Karina and I slid into our usual conversation whenever we were together: discussing some of our old childhood friends. It was lovely having a girlfriend with whom I could talk.

When the bullet train pulled up at Sendai Station, we quickly got off. We had to catch a local to Ishinomaki, the town which provided a ferry service to Cat Island. We followed the signs to Platform Ten, where our train had still not arrived.

Suddenly, music erupted from the level below us.

'What on earth?' Karina said.

'Let's check it out,' I said. 'Our train doesn't leave for another fifteen minutes.'

We walked to the mezzanine railing and stared down into the station concourse where a Japanese high school brass band had set up a live pop-up concert. Dressed smartly in their navy blue and white uniforms, a crowd of onlookers growing around them, the young musicians played music from the soundtracks of famous movies I couldn't name to save my life.

'*That* is what I love about this country,' I informed Karina. 'Just when you are getting yourself into a kerfuffle, a little surprise like this snaps you straight out of it.'

'Were you in a kerfuffle?' she asked.

I blushed. 'I was feeling a little guilty for the mix up with our seats. I should know all of our travel logistics.'

'You're doing great! I'm having a wonderful time. Really. Travelling is never perfect, and it shouldn't be. Unexpected things happen. Life happens.'

'Exactly,' I said. 'Until recently, I'd had a sort of love-hate relationship with Japan. Just when you begin to enjoy yourself, it can karate chop you in the face. When you're feeling down, it can thrill you with a forest of gold and red autumn leaves. Japan has the ability to stun you, surprise you, and occasionally ruin your plans. The trick, I've begun to learn, is not to sweat it. Like life, something good will come along in the end. This time, it's a brass band. The summer before last, it was a silver grey kitten trying to cross a busy intersection. I'm truly grateful for the fact that Japan is bringing out the best in me.'

'It's an odd place for an Englishwoman to find her true self, but I suppose that's what travel does: strips us of our usual comforts and safety nets and forces us onto our own resources.'

'All those resources we've ignored, usually for too long,' I agreed.

After the band finished playing their rendition of what sounded like the theme song from the movie *Rocky*, Karina and I walked to Platform Ten to wait for the next train.

After *twenty-two* painfully slow stops, the last ones at least giving us views of magnificent Matsushima Bay we finally reached the town of Ishinomaki in the Miyagi prefecture.

The city looked very flat and empty. Many of the shops had already closed, their shutters pulled down.

We stopped to photograph some of the statues of manga characters on the pavement just outside the station. This, after all, was the birthplace of the famous manga and animé writer and artist Shotaro Ishinomori, who created Japan's first super-powered hero team for the *Cyborg 009* TV series in 1963, and the popular *Kamen Rider* series in 1971, and who founded the Studio Zero animé company.

Karina was excited to see them, because, as it turned out, she was a big fan of manga and animé. Her favourite character was Totoro and she knew all about Studio Ghibli.

I was ignorant of all of this, and amazed that I had never known this side of my old friend.

I had been clever enough to book us into a nice hotel that was only a short walk from the station, but not so clever as to request better accommodation. Our room smelt heavily of cigarette smoke and it was next to a lift, which was noisy. After a very long day of travelling, I didn't really care. I was keen to have a bath in its large Western-style bath and get an early night, while Karina sent texts and emails on her iPhone and posted pictures of everything we had done so far in Japan.

The next morning, we jumped into a taxi and headed for the ferry port through streets lined by old, low-rise buildings. We got to the small port, paid our taxi driver, and stepped out into a day that was grey and overcast. Just outside the white ferry building, however, was a four-foot-tall statue of a grey cat that resembled Totoro. Near both the statue and door was a red mat on which sat a grey tabby with a white bib, who regarded us calmly.

'Oh, how cute!' Karina cooed.

I wanted to pet the tabby but she looked so peaceful I thought it best to just let her be.

We walked into the small ticket office where a middle-aged Japanese lady greeted us enthusiastically. She spoke as much English as I spoke Japanese. Still, she understood where we wanted to go, proudly showed us a long magazine article all about Cat Island (all of it in Japanese and unintelligible), and then pointed to a poster that had four rules for visiting the island:

1.   Don't Leave Cat Food on the Road Where Cat Residents Could be Hit By Cars

2.   Respect The Residents (Don't go into areas without permission.)

3.   Take Your Rubbish Home

4.   Don't Bring Animals to the Island

(signed) Tashio Island Cat Republic.

Once we nodded our understanding and acceptance of the rules, she smiled and handed us cat-shaped candies.

'I can't believe I'm finally here,' I said happily. 'I've wanted to visit Cat Island ever since I first read about it two years ago.'

Just a little over one-square-mile in size, Tashirojima, aka Cat Island, is mostly forest. It has had one industry for hundreds of years: fishing. During the Edo Period (1608 to 1868), many residents had also raised silkworms for their handmade textiles. Mice love to eat silkworms. So, the residents imported some cats to take care of the problem. The cats succeeded, and multiplied, prolifically, thanks in large part to the fishermen who fed them and cared for them because, like many in Japan, they believed that cats would bring wealth and good luck to anyone who crossed their paths.

In the twentieth century, the cat population continued to grow on the island while the human population dwindled, particularly when the silk industry collapsed. Today, there are only about one hundred (mostly elderly) people living on Tashirojima, and several hundred semi-wild cats, most of whom have been neutered and spayed to control the feline population. Most of the cats have what are called Identity Cards, which Dr. Kiyomi Kress, a visiting vet, uses every few months to check their health. She also treats any sick cat. She does all of this at her own expense, simply because she loves cats. She is, to my way of thinking, a heroine.

Tashirojima has two villages: Odomari Port on the north side of the island is quite tiny. Nitoda Port on the south side of the island is somewhat bigger and has several buildings, including Kamabutso Shoten, the island's only store, where some of the cats like to hang out.

About ten other people, mostly Japanese with one other Westerner, an American Goth teenager, waited with us at the mainland port, and then stood in an orderly line when the two-level blue and white ferry pulled into the dock.

The sky was still overcast and ominous, so Karina and I decided it would be wise not to sit outside. We went below deck and sat alone by a window toward the back of the ferry, looking out at the Pacific Ocean as the ferry set out for the almost an hour-long trip, rocking back and forth in the choppy grey sea. I popped one of the candies into my mouth, and gave Karina a mint to help her fend off seasickness, too.

When the ferry began gliding gently up to the dock at Nitoda Port, we hurried up to the deck and were the first in line to get off.

'Look, I can see cats over there,' I said pointing at small furry faces in the distance.

'So cute. I can't wait to meet them,' Karina said happily.

The ferry docked and suddenly the sun came out to greet and warm us. 'Clearly, we were meant to be here today,' I said with a smile as my feet touched the island for the first time.

'How cool is this?' Karina said as we stopped next to the welcome sign.

There were signs all over the place with pictures of cats plastered lovingly on them. Further along the path leading from the dock, there was a signpost directing us to go straight on to the cat shrine.

The village was small with old somewhat dilapidated wooden buildings, most just a single storey in height. Gardens and small trees were hidden behind fences and small walls. It was clear people lived here, there was washing hanging outside on clotheslines, but there wasn't anyone in sight.

Karina and I walked up a narrow street behind the other passengers, including several children dressed in cute cat-themed clothes who skipped happily in anticipation of seeing the island's cats. I wanted to skip right along with them.

The village's most important building was the store, located at the bottom of a hill. Eight wide steps in faded and peeling aqua-coloured paint led up to the entrance, which was bordered by two big bright red vending machines. Several cats – mostly a mixture of black, white, grey, and orange – were prowling the steps *waiting for us*. (We soon learned why. The store sold cat food, which tourists fed to the cats throughout the day.)

Karina devoted herself to petting every cat she could reach. I had packed some of Gershwin's dry food to bring with me, because I hadn't known how well-stocked the store would be. So now, I leaned down and spread the food out for the cats to eat.

'Remember, don't put it on the road,' Karina cautioned me as I was just about to do that very thing.

'Oh yeah, I forgot,' I said, chagrined.

The store was actually quite large inside, but very dim and musty-smelling. There were posters on the walls of women in traditional Japanese dress advertising coffee, and several aisles of different household items, including some nice looking biscuits, which Karina purchased to take home as a gift for some of her colleagues at work.

I led Karina up to the owner, a tiny elderly woman standing behind the checkout counter so overburdened with store items it was nearly impossible to see her. I spied her only because of her yellow headscarf, silver spectacles, and powder blue apron. Our conversation was hampered by my poor Japanese and her lack of hearing, but we were both game. I bowed and introduced myself and Karina. She bowed slightly and said that her name was Kato-san.

189

I bought lots of dry food for the island cats, drinks for Karina and I, and Karina paid for her biscuits.

We walked back outside into the sun and sat on the steps. Immediately, eight well-fed cats mewing in a very friendly manner came up to us, eager to relieve us of the cat food. Karina knelt down to feed them, petting each cat in turn as I smiled at a Japanese woman whose daughter, a young girl with dark bobbed hair, was petting a tiny tortoiseshell kitten.

'Excuse me,' the thirty-something mother said to me. 'Can you tell me, how do so many foreigners know about this island?'

'It's quite famous nowadays,' I said. 'There are newspaper and magazine stories about it, and it's popular on the internet.'

'Every time I come here, I see people from different countries,' the woman said.

With a little island and very many more cats to see, Karina and I tossed our empty bottles in a rubbish bin and began walking along a road past several dilapidated buildings that looked abandoned.

The land on either side of the road quickly became densely overgrown with trees and shrubs.

'What a perfect environment for cats to thrive,' I said.

'There probably isn't a mouse to be found on the entire island,' Karina said.

Almost immediately, we were joined by a gaggle of tabby cats who guided us up a hill to the centre of the island and their sacred place: *Nekokamisama*, a cat shrine that looked like a miniature house. It was just about five feet wide, with a slanted slate roof. A bright red wooden fence surrounded the shrine, more to draw the eye than to keep anything or anyone out.

Far from being erected for tourists, this cat shrine is quite old. One day, a cat who was a favourite with the fishermen was accidentally killed by a falling rock being collected for use with their fixed fishing nets. Grieving the cat's death, the fishermen honoured it by burying it on this site and erecting a shrine over it.

'Look at all the offerings!' Karina marvelled.

Spread on the ground in front of the shrine were everything from stones painted with prayers or good wishes or pictures, including paw prints; as well as cat dolls and figurines; cat toys; *maneki nekos*; and even flags from Australia and Canada.

'Some people are so organised,' I said in dismay. 'I never thought to bring offerings.'

'Neither did I,' Karina said, 'and I read all about the island before coming.'

'We'll have to improvise.'

We ended up scattering cat food near the shrine for a big black and white tomcat who had joined us. He tucked in while we took pictures of each other.

'It's impressive what an effort the islanders made to pay respect to the cat who died,' I said. 'I can't think of another country in the world that honours animals with shrines the way the Japanese do.'

We continued on our way towards the tiny village at the port of Odomari.

The village was much smaller than we had expected. It had a few white houses scattered about. A concrete dock jutted out into the bay. A couple of small fishing boats bobbed about in the water. The beach was almost completely covered in concrete as part of the seawall defence against tsunamis. Opposite the dock were a series of steep steps that led up to a temple for the villagers.

The village was absolutely deserted. There was no sign of human life, only cats.

Karina and I sat in the sun on the concrete beach and listened to the waves gently lapping what was left of the sandy shore. Then, a young black and white cat came up to us and sat on my knees, clearly requiring petting and the scratching of her chin. Her companion, possibly her brother stuck his head into our bag of cat kibble and promptly got stuck. I quickly freed him. He sat down and began cleaning himself, completely unfazed by the experience.

By this point, Karina had attracted four black cats whom she was happily hand-feeding and photographing.

I could have stayed all day listening to the delicate purrs of the contented cat lying on me. Finally, though, I stood up (reluctantly) with Karina and continued walking to the other side of the island. We had one more sight to see.

The island has a small resort on the top of a hill with fantastic ocean views. The white and red horizontally-striped guest cottages are cat-shaped, complete with ears projecting from the roofs over the front doors. In and around the buildings are cat-themed paintings and sculptures by famous Japanese manga artists, including Shotaro Ishinomari. That's why this part of Tashirojima has a second nickname: Manga Island.

'That is so cool. Look at the back of this house,' Karina said, pointing at a large yellow cat that was painted over the top of a door. 'The house even has blue whiskers!'

We continued hiking up to the main house. In front of it were three boxes: a cardboard box with a hole in it, a brown and white wooden box with yellow cat ears and eyes drawn on, and a cardboard box shaped like a house with a window drawn on the side. In front of these were dishes filled with dry biscuits and water bowls. One of these boxes was clearly the home of the kittens and mother cat.

They jumped up onto a wooden picnic table and allowed Karina and I to pet them.

'I want to take one of the twin baby kittens home,' Karina announced.

'But it looks like they have a nice life here,' I said.

As we rode back to Ishinomaki on the ferry, watching fishing boats bobbing up and down in pursuit of the last of the day's catch, the sun disappeared behind the heavy clouds, the sea turned charcoal grey, and cold replaced warmth. Once again, as was usual for me in Japan, I was the only person unsuitably dressed. I had only a light rayon cardigan to protect me from the cold, the wind, and the rain that began to fall.

'Let's get below deck.' Karina said.

'You go ahead,' I said. 'I want to stay on deck a while longer.'

'You're crazy! You're gonna get wet.'

'I don't care. I want to make the most of this experience.'

'Well, don't blame me if you get sick,' Karina said as she headed below deck.

Soon, I was rewarded as the sun reappeared, its golden rays glistening on the Pacific Ocean. Suddenly, a rainbow appeared in the sky behind the southern mountains in the direction of Fukushima. I smiled. Maybe there *was* a pot of gold there after all.

When the ferry finally docked, Karina and I took another taxi to our hotel, collected our things, and then walked back to the train station. This time, we made sure we took an express train.

At Sendai Station, while we waited for our bullet train, we watched four uniformed cleaners with striped shirts and little white hats bow with robotic precision at an incoming *shinkansen* demonstrating what's known as, *omotenashi,* the spirit of selfless hospitality.

Plink-plonk music signalled the approach of another train, our train. This time, I made sure we got into the correct carriage.

We returned to Tokyo that evening and checked into a slightly more upmarket hotel in Asakusa that had a pool, and spent the rest of the night swimming and talking.

The next morning, Karen left for the airport and I had a few hours left before I caught the train back to British Hills.

This had been, for me, a soul-satisfying visit. I had finally had the opportunity to share with a close friend not only the country I had chosen for the last two years, but also the changes it made in me. I was less impatient than I'd been when Karina and I were growing up. I was much more open to new people, places, and things.

I thought about all the things I had wanted as a child, I had none of those things and yet, I realised as the Japanese countryside swept past, I *was* happy. I was a bit like the Japanese bobtail cat. It didn't matter if I had a tail or not. I had found my own way, my true path to happiness, with Ryan, Gershwin, travel, and the understanding that I could marry my passion for animals with a new career.

And that's when I reached my *ikigai*. All I needed to be happy were my cats, travel, and my family. And I was already doing that!

Chapter 22: A Flea in a Cat's Teeth

猫の歯に蚤 / Neko no ha ni nomi

Back at British Hills, I returned to my usual routine at work and continued planning our move to Australia in April, five months away.

On Monday, my first class of the day was a painting lesson in one of the grand rooms of the Manor House. It had tall windows at one end, an old fashioned blackboard at the other. I diligently placed newspapers over the antique desks to protect them and set out the art supplies. I had got an 'A' in a night school art class but that was primarily a photography class, not a painting class. Needless to say, I was more than a little concerned as I tried to figure out how to fake it in front of the teenagers.

Ten high school girls piled into the classroom excitedly. It took me a moment to settle them down, then I explained the different types of materials on their desks, from oils to watercolours.

'Please paint something that reminds you of British culture,' I said. 'It could be something you've learned here at British Hills, someone you've met, or even something you've seen on the telly or in a cinema.'

They immediately began creating mini-manga masterpieces. I walked around the room slowly, inspecting their artwork. 'This is great,' I said in amazement as I looked over a manga-style picture of a girl in school uniform sitting at a desk at British Hills. (I suspected this was a self-portrait.) The girl, who had short bobbed hair and a slightly chubby face, nodded her head modestly.

What, I wondered, made these girls so creative? Was it simply because they grow up surrounded by manga and anime or something else? Whatever the reason, their drawings were far more imaginative and technically skilled than anything I could ever attempt.

While I could never reach their artistic heights, their joy in creating something new did inspire me. I, too, could create something new. Not art, but service. Perhaps even the start of my own *ikigai* inspired project. After seeing how the cats on Tashirojima were so highly regarded by both residents and tourists, I wondered if I could help homeless cats and dogs by raising money for an animal charity. I knew animal shelters were few and far between in Japan. As far as I was concerned, they were doing

God's work, so if I could raise some money for one of them I would.

There was one animal charity that I knew about which was based in Osaka, Arkbark, which had offered me advice when Ryan and I had first found and were trying to re-home Gershwin.

I thought of different kinds of fundraisers, from 5K runs to bazaars. Then I remembered reading about people who had organised sponsored swims to raise money for charity. How difficult could that be to arrange? All I needed was a pool, some swimmers, and people willing to donate money.

At the same time, as far as I was aware, things like sponsorship and fundraising were far from being as prevalent in Japan as they were back home. Then there was the language barrier. Could I explain my project without the necessary linguistic skills to get approval for it *and* raise money?

The next day, I got busy researching how to run a swim-a-thon and how to create forms that would register sponsors and their donations.

With the swimming pool in the Manor House free most evenings, I thought it would be the perfect place to hold the event. I printed out some samples of the sponsorship forms and took them home to review. I also sent an email to Arkbark telling them what I wanted to do and asking their permission for them to be the designated beneficiary of the swim-a-thon. I heard back from them just a few days later.

Dear CJ,

That's a great idea! We don't have forms to sponsor people nor certificates, but I am sure we could make some. Please let me have more details such as the length of the swim, the date, and of course the swimmers' names. Be sure to take pictures. We can run them in our newsletter.

Elizabeth Oliver

The only thing left to do was to get approval from Yasuda-san, my boss. He remained largely disconnected from the Western staff, even going so far as to sit far away from us on the other side of the office. The only time I had ever spoken with him was the day Ryan and I had first arrived on the campus. It had crossed my mind to hold the event in secret without informing the upper echelons. Between the working holiday staff, the English teachers, Japanese cooks, and administrative staff, there were enough people to raise money without involving management. At the same time, if I was discovered by an uncharitable member of the British Hills hierarchy, they could kill the swim-a-thon before it began.

You might think I was thinking crazy, or acting paranoid, but the fact of the matter is that the Japanese have an entirely different view of charity from the West. Their culture doesn't seem to have the same Western mania for using swim-a-thons, and 5K runs, and bazaars to gather donations for every charity or need on the map.

I was particularly wary, because I'd witnessed first-hand how Golden Week had been run at British Hills.

Rather than holding a big public event to maximise profit or exposure or both, management kept everything very low key. We had an open day for local residents to come on campus and walk around to their hearts' content and free classes for parents and children. But it was not widely publicised, so not many people came.

As far as management was concerned, hosting a charity event would not add any lustre to British Hills' reputation. Then there were British Hills' high-paying guests. They would not look kindly on being denied any amenity or privilege of their stay, even if it was just for an hour or two.

That was the environment in which I was planning a charity swim-a-thon.

I was reminded of the saying they have in this country like *a flea in cat's teeth*, which means small things are difficult to catch, and it was a apt description of the impossible task I had ahead.

But if I wanted enough people to make contributions to really benefit Arkbark, I couldn't hide the event. So, a few days after Arkbark gave me their blessing, I plucked up the courage to approach Yasuda-san.

I walked up to his desk and bowed. '*Sumimasen*. Excuse me. I have a question.'

Yasuda-San motioned for me to sit down.

My throat a little dry, I continued. 'I want to hold a charity event to raise money for an animal shelter based in Osaka. Could I please use the swimming pool one evening for a competition? Is it possible?'

He considered a moment without actually looking at me. 'A swimming type of competition would be okay,' he conceded. 'If our paying guests want to use the pool, however, you will have to leave and postpone the event.'

'I'll make sure to hold it later in the evening, then, when our guests will be dining in the Refectory so they won't be inconvenienced.'

'Very logical. You may go ahead.'

'Thank you so much! This means a lot to me.'

He had nothing to say to that, so I bowed and left.

I decided to keep the swim-a-thon a small-scale event. I knew from past experience that if a *gaijin*-sponsored activity drew too much unwanted attention, it could garner the opposite of the intended result. Unlike a swim-a-thon in England or Australia, it was not a case of the more people you get to swim, the more money you raise. It was a case of less is more, or the whole event might have been kiboshed.

Ryan, eager athlete that he is, had been looking over my shoulder while planning the event and instantly volunteered to swim for Arkbark. Miles, a teacher from Liverpool who heard about my plans, also volunteered to do his bit for shelter animals. I really didn't want to get anyone else involved. This was a personal event for me. Besides, donations would be coming from a small finite pool of people on the mountain. More swimmers would not have generated more donations.

I printed out flyers in English and Japanese with some information from Arkbark's website and started to approach people on the campus to raise donations – whatever amount they chose for each lap swum – telling everyone what a great job this charity did for animal welfare. I was surprised at how positive the reaction was, even from the Japanese staff. Particularly generous was Simon, who was a kind sweet-hearted soul and supported anyone who tried to do anything for a charity or local community.

Just before eight o'clock on a Thursday night, two weeks after getting approval from Yasuda-san, I stood at one end of the British Hills swimming pool with a clicker in hand, which I'd borrowed from the sports desk to count the laps, and a whistle around my neck to start and end the event. We purposefully hadn't decorated the pool for fear of raising unwanted attention.

Because the event was being held at night, many of the Japanese admin staff who had pledged their donations had already gone home. The Western working holiday staff were either in the pub or serving dinner in the Refectory. Most of the regular teachers were also in the pub, unwinding after work. So, there were few spectators, which I was happy about. Too many *gaijins en masse* also might have raised unwanted attention. (In the past, some Westerners had acted poorly at British Hills, leaving the Administration suspicious of the rest of us.)

I had set up a few chairs for spectators, currently filled by four people: Hayley, Stefan (Gloria), and Sinead.

Ryan and Miles walked in, to the cheers of the four spectators. They took off their robes (which garnered some whistles from the four spectators). 'British Hills teachers like we've never seen them before,' Hayley said with a grin and a nudge as the boys jumped into the pool. Arkbark had asked for pictures and she had agreed to be the event's photographer.

I stood ready with whistle in hand, and nervously counted down to the official start time: eight o'clock. When the minute hand reached twelve, I blew my whistle, the sharp sound echoing a little as Ryan and Miles pushed off from the end of the pool. The Arkbark Charity Swim-a-Thon had begun!

After a few laps, the boys found their pace. Officially, they weren't racing each other. They were just trying to swim as many laps as possible – 'Let's see how many we can do,' Ryan had said and Miles had instantly agreed. I suspect, however, that somewhere in their male psyches neither wanted to be outdone by the other.

Back and forth they swam, the laps mounting up as I worried I wasn't counting properly. My thumb pressed the clicker in my hand again and again. 'That's fifty!' I shouted excitedly to the boys as they swam past me. 'You've completed fifty laps already! Keep going!'

On and on Ryan and Miles swam. They seemed to have enormous stamina. Their pace never slackened. The spectators were clapping and shouting their own encouragements.

Much sooner than I had expected, I shouted to the boys 'That's it! That's 200! You've done it! You can finish!'

But they weren't ready to finish. Spurred on by adrenalin and cheers, they looked at each other and immediately agreed to get in another fifty lengths, which brought more cheers from everyone and earned some additional shots from Hayley's camera.

When they finally swam their two hundred and fiftieth lap everyone cheered them down to the end of the pool. Panting heavily, Ryan and Miles stood up, shook hands, and heaved themselves out of the water: wrinkled, red-faced, and triumphant. I rushed over with towels for them both as the spectators continued to applaud and Hayley snapped photos wildly.

'You guys are awesome!' I cried. 'You swam two hundred and fifty laps! You've raised much more money than we'd planned. Thank you both so much.'

'Pleasure,' Miles said, draping himself in more towels.

'I'm ready for a beer after that,' Ryan declared.

'Me too,' Miles said.

Hayley, Stefan, and Sinead crowded around congratulating them.

'You sure you don't want a bit of a lie down after all that?' Gloria asked with a wink at Miles.

'Maybe later,' he said, chuckling.

'I want a picture of me with the boys with their tops off,' Sinead said.

The boys and Hayley obliged.

I was ecstatic, not so much about the money we had raised, but about everyone coming together for the occasion, generously donating their cash and time for an event close to my heart. Hayley and I put the chairs back while the boys went to the dressing room to change.

Hayley posed all of us for a final group photo outside the main entrance to the Manor House under the Union Jack and Japanese flags, then we walked over to Falstaff's. Hayley was joined at the hip with Gloria, who had a pink feather boa wrapped around his neck. They were inseparable friends and now they were talking and whispering and laughing together.

'Those little cats and dogs are going to be so happy with the work you've done,' I said to the boys on either side of me.

'I'm glad to have helped in any way,' Miles said.

'Happy to be a part of it,' Ryan said.

I opened the pub door and a roar went up from the crowd inside. 'Here come the champions!' Canadian Simon shouted (he was always one of the most vocal teachers). 'Yeah, baby, yeah!' (Austin Powers was in the house.)

People were shaking Ryan's and Miles's hands and congratulating them. The boys were beaming.

'How much has been raised?' someone called out.

'I haven't added it all up yet,' I said, 'but with the fifty extra laps they swam, I'd say they raised over thirty thousand yen.'

This earned more cheers.

My eyes welled with tears. I was speechless at such unexpected generosity. This meant we'd have even more money to send to Arkbark. It was the perfect boost to my *ikigai* journey as the countdown continued to Australia, and the perfect reminder of how many people I would miss when Ryan and I finally left British Hills.

Chapter 23: Like Silver Vines to Cats

猫にマタタビ / Neko Ni Matatabi

A fortnight later, I was sitting on a *shinkansen* heading south to Tokyo again, this time with Nyan-chan in tow. I was taking her to Takayama and her forever home with Sayuri's grandmother. Like Gershwin, she seemed soothed by the gentle rocking of the bullet train, and she certainly enjoyed the attention and praise from the other passengers.

Going back to Takayama without Ryan or Gershwin was strange, even a little disorienting. Fortunately, Sayuri met me at the station.

'*Ohisashiburi,*' (Long time no see) she said as she hugged me and took my bag.

'It's so good to see you.' I said gratefully. 'This is Nyan-chan.'

Sayuri knelt down to see the calico cat. '*Hajimemashita*, nice to meet you,' she said. 'She's very *kawaii*.'

'She *is* very cute and cuddly,' I agreed. 'I only hope your grandmother likes her.'

'Of course, she will. She loves animals, and Nyan-chan is super *kawaii*.'

Because Nyan-chan had not yet been de-sexed, we had agreed that she would stay temporarily with Sayuri until she had the operation, which I would pay for and Sayuri would oversee, to avoid producing any unexpected and unwanted litters of kittens at Sayuri's grandmother's house.

Sayuri drove us to her home, which was just a couple of blocks from the station. Takashi, who had been napping on the bed, raised his head as we walked in, recognised me immediately, and ran over to give me an ankle rub.

'Hi, Takashi-kun! *Genki desu ka*? (How have you been?)' I said as I pet him. The answer, of course, was clear. He was quite plump and content.

He was also very curious about the cat carrier. This was the moment. After all the strangeness of a lengthy train ride, Nyan-chan now had to meet Takashi.

I opened the carrier door and let Nyan-chan out. She padded quietly over to Takashi. Without any hissing, the two cats touched noses and smelled various parts of each other's anatomy.

Satisfied with her new roommate, Nyan-chan then walked back and settled down next to me on Sayuri's futon.

Unfortunately, I would miss Nyan-chan's introduction to Sayuri's grandmother as she lived on the other side of town. There just wasn't time for me to meet her. My work at British Hills didn't allow a longer stay.

The next morning while Sayuri was at work, I walked around the town I loved, only to find that much had changed in only a year. Most of our ALT friends had returned to their home countries. Bagus, our favourite reggae bar, had changed hands. My old apartment was empty. I felt like a stranger in Takayama.

I could not even enjoy my favourite activities in the city: cycling through the town at a leisurely pace and dropping in on friends. My time here was extremely limited. I had this single day to pack in my final memories of Takayama. Tomorrow, I would be back on the train and returning to British Hills to resume teaching with one less cat in the house.

I decided to do something I had often wanted to do, but had not: I went for a hike on the Higashiyama Walking Trail, which encompasses several Shinto shrines and Buddhist temples and graveyards on the eastern edge of the city.

When I had lived in Takayama, I had generally avoided the city's touristy destinations and activities, like the cultural workshops and craft lessons. I had told myself they were a bit lame and too much of a cliché.

The truth, I think, was that I had been reluctant to fully embrace Japanese culture, mainly due to my Osaka misadventure and the country's often rigid work practises and social customs. I didn't want to look like a typical *gaijin* tourist to the residents of my new home. Fortunately, living two years in Japan had taught me to be much less self-conscious.

Of equal importance, with Ryan's and my departure from Japan drawing near, I was ready to immerse myself in some of the things I had avoided while living in Takayama. I was no longer a resident, I *was* a tourist in the city.

While living in Takayama, Ryan and I had often used the Higashiyama Walking Trail as an easy travel route to reach the apartment. I had allowed myself to admire the architecture and craftsmanship of the old buildings we passed without letting my appreciation go any further. This time, however, I was ready to see past the buildings' exteriors and value the spirituality and belief system the temples and shrines embodied.

As I set out walking, I finally acknowledged a deeper truth: I had fought against my own spirituality and the emotional impact of this trail, because my family had such a chequered history with religion. My relatives ran the gamut from fair-weather-Christians to overly-pious Jehovah's Witnesses. One side of my father's family was descended from French Huguenots. They had swapped one joyless religion for another. On the other side of my family, my lapsed Christian Grandmother had married a man with a Jewish surname, which led the ignorant and the anti-Semites at school to tease and occasionally torment my mother and Aunt Cora, which had put them off religion.

As a result, I was never a particularly religious person growing up. I'd learned not to be heavily influenced by any one single idea about religion, so I carefully avoided subscribing to any one particular belief.

That's not to say I didn't have an interest in religion, and more particularly in spirituality. In my secondary school days, I had enjoyed my mandatory religious education class immensely. At university, I was drawn to the philosophical aspects of Taoism. Now, in Japan, I had been slowly working my way deeper into Buddhist and Shinto thoughts and practises, particularly meditation.

Unfortunately, on my one full day in Takayama, all of the Higashiyama Walking Trail temples and shrines were closed. I could not go inside. But as the late afternoon sun descended, casting golden beams on the timber buildings, the perfectly raked Zen gardens, and the row of Buddhas with tiny red caps on their heads inside a small wooden shrine, I felt increasingly aware of the sacredness of this place.

I stopped first at the calligraphy shrine – a big stone monument (it looked like a tombstone) with Japanese writing on the side. Many visitors before me had left their old pens and calligraphy brushes to the side of the shrine on a small tray as offerings to help them become highly skilled in their future writing practises. That was certainly for me. I searched in my backpack and pulled out an old pencil. I grimaced, but it would have to do. I added my pencil to the offerings, placed my hands together, and said (lightheartedly) 'Please give me the writing skills I'll need in the future.'

Walking amongst the towering trees and the centuries-old temples and shrines, I felt more at ease with myself than I had for a long time. My neglected spirituality began to spark within me. I vowed that I would make more time for it in each of my coming days. I wanted to learn more about the ancient practises of Zen and meditation and get more balance in my life, instead of worrying all the time.

On my return from the *teramachi* (temple district), I stopped at a crossroads about three blocks from Sayuri's house and suddenly realised that I was standing where Ryan and I had first found Gershwin. I retraced our steps and, to my amazement, I found myself standing outside Zenkoji, an old Buddhist temple on Tenman-machi Street. Gershwin had been waiting for us in front of a *temple*!

Surrounded by residential buildings on a busy street, Zenkoji had reddish roof tiles and wooden steps leading up to the tall wooden main doors. The grounds were lovely and peaceful.

There was a plaque outside the wooden structure, which I read intently. Built in 1894, Zenkoji was also run as a guesthouse where visitors, mainly backpackers, could stay and learn more about the Japanese culture in return for a small donation.

How could I have been so oblivious to this temple when I had lived here? It was literally across the road from our old apartment. I had passed it several times a week, but my old self had been blind to the possibilities of personal growth.

Hungry to learn everything I could about the temple that had brought Gershwin to me, I slid open the panel glass doors of the guest house to the right of the main temple and peeked inside. No one was around, so I stepped inside, removed my shoes, and placed them on a wooden shelf before walking into the reception area. It was deserted except for about six pairs of stacked shoes and a friendly-looking cleaner in her late twenties.

'May I look around?' I asked in English

'Sure,' she replied in English. 'You can go in the garden, too, if you like.'

'Thanks,' I said with a grateful smile. 'I will.'

I walked up to the plain white shoji screens, slid them open, and walked across tatami mats into the main hall. Even though no incense sticks were burning, I could still smell their musky smoke. It must have been seeping into the walls and ceiling for centuries.

The rectangular main hall was about eighty square metres in size. It had tatami mats on the floor, and six cream-coloured stools arranged in an orderly fashion in front of a half-metre-tall gold Buddha. In front of the altar was a large purple banner hanging down. At the top of the banner was a triple hollyhock (or possibly wild ginger), which I'd seen before in Japan as a family emblem.

I saw in the far right hand corner of the room a sign. I walked over to read it.

'You will find a staircase leading to a dark passage. You will go down the stairs into the dark passage. Directly under the Main Altar of the temple, you will find a sacred lock. The goal is to find this lock, which is known as the Jodo no Kagi, or the Key to Paradise. We human beings live in light. We take it for granted. We are not thankful for the light. By entering the complete darkness, we must use faith to guide our steps.'

Taken aback, I re-read the sign carefully. Had I been living in and taking for granted the light so much that I had missed all that was most important around me?

I grimaced. The truth was, I had always been distracted, intentionally so. I had used the distractions of school, money, work, stress, and the pursuit of false happiness to avoid myself: my deeper thoughts and feelings and needs and pain. I had used distraction to avoid being moved by the beauty, and joy all around me.

Still, this had been changing, *I* had been changing, since I had first come to Japan. I *was* noticing things, like this temple, and I was learning more and more every day. I felt more settled than I had ever felt before, which was ironic considering Ryan and I were about to completely unsettle ourselves by moving to another country where our lives were bound to be in a state of flux for some time.

But the prospect didn't worry me as it had in the past. The old parasitic voice inside my head had not spoken for some time. Most importantly, in going to Australia this time I wasn't running *from* anything.

Standing still in the silence of this charming old temple that I had passed so many times before and ignored, my mind felt less cluttered than usual. I remembered the words of the Chinese writer Lao Tzu: *'When I let go of what I am, I become what I might be.'*

'I can't believe I never took the time to visit these places before,' I told Sayuri that night as we set the table for dinner. 'I saw so many things today that I'd never seen before, even though I'd lived here for a year. To think I passed that temple almost every day, but never knew anything about where Gershwin was found.'

'You were too busy doing other things,' Sayuri said and smiled.

That was becoming increasingly clear. Throughout my life, I had been too busy with unimportant things to notice the many things of significance.

I returned to British Hills the next day, sad at saying goodbye to Sayuri for the last time, my head filled with all I had learned about myself on this trip, which had been, as the saying goes, *as effective as a cat drawn to Matatabi* (Japanese cat nip). I vowed to hold on to those lessons over the Christmas holidays, which Ryan I spent in the same way as when we first arrived at British Hills.

Chapter 24: Want to Borrow a Cat's Paw

猫の手も借りたい / Neko no te mo karitai

Bolstered by all I had learned on my last visit to Takayama and by all the holiday festivities and silliness, I got down to the business of getting Ryan, Gershwin, and me to Australia.

When Ryan and I had made the decision to move to Australia rather than England, I had immediately contacted the relevant organisations Down Under and booked Gershwin into the quarantine station where he would have a short stint after we arrived. After that, I kept checking the details of Australian customs rules again and again, making sure I hadn't overlooked anything important. I felt like I needed a thousand hands (and paws, as well) to finish everything.

As I started to delve deeper into international pet regulations, I grew a little envious of Gershwin's relative travel immunity. While Ryan and I both had to prove not only our relationship together but also our qualifications for work – which involved endless photocopies, certified documents, and requests for references from former employers – my little furry friend was a cat and that meant he was free of language tests and work-related checks. With everything I was doing on his behalf, he could actually travel to all three countries in which I'd lived. He was a cat who had three passports in the bag.

I had been corresponding regularly with my Aunt Lydia without unleashing an emotional tsunami on her. I had so many questions I needed answered about my family, but I was still afraid to ask. I wanted first to rebuild our fractured relationship before I dug any deeper.

Aunt Lydia had asked me to email a photo of Gershwin to my cousin Jessica (her daughter), who was also a cat lover. Jessica responded immediately:

'He's such a majestic looking cat. He's got quite a thoughtful air about him. You could imagine he's thinking deep thoughts.'

I smiled and quickly typed a reply: 'I know. We nick-named him Buddha-Pest.'

When I sent Aunt Lydia an email mentioning the turmoil I was feeling, not only about starting another new home, but also bringing a pet along for the first time, she quickly replied:

'Don't worry. I know it's scary when a little furry creature – and one of the family – depends so much on you, but it will be OK. The first time I did it, I shook and was generally very ill because of stress. You will be fine. I am positive you have done it all the correct way.

LLx'

Her email was so encouraging. Unlike the monster I had been led by certain members of my family to believe she was, Aunt Lydia was actually a sympathetic and soothing confidante whom I desperately needed at this point. I sent her my thanks and closed the email feeling that, finally, there was at least one person in my family with whom I could talk, even though she was on another continent.

But there was still more to do.

Before Gershwin was allowed to travel, I had to prove that his vaccinations against cat flu, feline enteritis, feline rhinotracheitis, and feline calicivirus were up-to-date. Once I had all his vaccinations certificates in order, I was finally able to apply for an entry permit. With that in hand, the final onslaught of Gershwin-related tasks would not come until the day before and the actual day of our flight.

On those days, and not before, we had to have his health checked by an official vet, and we had to have him treated for parasites. I searched various ex-pat community blogs in Japan for some guidance on which vet to choose. It was quickly apparent that I wasn't the only one planning on taking a pet overseas. Many people on the blogs were asking for advice about international pet travel. It was comforting to see I was not alone in my ignorance and worries.

From the blogs, I learned that Angel Memorial Hiroo Central Hospital in Tokyo was the most familiar with the pet emigration process *and* it had English-speaking staff. My anxiety level dropped considerably.

At the Narita International Airport, we would need to take Gershwin for one more final check by another official veterinarian before finally taking him to the cargo terminal where I would have to produce two official copies of his entry permit: one that travelled with Gershwin and one that I had to keep and produce at a moment's notice.

All of this meant that we couldn't just take a train to Tokyo on the day of the flight and head straight for the airport. We had to get there a day early for the first of the two vet checks and the parasite treatment, which meant we needed a pet-friendly hotel and easy transportation to and from Angel Memorial Hiroo Central Hospital.

I studied the map of the Tokyo subway. It was a mammoth maze of coloured lines with unfamiliar place names. I narrowed my search to stations between Ueno Station (where we would be arriving on the bullet train) and Minato, which was the closest station to the veterinarian. Then I looked for subway lines that wouldn't require a lot of changes onto different train platforms. Within that narrow band, I began my hotel search.

Not only did the hotel have to be in the centre of Tokyo and convenient to the subway lines, it had to be comfortable, pet-friendly, and affordable. Finally, I found *Hotel Sumisho*. It ticked all the boxes. Perfect! I quickly booked a room for the three of us and went to bed with a major weight lifted from my shoulders.

Now, all I had to arrange was getting all of our belongings to the airport, and then Ryan, Gershwin, me, and our backpacks from British Hills to the Shirakawa train station without the use of a school car.

One of the Japanese staff, Yurie, recommended we use *Ta-Q-Bin*, a nifty delivery service that would pick up our luggage and deposit it at the airport for a very reasonable fee. So, all we needed to take to Tokyo was an overnight bag and a cat carrier. I'd seen the little yellow trucks with the black cat logo on the side drive up and down the mountain many times. This time, they would be coming for us. Or at least our things.

Big T, an Australian teacher in his forties, volunteered to drive Ryan, Gershwin, and me to the train station. He had dark curly hair and blue eyes and he was Big T, not because he was tall (he wasn't) or burly (he wasn't), but because he was a lovely human being with a big heart and a gentle soul. He was also a big fan of Gershwin. He wanted the chance to say a final goodbye to the cat who had successfully hidden from management for over a year.

We were all set.

Chapter 25: It Will Work Some Meow (Somehow)

何とかなるにゃん / Nantoka naru nyan

Gershwin, as clever as he was cute, knew that something dramatic was up. We had spent the last few weeks clearing out old belongings and packing boxes that would be sent to Ryan's new company in Australia to hold for us. During these days, Gershwin spent most of his time jumping in and out of the boxes, while I pondered over what to take and what to leave behind. In my mind, I was already planning the neighbourhood where we would live in Sydney, the type of apartment we would have, and even the colour of furnishings. I had to keep reminding myself not to live too much in the future. These were my final weeks in Japan. I needed to pay attention and not let them slip past like a leaf carried away by a river. I had to enjoy what time I had left in the country that had transformed so much of my life.

I also wanted to enjoy every second of the time I had left with the people who had been strangers only a year ago and were now good mates and people I could rely on.

Near the end of our stay, our friends organised a special meal in our honour one night at a restaurant named Piranha on the outskirts of Shirakawa. It was a small modern building with a few plant pots by the glass front doors. Inside was equally modern, with an industrial design and an exposed ceiling. The skinny forty-ish owner and chef stood behind a metal counter preparing all of the food for his customers.

The restaurant's only waitress led us to four tables pushed together where our friends had already gathered: Ryan's best bro Canadian Simon, bubbly Sinead, Stefan, and Hayley.

'Good evening,' Ryan and I said together with our best Japanese bows.

'How many rounds have you already had?' I demanded.

'You're late, love!' Gloria shouted. 'You're a round behind.'

We ordered drinks and lots of them. We ordered food and lots of it. We were all preoccupied with leaving, so conversation ranged from who would be the next off the mountain after us (Hayley), to wondering if we would miss British Hills when we left.

'It's a crazy place to live and work, but I'll miss it,' Stefan said.

'I won't miss the Japanese work ethic and being told what to do every minute of the day,' Simon said.

There were no misty eyes. We were all ready to get away from an English fantasy-land with its 24-hour-a-day scrutiny and back to the real world.

On a cloudy cool Thursday morning in April, *Ta-Q-Bin* arrived right on time (of course). With Gershwin safely secured in his cat carrier to keep him running out the door, or leaping into the van for an impromptu jaunt, two uniformed men collected all our luggage with impressive efficiency, and drove off just thirty minutes later.

I looked around at the house that had been so welcoming and was now so bare, save for the blue two-seater sofa, bookcase, and TV.

'Will we ever be so lucky to live in a place like this again?' I asked.

'There will be other places just as nice, you'll see,' Ryan replied.

'Gershwin is going to miss this place. I will, too.'

'I'll miss snow-boarding with Canadian Simon.'

'And I'll miss having a swimming pool and steam room at my disposal.'

'I think the hardest part for me will be living so far away from nature, from being able to walk for hours without seeing anyone.' Ryan said.

'Yes,' I agreed. 'That will be hard for me, too. Japan and Gershwin have turned me into a walker, but it's walking in Nature I love, not tramping through city streets.'

'Still, there'll be ocean beaches you can walk on.'

Just before eleven o'clock that morning, Ryan and I climbed into our metallic silver Nissan Laurel and drove up to the Manor House one last time.

I stared out the window at the golf course with its lush green fairways and greens that lured golfers from the Tokyo heat to be tormented by eighteen holes of golf and get so drunk at the golf club bar that they routinely drove through hedges and crashed their cars. Gershwin and I had avoided the golf course on our walks, preferring to go down by the lake and sit in silence together and watch the eagles flying overhead. In winter, we had observed the curious and heretofore unknown sport of ice-fishing. Regret and tears welled within me at ending the life Ryan and I had built here.

He parked the car next to the Admin building. The April morning was a clear and bright and I had no sunglasses to hide my red-rimmed eyes.

We walked into the Admin building and said goodbye to the Japanese staff. 'I want a group photo of all of us together,' I declared.

They were so used to this sort of request – so many teachers had come and gone – that they promptly filed into their usual formal pose. We got into the middle of the line of the Japanese staff and Suzuki-san snapped a few quick pictures. Sadly, 'K' was nowhere to be found. I wished I had thought to take his picture before this.

To our utter surprise, Yasuda-san walked up to us. 'Thank you for your contribution to British Hills,' he said with his usual formality. 'We hope you enjoyed working here.'

'Yes, we did. Very much,' I said.

'We hope to come back one day,' Ryan said.

'You will be welcome.'

With time sprinting by, Davina and Simon came into the office, their morning classes over.

'We need some final group photos,' Simon declared. He was always trying to unify people.

The location for our photo shoot was obvious. We trooped over to the steps of the Manor House next to the Shakespeare statue, minus the Aussie flag that had greeted us on our first day.

Twenty-one people gathered on those steps. Simon volunteered to serve as photographer, using Ryan's camera. The Japanese Admin staff stood in front, and everyone else filled in. Simon instructed Ryan and me to stand in the centre. Sinead stood beside me and draped her arm around my neck. Ryan, who was crouching down, gave the obligatory peace sign.

I marvelled at how many people had come to bid us farewell. My eyes welled up again as we took one last group photo.

It was a funny assortment of people who stood together. We had come from all corners of the world, from the UK to Australia, from New Zealand to Northern Ireland, plus, of course, the Japanese – a mixed bag of people thrown together on this isolated mountain-top. We had formed bonds and alliances and seen each other through myriad strange manifestations of 'cabin fever,' because we had never really been free to escape the school and each other when we wanted.

Now, we were parting forever and I suddenly longed to go through cabin fever all over again.

'Let's keep in touch,' Hayley said giving me a hug. 'We'll see each other Down Under.'

'I'll Facebook you when we've settled in,' I said.

'You know, we call Australia the lucky country, but with you lot moving in, maybe it isn't so lucky after all.' She winked.

Ryan guffawed.

Davina came over next and hugged me. 'Stay cool, Miss. Just remember: stay true to you and you'll do great!'

Finally, Simon walked up to me. 'So, we'll all be back to work here in a few years, because we'll be broke. And don't forget the ten-year reunion.'

We both laughed, mostly to hide the sadness, because we knew everyone would be scattering to the four corners of the earth and we would never be a group again.

I choked back my tears as I hugged my friends from different countries and backgrounds one last time.

Then, I got into the back seat of the car, wiping the tears from my eyes as I looked back at all the smiling faces of my friends. 'I'm so grateful for all of this,' I said. 'This year at British Hills, our time in Takayama, all of it.'

'Me, too,' Ryan said from the front passenger seat. 'And to think we mightn't never have even come back to Japan.'

'Thank you for talking me into it,' I said with a watery smile.

'No worries, mate,' he said dryly in a mock-Australian accent that made me laugh.

Big T climbed into the driver seat. 'Are you guys ready?'

'Let's go,' Ryan said, because I wasn't able to speak.

He drove us quickly down the mountain to our house. Ryan and I hurried inside, scooped up Gershwin, slid him into his cat carrier, grabbed our overnight bags, carried them out to the car, and then Big T drove us to the Shirakawa train station.

'I'll miss this place so much,' I said.

'But remember, you're getting your freedom back,' Big T said with a smile. 'You can slip away without management breathing down your neck. You won't have to hide Gershwin. And you can go wherever you want without having to fight over who has the Nissan Laurel.'

'That's true. I won't miss the car politics,' Ryan said.

At the station, Big T climbed out of the car for a final goodbye. 'We'll see you in Sydney,' Ryan said.

'For sure,' Big T said.

I hugged him one last time. 'Bye,' I said, getting teary-eyed again.

Then we carried Gershwin and our backpacks onto the platform to catch our final *shinkansen*.

Gershwin was sitting upright in his carrier, ears pricked, as he breathed in the unfamiliar smells of the city. 'It's okay Gersh-kun,' I said, peering into the carrier and blinking affection into his green eyes. 'You're safe. This is only half of one day being cooped up, I promise.'

The train, of course, arrived right on time. We easily found seats in the last carriage and settled in with Gershwin beside me in the window seat. We heard the usual public announcement, and then the train engines began to move us forward. As the bullet train sped out of Shirakawa, I felt both a deep sadness at leaving and a growing excitement. I was starting a new life.

'Let's order some drinks from the trolley to celebrate our new adventure,' Ryan said.

'Great idea,' I said with a smile.

Two hours and twenty-three minutes later, the train pulled into Tokyo's Ueno subway station, which was just as crowded and busy as before, but I didn't mind, not even with a cat carrier in hand.

Ryan and I split up. He took our bags to check into our hotel, and I carried Gershwin onto the Grey Line to take him to the first of his two vet visits. I confess to some anxiety simmering quietly within me as I navigated the Tokyo subway alone with Gershwin. I was responsible for getting us to the vets on time and for then getting us safely to our hotel.

'This is a good opportunity to practise being more Zen and living in the moment,' I kept telling myself and, occasionally, Gershwin. *'Shimpai shinaide* (Don't worry),' I whispered to him as he sat in his carrier on my lap. 'It's going to be okay.'

With his usual aplomb, he sat quietly in his carrier on the subway, taking it all in his stride, and enjoying the friendly stares from the other passengers.

Getting off at Shirokanedai Station with what felt like hundreds of other people, I carried him out into the rushing city and excitement grew within me. When we stopped at a crosswalk and the traffic lights started to sing, I couldn't stop smiling as it reminded me of my first time in Japan.

Angel Memorial Hiroo Central Hospital was an easy four-minute walk from the subway station through an affluent area with tree-lined streets and stylish cafes. A large red and white sign hung over the vets door. I carried Gershwin inside and was surprised to find that the waiting area was smaller and not as well lit or as welcoming as our beloved veterinary in Takayama, or even the one in Shirakawa. There were no other people in the waiting room, just two receptionists who were busy working behind a counter. I walked up, checked in, and it wasn't long before Gershwin and I were ushered into an exam room: small, square, featureless. For my first time in Japan, a female Japanese vet walked into the room and then greeted me in perfect British-accented English.

'Have you studied in the UK?' I asked.

'Yes, I studied at Royal Veterinary College and worked in the UK for many years,' she said with a smile. She examined Gershwin's documents. 'So, you will all be moving to Australia?'

'Yes, tomorrow.' I said.

'Let's get him out of the cat carrier so I can examine him.'

I opened the carrier door and Gershwin sauntered out onto the exam table.

'He's a handsome cat,' the vet said, stroking him with one hand. 'What breed is he?'

'He was a stray, so we don't really know.'

Gershwin didn't seem scared of this stranger, or annoyed at my pointing out his uncertain ancestry. He sat in front of her calmly.

With skilled hands, she quickly and expertly examined Gershwin and pronounced him in excellent health. Then, she opened his mouth and with practised skill popped a parasite treatment down his throat. It was done so fast, that Gershwin didn't even realise what was happening.

Just thirty minutes after we had entered the veterinary hospital, I was walking back out the door and heading for the subway station, required vet documentation in my bag, cat carrier in hand. The experience at the vet had been so smooth, that I couldn't believe I had spent so much time worrying about it.

'This,' I told myself, *'is yet another lesson in the wasted energy and stress of catastrophising.* A visit to the vet is simply just a visit to the vet.'

Setting my worries firmly aside, I carried Gershwin back onto the Grey Line heading in the opposite direction to the Ningyocho subway station, which was near our hotel. I guess it's not every day that Tokyo-ites see a blond *gaijin* carrying a silver tabby. We were drawing attention and Gershwin couldn't have been happier.

'What's her name?' a middle-aged Japanese lady with a designer handbag asked with a smile.

'His name is Gershwin,' I replied with my own smile.

'Oh, a boy! He's so cute.'

'He certainly thinks so,' I said with a grin. 'Tomorrow we're moving to Sydney.'

'He's a very lucky cat to be so well-travelled,' she said.

Squeezed between another hotel and a nondescript office block, Hotel Sumisho didn't look like the cheap hotel I was expecting. It had four large windows next to the entrance, white tiles on the upper façade, and a sort of miniature Zen garden with some small potted plants and stone pebbles on either side of the door. The grey lobby was very compact, clean, and quiet without the fuss of a big hotel. It was modest but likeable. This was a pet-friendly hotel, so no one looked at me oddly or suspiciously for carrying a cat carrier, which was reassuring. The front desk clerk gave me a key to our room, Gershwin and I got into the lift, and up we rode to the fourth floor.

Ryan let us into our room before I could even use the key. 'How did it go?' he asked.

'It couldn't have gone better. The vet trained in London,' I said.

'Is he okay? Was he scared?'

'No, he was absolutely fine and he got some attention on the subway, which he seemed to lap up.'

'I can imagine.' Ryan said with a knowing smile.

I looked around. The room was as advertised: no frills. It was small, with an en-suite bathroom and one window, which provided views of more buildings and very little sky. It was cramped and I could smell nicotine, but it didn't spoil my mood. Just one hurdle left and we were on our way to Australia.

Ryan went back to setting up the Wi-Fi on his laptop computer on the desk while I let Gershwin out of his carrier.

Rather than being scared, he set out with both confidence and curiosity to inspect his new surroundings while I busily went over all the last minute details: re-checking all of Gershwin's paperwork, train times, and our route to the airport.

That night, with Gershwin sprawled on our queen-sized bed sleeping off his dinner, Ryan and I walked to an Italian restaurant just a few blocks from the hotel.

After dinner, we hurried back to the hotel, concerned for Gershwin after leaving him alone, and concerned for the hotel room in case he had decided to become Ninja Attack Cat in our absence. We needn't have worried. We walked into the hotel room and there was Gershwin still sprawled on our bed. He raised his head slightly and blinked at us, as if to say 'What's all the fuss?'

The next morning, I was too nervous for breakfast, so we drank powdered green matcha tea in our room. I applied a light lavender spray that Davina had given me all over Gershwin's blanket to help him stay calm over the next trying twenty-four hours, then I loaded him into his cat carrier and we checked out. The train ride from Ueno Station to Narita International Airport was both quick and painless, but my nerves were still on edge. I was about to hand over my beloved cat to strangers.

Finding the cargo terminal at the vast airport was not easy. It wasn't far from the subway station, but we took several wrong turns, even stopping at a place where meat is checked before being unloaded and dispatched to stores and restaurants, which did little to ease my anxiety.

'Remind me never to travel internationally with a pet again,' Ryan said when we finally found the airport's official veterinarian in a tiny nondescript stand-alone clinic in the commercial cargo area. The vet, a very old Japanese man with glasses, said maybe two words to us. He was not particularly friendly and did nothing to ease my nerves about handing my precious cat into his hands. He gave Gershwin a cursory glance, signed our documents, and sent us on our way.

We were in and out so fast, I almost had to catch my breath. 'Yet another lesson in the futility of catastrophising,' I said wryly.

'We could have slept in this morning,' Ryan said.

The offices of Nippon Express were almost next door to the vets. This building, however, was big and clearly labelled. Although Gershwin would be flying with us to Sydney in the cargo hold of our plane, for some reason he had to be checked in hours before us.

'Why they can't have pets checked in at the normal airport I'll never know,' Ryan said with a sigh.

'I know. It's *mendokusai,* a real pain,' I said.

The Nippon Express offices were in a nondescript block close to a runway, which meant we were buffeted by the constant roar of jet engines, which put both me and Gershwin on edge as we walked through the bland lobby and up a flight of stairs.

'Gershwin isn't cargo,' I muttered. 'He's a cat, he's part of our family, and should be treated better.'

'International travel rules suck,' Ryan agreed as we walked into the main office, a large open-planned room that was empty, except for two Japanese employees: one in his twenties and the other middle-aged. Large windows provided views of the airport runways and large international jets talking off in the distance.

To my surprise, Kota – the man with whom I had been speaking for months on the phone, the man who had done his best to ease my travel fears about getting Gershwin to Australia, was not the middle-aged man, but the slim young man wearing a company tee shirt and sitting at a desk working quietly.

I introduced myself and Ryan and Kota's dark eyes lit with a smile of recognition. He walked up to the counter with a smile. 'Hi, CJ. Nice to finally meet you,' he said, shaking my hand.

'This is for you,' I said pulling a small package from my backpack. 'For all the kind emails you have sent me over the last few months. You really put my mind at ease. Thank you.'

I had bought a small tin of Scotch biscuits at British Hills for Kota, which I had specially gift-wrapped, as is custom in Japan, in green-coloured paper.

'Thank you. That's very nice of you,' he said graciously. 'May I have Gersh-kun's documents?'

'Of course,' I said, pulling the papers from a manila envelope and handing them to him. (I had made many copies as a precaution, probably enough for every Nippon Express and Qantas employee.)

'Great. It looks like you have everything in order,' Kota said as he slid our documents back into their envelope.

He made a quick phone call and almost immediately an older gentleman in his fifties wearing a navy Nippon Express tee shirt walked into the office. His face was kind as he smiled awkwardly at me.

'May I have Gersh-kun, please?' Kota said.

'Oh,' I said, 'so soon? *Ki o tsukete* (take care), Gersh-kun. Look after my little friend,' I said as I handed the cat carrier to Kota, who transferred Gershwin immediately into the hands of the older man. I was battling against huge tears trying hard to fall.

'We'll see you in Sydney,' Ryan whispered through the carrier to

Gershwin.

Far from his Takayama birthplace and the remote mountains of Fukushima, roaring jumbo jets taking off overhead, Gershwin looked up at me with sad green eyes.

'Here, take my scarf and put it over his cage to keep him from getting scared,' I said to the Nippon Express handler as I handed him my black pashmina. I'd read somewhere that both the familiar scent and limited view of an article of clothing draped over a pet carrier could ease stress.

'I won't be able to return it,' Kota said.

'Don't worry. His comfort is more important than the scarf.'

As I said this, my throat tightened and a multitude of worries and anxieties filled my head.

'You'll be okay, my little friend,' Ryan said. I could tell he was trying his hardest not to react to our separation from Gershwin.

'We'll see you soon,' I called to Gershwin as the handler carried him away. Turning my back, I barely made it to the door. Gershwin's tiny cries were tugging me back into the office.

'We'd better check in ourselves,' Ryan said.

'Right.' Tears sliding down my cheeks, I glanced back at Gershwin, feeling fragile. This would be the last time I would see my friend in his native Japan.

'He'll be fine, CJ,' Ryan reassured me as we walked back downstairs.

'In less than twenty-four hours we'll be together in Australia,' I said, trying not to think of all the things that could potentially go wrong.

We took the subway to our international passenger terminal. Because of having to get Gershwin to Nippon Express early, we had a few hours to kill before our flight so, by mutual agreement, we found a bar in the terminal.

'I'm going to find out where the showers are,' Ryan said. 'It will help us both feel comfortable for the long flight.'

'Great idea,' I said.

While Ryan went looking for showers, I thought about our time in this amazing country, with its kind people and their impeccable manners, its crazy *kawaii* culture and beautiful natural landscapes. I thought about how much I had learned about myself, and changed, and grown because of Japan. Weaving through all of our time here was Gershwin. He was our touchstone, our connection to the rice paddies, narrow streets, and cats curled under a *kotatsu*. As long as Gershwin was with us, we would always be tied to this land unlike any other.

Epilogue: The Cat's Repayment

猫の恩返し / Neko No Ongaeshi

After living in beautiful Takayama with its thoughtful people and in the surreal quasi-English amusement park that was British Hills, I soon realised as Ryan, Gershwin, and I settled into Sydney how much I would miss the wonderful and always surprising randomness of Japan.

I missed Japan's distinct seasons, the powdery white snow that dumped so massively overnight that I had to wait until a little man in his yellow truck came to set me free just in time for work. I loved the long spring walks where I could see beyond the clouds. I had even learnt to love the cold. I loved the fact that vodka in Yamaya, the local store, cost half the price it does in Sydney or London. I loved the fact that I could walk home no matter how late and never feel in danger. I did love Japan. I just didn't realise how much until I left it.

In the time I'd been away from London, I had changed. I felt more at ease with loss and death. When I used to think about lost relatives and friends, I'd often worry about losing more. No longer. I had learned to live more in the moment and to appreciate everything and everyone I had while I could. Those changes stayed with me. Now, I am more at peace with myself.

Before going to Japan, I had spent too much time and energy thinking about what was lacking in my life rather than focussing on what I did have. I had taken basic things for granted, like how fortunate I was to be born in a country with universal health care, a country that housed and educated me when I was in need. I hadn't fully appreciated what I had. I had taken simple things for granted, like the fact that being able to speak English fluently can get you a job in many other countries, while people in the non-English speaking world have to spend a great deal of time and effort and money learning my native language.

When I'm asked what I've learnt from my travels, I say it's more what I've *un*learned. I let go of the negative patterns of behaviour that made me believe things I wanted to do were impossible. I've fully extinguished that parasite in my mind that was always telling me to run. I've learnt to jettison the dark thoughts and behaviours that felt tight and restrictive, so tight that they often prevented me from following happiness. Living and working in Japan had not just opened up my heart, it had opened my mind, too, and for that I was and am truly grateful.

In the popular Studio Ghibli film *Neko no Ongaeshi,* Yuki a white kitten is saved from starvation by a girl named Haru. The white cat returns her kindness by rescuing her later. In many ways, I felt Gershwin had also rescued me. Gershwin didn't listen to what people told him, he just did what he wanted, and that's what I started doing.

The truth is, if it hadn't been for Gershwin, Ryan and I probably would have left Japan after the first year. While we needed to reduce our debt, we really stayed for Gershwin. Because of staying longer, Gershwin and Japan had time to open my heart and teach me – by actually experiencing people from around the world and customs and a society completely foreign to me – that I didn't need to fear the world.

Gershwin had inspired me to do the swim-a-thon (I had only learned about Arkbark while trying to re-home him) and, through that, he taught me that the world was a place of possibility. The only thing holding me back was myself. I now try to see the world through new eyes. It is not a place to run from, but a place of transformation.

Seeing *ikigai* at work in Takayama and having so much time to meditate on what made me happy, I decided to start documenting Gershwin and my travels. It had been a while since I'd done anything creative. The first time in a long time had been writing an article for the Arkbark newsletter about the swim-a-thon. So, it came as a big surprise when my first article in Australia was published. As the old adage says: *Write what you know.* For me, that meant writing about travel, and of course cats.

When the opportunity came up to document my travels for a website, I jumped at the chance. I had discovered when planning to transport Gershwin from Japan to Australia how many other people were starved for even the most practical information. So, I decided to share what I knew. I wrote an article for a UK magazine about the international pet travel process, and other features about different places to take your puss. Since returning to Sydney, Ryan, Gershwin, and I had made several trips up and down the coast. So, I put those experiences and what I had learned into an article.

Gradually, I gained confidence in writing articles, and I collected my articles into a book manuscript and, somewhat naively, set about contacting publishers.

The second publisher I contacted gave me a contract, which I later learned was rare.

I accomplished all of this because of a silver green-eyed Japanese kitten.

My ties with my Aunt Lydia have grown ever stronger. She has visited me in Sydney and Ryan and I took a two-week holiday to her home, where I finally got to meet all of her rescue dogs.

Although my relationship with my father is still distant, we communicate via email on birthdays and Christmas, I am fortunate enough to have a large circle of friends on three continents. Sayuri and I use Facebook® to stay in regular contact.

Ryan and I have returned to Japan three times since we left. On our last visit, I got the chance to meditate with a Zen Buddhist monk in Gershwin's home town. We did not go back to British Hills because it never had that feeling of home that Takayama had and, besides, all our friends there had spread out around the world.

So, Ryan and I have gone three times to Takayama to visit old friends and make new ones.

Japan will always feel like a second home. That wonderful country and one special silver tabby have left an ever-lasting paw print on my life.

Acknowledgements

While this book is dedicated to Gershwin, there are some humans I would like to thank who have helped make this book possible and without whose support and advice it would not have happened at all.

Thank you to: Minuella Chapman, Zanah Michelle Martin, Valentina Dordevic, Sarah Ingraham, Louise Carter, Karen Dench, Michiyo Miyake, Kathy Nunn, Gaiti Rabbani, Margarita Steinhardt, Chie Tokuyama, and to my wonderful family – you know who you are. A special mention to Sayuri for being a true friend and Dr Iguchi for his expert advice and support.

Organisations such as ARK Animal Rescue Japan, Arts Law Centre of Australia, The Japan Foundation, and the Takayama Tourist Office all of which have been a vital source of information on this journey.

Finally, thank you to all the people I met in Japan and who to this day remain genuine friends, to my amazing partner, Ryan, who travelled to the other side of the world with me (and back!) and to all of my inspirational pets past and present.

About the Author

CJ Fentiman is a freelance writer and animal lover and resides in Sydney, Australia with her partner and 2 cats. This is her second book. Follow @ catwith3passports.

Printed in Great Britain
by Amazon

37265354R00131